FACES OF HONG KONG

AN OLD HAND'S REFLECTIONS

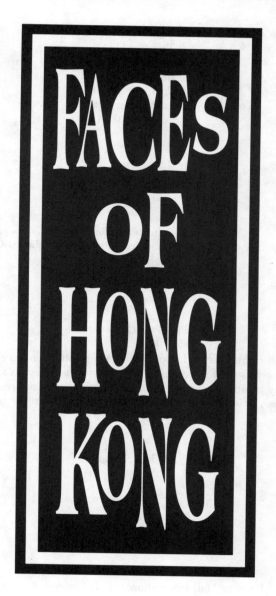

FACES OF HONG KONG

DAN WATERS

PRENTICE HALL

New York London Toronto Sydney Tokyo Singapore

First published 1995 by
Prentice Hall
Simon & Schuster (Asia) Pte Ltd
Alexandra Distripark
Block 4, #04-31
Pasir Panjang Road
Singapore 0511

Simon & Schuster (Asia) Pte Ltd
A division of Simon & Schuster International Group

Printed in Singapore

2   3   4   5   99 98 97 96 95

ISBN 0-13-324757-0

Prentice Hall International (UK) Limited, *London*
Prentice Hall of Australia Pty. Limited, *Sydney*
Prentice Hall Canada Inc., *Toronto*
Prentice Hall of Hispanoamericana, S.A., *Mexico*
Prentice Hall of India Private Limited, *New Delhi*
Prentice Hall of Japan, Inc., *Tokyo*
Editora Prentice Hall do Brasil, Ltda., *Rio de Janeiro*
Prentice Hall, Inc., Englewood Cliffs, *New Jersey*

This book is dedicated to all cross-cultural
marriages and to Eurasians everywhere

Acknowledgements

I am grateful to my son, Barry, for his comments on an early draft which helped me shape this book. Similarly, I must thank the Reverend Carl T. Smith, Hong Kong historian, upon whose considerable research, especially that into 'protected women', I have drawn. Innumerable people to whom I am indebted are named in the text. There are also countless acquaintances, friends and relatives who, knowingly or unknowingly, in either major ways or merely by a few words or a simple act, have assisted me. To all these persons, as well as to the authors and publishers named in the bibliography, my sincere appreciation.

A special thank you must go to James Hayes, himself an Old Hong Kong Hand. Not only did he write the Foreword which starts the book off on the right note but he also read through my typescript and made a number of valuable suggestions.

CONTENTS

FOREWORD

When Dan Waters asked me to write a foreword for his new book I was not sure what to expect. In fact, I never imagined it would be such a wide-ranging account of Hong Kong, and less about my friend's career and experiences than about the place itself as a living entity. Consequently, it is not surprising that the book has the breathless, nervous energy that is so typical of Hong Kong and its people, past, present and, to be sure, future.

It is, nonetheless, the man and his experiences within the family circle of relatives of his Chinese wife, and their friends and interests over his forty years in Hong Kong, which provide the thread that links and binds the whole. The book gains extra balance and counterweight from Dan's roots in Norfolk and the old house that has been home to the Waters' family for five generations.

Through Dan's eyes, the Hong Kong scene and its overseas extensions are recreated for other 'Old Hong Kong Hands', and are also made available to the international reading public. The book does not rest in the present but is also concerned with, and for, Hong Kong after 1997. Born in 1920 Dan is still going strong, full of life and energy, and is probably doing more today than when he retired in 1980. He and Hong Kong will both surely outlast 1997!

James Hayes ISO
MA (Lond.), PhD (Lond.), Hon. DLitt (HK), JP
Historian and former member of the Administrative
Grade, Hong Kong Civil Service, 1956–88

PREFACE

Hong Kong, pimple on the posterior of China, is to be handed back to its motherland. In the run-up in Britain, debate largely centred on how many passports should be granted to Hong Kong residents and how the colonial power can save face in spite of handing over more than three million British subjects to a totalitarian regime. But what of Westerners?

I, Dan Waters, am one of the so-called 'Old Hong Kong Hands'. Having lived in the Territory for four decades I have become a 'cultural Eurasian'. With the takeover of *Xianggang* (People's Republic Romanisation of 'Hong Kong') what will all this mean to me, a white-haired 'barbarian' with a Chinese wife? Will I be forced to return to my native England which I miss when it is sprinkled with the first winter snow?

Writing a book is the nearest a man can get to giving birth. I have lived through calamities and enormous changes in this extraordinary, exciting, city-state of Hong Kong. All that was necessary was to record what I have seen, heard, felt, smelt and tasted. The 'story' also incorporates episodes from my earlier life and it is thus a compression of experiences, a catharsis, which needed 'expelling' from my system.

For *Putonghua* (Mandarin) words and place names in China, apart from well-known cities like Peking and Canton, the more easily identifiable *pinyin* system of Romanisation has been used. But otherwise, because 95 per cent of Hong Kong's population understand Cantonese and 75 per cent regard it as their mother tongue, local transliteration, the Hong Kong Government's *Gazetteer of Place Names* and the *Student's Cantonese-English Dictionary* have been followed, omitting tonal indicators.

Because white Americans, Australians and other Whites originated from European stock, the term 'European', to cover all 'Westerners' or 'Caucasians', is common in Hong Kong.

As at summer 1994 US$1.00 equals approximately HK$7.73, and £1.00 equals about HK$11.86.

Dan Waters
Hong Kong

PROLOGUE

Beautiful, ugly, contradictory, conflicting Hong Kong, that old prophecy, 'and a myriad of lights shall glow', has long come true: now, Lord Palmerston's 'barren island' has many magnificent mansions and countless rickety squatter huts perched precariously upon it.

Glorious November days with superb seascapes on Victoria Peak contrast with hot sticky May in overcrowded, steaming Mong Kok, a festering concrete jungle with barely a blade of grass. Here the world whirls fast. Noisy commercial conversations complement clattering mahjong tiles. Wreckers' hammers take their toll.

The levelling of Chek Lap Kok, an outlying island with pitcher plants and tiny Romer Tree Frogs, a unique species found only in Hong Kong, has made way for a new airport. This single civil engineering project, including sea port facilities, is the largest and one of the most complex and creative ever undertaken anywhere in the world.

Materialistic, glittering, vulgar, gaudy, overbuilt, stressful city; with abundance, privilege, flaunting of wealth, waste, want, squalor, rickshaws, gold-plated Rolls Royce, gold-coin-inlaid lavatory seats, sumptuous banquets, cancer-causing salted fish, bitter herbal medicines and bone setters.

Crown Colony founded on opium; money-making machine embracing international big business, nepotism, rackets, greed, graft, face and *feng shui* (geomancy). O miracle that is Hong Kong, your economic importance far outweighs your size! With ambition and good joss an aspiring foreman knows that, by striking out on his own and working all hours sent by *Ts'oi Shan*, the God of Riches who rides a black tiger, he too can become wealthy.

Men-on-the-make, loving kindness, generosity, charity, donations, philanthropy and puritanical morals co-exist with man's inhumanity to man, heroin addicts, loan sharks, triads, vice and prostitution. A fourteen-year-old virgin has her price. More Mercedes and Rolls Royces per mile, more Scotch salmon, 'Sunkist' oranges and French brandy consumed per head than in any other place.

Anachronistic, incongruous outpost of Empire. British administration, justice and free speech prevail alongside outdated remnants of Ching Dynasty law, male succession in the New Territories and kowtowing.

In the twenty-first century, free-wheeling Hong Kong, with its free port and six million souls, will be part of centrally controlled, communist China. No goodwill will be paid for this last jewel in the crown. In this city of immigrants, and sons and daughters of refugees, British-born subjects are no longer entitled to reside in the United Kingdom. Although a few requested 'barren island off the coast of Scotland to develop into new "economic dragon with shrunken horizons"', for most, 'Pearl of the Orient' is the end of the road.

Notwithstanding, masses of wealthy and middle-class Chinese, as well as loyal 'Queen's Chinese' bedecked with medals, have found new homes in Canada, Australia and the United States. Yet for many, no country can replicate Hong Kong. It is still a blessed place. It is wealthy, it is impoverished; it is compliant, it is dogged; but, above all, it is a success.

After the sun has set will an 'Old Hong Kong Hand' who has experienced the golden years of the Territory be able to continue living here? Will he want to watch it all come to an end? And, if so, 'with leaves returning to the roots of the tree', will he choose, later, to leave his bones where black-eared kites wheel under a dusty-blue sky in what will be Chinese soil?

Learn from Hong Kong

Where and how did I get my revolutionary and modern ideas? I got my ideas in this very place; in the Colony of Hong Kong. More than 30 years ago I was studying in Hong Kong and spent a great deal of spare time in walking the streets of the Colony. Hong Kong impressed me a great deal because there was orderly calm and because there was artistic work being done without interruption. I compared Heung Shan with Hong Kong, and, although they are only 50 miles apart, the difference in the governments impressed me very much. Afterwards I saw the outside world and I began to wonder how it was that foreigners, that Englishmen could do such things as they have done, for example, with the barren rock of Hong Kong, within 70 or 80 years, while China, in 4,000 years, had no place like Hong Kong ... My fellow students, you and I have studied in this English colony and in an English university, and we must learn by English examples. We must carry the English example of good government to every part of China.

Dr Sun Yat-Sen
Speech to Hong Kong University students, 1923

Dream of the Yellow Peril

Truly, I often wonder whether the dream of the Yellow Peril is not likely to come true some day, and the Chinaman by sheer ability and industry will dominate the commerce of the world.

Sir Frederick Lugard
Governor of Hong Kong, 1907–1912

CHAPTER ONE

NORFOLK

A LONG the tram tracks in Hong Kong I ambled, past my Chinese wife's grandfather's salt-fish shop. Although not entirely unpleasant, once smelled that indescribable reek of preserved fish is never forgotten. Strangely, it was present in my dream.

Suddenly, I was pinned down on my back in the yoga 'death posture' with a weight on my chest. My limbs were immobile like a Shanghai fresh-water hairy crab, claws and legs bound to prevent escape, destined for a Hong Kong gourmet's table. Sweating and afraid I lay, partly 'submerged' in the Edwardian feather bed which enveloped my body like a bulbous white shroud.

The danger was that the long imaginary string, attached to my torso and to a huge paper kite resembling a ferocious dragon pitching and tossing furiously high in the sky, would be severed by an all-powerful God. The kite representing my soul would, if I had performed good deeds on earth, then soar upwards to what the Chinese call that 'supremely happy world'. 'Don't want to die!' I bawled in Cantonese, and awoke in a sweat, shaken but relieved to be in our 140-year-old clay-lump house in England, as the seven-foot-high, oak-cased, century-old grandfather clock in the hall struck two.

'Many Chinese believe in "sitting on body ghosts",' my Cantonese wife would have exclaimed had she been there.

'Probably caused by paralysed wakefulness. Not the first time it's happened to me!' I would have answered, tactfully, so as not to mar race relations.

1

The motor section of the brain lags behind the intellectual and sensory parts when waking, medical books inform us.

She would likely then have repeated the tale of the devout Buddhist who had severe stomachache. In his sleep, a large turtle suddenly appeared on his abdomen.

'A small hole bored at the rear of its shell signified it was holy. Fishermen know,' my wife would have continued, 'if they catch one like this, it must be released.'

Anyway, the devotee realised that the turtle sitting on his chest was the one to which he had donated money – in a red 'lucky envelope' with the Chinese character for 'blessings' on the front – for the reptile to be released back to the sea. Luck is 'accumulated' by doing good deeds and one's life can be lengthened if animals are set free. Chanting Buddhist monks, who believe it is wrong to kill, had been present wearing long, red or saffron, loose-fitting, flowing robes, with peculiar, black, angular, flat-topped hats. Some struck percussion instruments such as hollow, sonorous, 'wooden fish', which are smooth and rounded, with big gaping 'mouths'. They do not look a bit like fish but make a lovely, dull, 'plopping' sound when tapped. There were also other Chinese musical paraphernalia, including flutes, drums, cymbals and gongs.

'And when the fervent Buddhist awoke the ghostly turtle had disappeared,' my wife chipped in, 'and the belly pain had miraculously left him.'

Chinese have countless fables and mysterious beliefs, like 'sitting on body ghosts', and others bordering on the more scientific, like *yin* and *yang*, meaning, literally, 'shade' and 'sun'. Things are paired, including not only moon and sun, earth and heaven, gentle and aggressive, mind and body, intuition and reason, subconscious and conscious; but also south and north, positive and negative, even and odd numbers, foods that cool and those that heat one's system, and so on. In every being there is something associated with, and affected by, currents and the ebbs and flows of tides, and changes of seasons.

This limitless circle in the universe contains *yin*, the female principle, and *yang*, the male principle, and these complement and enhance each other and provide balanced wholes among the cosmic forces. *Yin* is seen as bestowing fertility and being capable of giving and maintaining life, grace and patience. *Yang*, sometimes portrayed as a winged dragon in the heavens, is vigorous and initiates. The concept is not so much about polarity in examples like white and black, below and above, and no and yes, as about basic harmony. There is no inherent contradiction between the two.

Nor does the theory imply a static state but rather one that is relative and dynamic. As written in the bible of Taoism, the *Tao Te Ching* (meaning 'the way and the virtue') attributed to Lao Tzu (369–286 BC), although this name could have been a pseudonym:

> By blending the breath
> Of the sun and the shade,
> True harmony enters the world.

In Chinese culture man tries to harmonise with nature and sees himself as part of it. Many of Lao Tzu's hermit followers renounced all worldly ambitions and lived only for death. In western culture, so often we pit ourselves against nature aiming at conquering it.

But even in the West the Greek theory of humours, with correct balances of blood, yellow bile, phlegm and black bile, dominated medical thinking for 2,000 years. This assumption underwent a scientific change with the development of homeostasis or internal constancy in the early nineteenth century. The 'four humours' is strikingly like Chinese medical theory but it evolved quite independently.

'That explains it!' I muttered to myself thinking again of the two complementary forces. Father always said one hour's sleep before midnight is worth two hours later. At eleven o'clock, according to Chinese belief, night changes to *yin* or passivity. To lie abed after daybreak, when cyclic change has returned to *yang* or activity, does not harmonise with nature.

But although I was in bed before eleven last night I slept fitfully. We all have gnawing problems at some stage in our lives. Mine now is, 'Where will I live after 1997?' The Year of the Ox, when Hong Kong reverts to China.

'What do we do?' my distressed wife racked by outrage and insecurity exclaimed after the massacre of chanting students in Tiananmen Square. Accompanied by the Goddess of Democracy they had worn white headbands and made 'V' for victory signs in Beijing (Peking), on 4 June 1989, before some were mown down by gunfire. My wife feels strongly that she and I should stay on in Hong Kong after 1997, but, on that occasion she acted out of character.

'We remain here; unless the situation gets worse!' I muttered, trying to console her and appear resolute.

'What about Singapore?'

'Alternatively return to England,' I retorted. 'You'd be happy there?'

'HK superstar, UK nobody,' I thought to myself. Many Chinese emigrate and then fail to adjust to western culture, high taxes and life without amahs (maids).

'It'll work out,' I had optimistically assured her.

Now, several months later, having been at Loughborough University doing research, I knew I had to return to Hong Kong to see what the situation was really like. The urge was there to walk familiar paths bathed in sunshine; to see old, creased, chestnut Chinese faces that have weathered. People I have known since they were young. To drive around the now commercialised New Territories, with high-rise, nondescript buildings and acres of ugly, piled-up, massive shipping containers.

I need again to sample simple things. Like *yau tsa kwai* (oil-fried devil), one-foot-long pastry sticks, which are broken into pieces and dunked in *congee* (rice gruel). To smell chestnuts being stir-fried, by street hawkers, in a mix of coarse sugar and sand in a large Chinese wok. I need to savour the revolting 'pong' of fermented beancurd being cooked.

Hong Kong is a city of contradictions. The story of my wife and me followed the oldest theme – of Romeo and Juliet. Of two different kinds of persons, occasionally ostracised by Europeans. Vera's father, like many old-fashioned Chinese, objected up to his death in 1959 (one year before our marriage) to his daughter going out with a *gwailo* ('foreign devil'). Mixed marriages were less common then. In spite of that romantic, Chinese stuff about the *kwong long* tree (the sugar palm with a long, straight, unwavering heart), marrying across ethnic boundaries means involvement in each other's culture. What is accepted by society is largely what has developed and been permitted by circumstances.

The hazards of love have brought together diverse races, civilisations and cultures, with resulting difficulties in adjusting to country, lifestyle and cuisine. For a western woman taking a Chinese husband, especially, it means marrying the extended family, not just the spouse. A mixed marriage, even more than others, takes a lot of hard work to make it work.

In our case, too, my wife prefers late nights, city life, the 'buzz' of crowds. I receive inspiration from the magic of sunrise, the breeze and the stars, the hum of insects and the music of the waterfall in spate on Victoria Peak. But my wife's and my differences, like *yin* and *yang*, complement. We follow in others' footsteps. Although mixed weddings were uncommon in earlier times, liaisons between Europeans and Chinese have existed for centuries.

When I first saw the 'Pearl of the Orient' on that cool, clear, winter's day in the mid 1950s I was not overly impressed. Then in my mid-thirties, with the 'vitality of a dragon or a horse', the Colony was absorbing its lifeblood – refugees from China. Because that country had erected the bamboo curtain, Hong Kong had little entrepôt trade. This meant the Crown Colony, which received no financial aid, had to change to manufacturing and exporting.

But the Territory grows on you. When I close my eyes in England I see Chinese mothers wearing plain, trouser-suits, carrying cuddly babies, piggyback, in psychedelic cloth 'slings'. I hear the 'Noon Day Gun' at midnight and the cacophony of ships' horns in the harbour welcoming the new year. Green, poisonous bamboo snakes slither across Conduit Path. I recall Hong Kong's floral emblem, the orchid 'butterfly trees' (*Bauhinia Blakeana*, named after Governor Blake who took over the New Territories in 1898) in winter along Bowen Road, with large, purple-red flowers shaped like camels' hoofs. In late summer, swarms of dragonflies on Victoria Peak hatch more rapidly on the approach of a storm.

'Can't wait to get back!' I murmured aloud.

Insomnia is not really the villain it is made out to be. In the dead of night the *yin* and the blackness offer an opportunity to ponder. I lay awake and stared at the old reeded ceiling skimmed with lime plaster.

Our house in Norfolk, with its patina of mellowed age, has character. Five generations of the Waters family have lived there. For a septuagenarian, it offers a distant anchor and a reassurance to counterbalance the bewildering change I meet in Hong Kong. While the quill pen should not reign supreme, the Chinese sages believe a person who cuts himself off from his roots is in danger, emotionally.

There have been bawling, wriggling, newly born babies; and stiff dead bodies of the Waters family have lain in our house. My wife senses the place is haunted. Chinese are more attuned to the spirit world. 'Happenings' may have been absorbed into the structure. Perhaps, when atmospherics and other conditions are favourable, years later rays or vibrations can be picked up by a psychic person. Everywhere one leaves a shadow of oneself, and, at given intervals, scenes are re-enacted. Then, when we die, we collect them like snapshots and take them into the next world. Are there any Chinese ghosts in East Anglia, I wonder?

Visiting Mother gives a sense of belonging. That my grandfather slept in the same bed that supports my 5-foot-9-inch, 172-pound frame there would be unthinkable in Hong Kong. With 98 per cent of all buildings post-World War II, contractors in the Territory are expert at pulling them down. All I have ever lived in there are concrete, box-like flats, where a saying has it, 'Greedy for the new forget the old'. One cannot help but make comparisons between two worlds.

At Watton the full moon, signifying the fifteenth day of the

lunar month by the Farmers' Calendar, is shining. A brown owl
hoots, perched on his favourite, partly hollow, English oak. My
thoughts leap one-third of the way around the world to Hong Kong
University campus. Gaggles of black-faced laughing thrushes
congregate there in winter among the dense clumps of tall, erect,
yellowish-green, bamboo, with classical, delicate leaves like fine
painting on porcelain. Admired by Taoists for its resilient beauty,
tenacity and flexibility, bamboo symbolises endurance and the
lifestyle of an upright man. It bends but seldom breaks. Its
unbounded usefulness means it is used to make utensils like
chopsticks, pillows and divination blocks in temples. The elderly
will have slept in bamboo cradles as children. They will be
conveyed to the grave by bearers using bamboo carrying poles. Will
I depart in the same way?

The same moon outside, in Norfolk, shines over Hong Kong.
My wife's late father liked to go into the street at *Uet Tong Tau*, on
the fifteenth day of the Eleventh Moon, when it is directly overhead
and casts no dark, sinister shadow. It is an auspicious time.

Nonetheless, he died a bitter man. He had three daughters, but
no sons to 'buy water' at his funeral to ensure continuation of
lineage. 'Women spell disaster', was one of his expressions. Did he
ever visit the thirty-foot-high 'Boulder of Pre-ordained Marriage',
which is said to resemble an erect phallus in Bowen Road, I
wonder? Chinese girls believe, 'Marry a dog, follow a dog'. They go
to 'Marriage Rock' to burn joss sticks, to pray they will wed good
husbands and give birth to sons. They beseech happiness in
matrimony. A young Chinese girl and an Englishman committed
suicide together by drinking poison in the shadows of Maiden's
Rock, earlier this century, because the girl's parents forbade them to
wed.

As I lie in bed first light dances in the bushes outside. The
dawn chorus dies and the life-giving sun, which the Chinese regard
as *yang*, comes up over the horizon like a huge red ball. Old folk in
Norfolk carry the adage 'red sky in the morning shepherd's
warning' a stage further. If the red is only in the east, only then does
it foretell bad weather.

'If the red goes right over, so it is also red in the west,' an old
bricklayer once expounded to me, 'it's a sure sign of a fine day.'

The Chinese, of course, have their sayings, and they also watch
animals and birds for signs. In the mid 1970s, an armada of boat-
people sailed into Hongkong harbour from Fujian Province.

'Avoid earthquake!' they chorused. They had been observing
frogs, which, like some other creatures, have early-warning systems
of forthcoming disasters. Neither Hong Kong nor Guangzhou

(Canton) meteorological stations, with their scientific instruments, had knowledge of any impending earthquakes. As illegal immigrants, these boat-people were consigned back to China before the quake struck. Fortunately, it was not severe.

Visiting my home town is evocative of boyhood days. In 1921, the year after I was born, the parish had a population of 1,331 souls and eleven public houses. But Watton is far more than an area of flat land, two miles by one-and-a-half miles with broad horizons, with low average annual rainfall (London has about 23 inches), less than the 27.44 inches which fell on Hong Kong in twenty-four hours in May 1889.

Watton is lazing in the long grass at haysel (hay-making time), watching a skylark take off from its nest, rising vertically, singing, until it disappears. Watton is lying on the banks of the Wissey catching sticklebacks in a jam jar, near where Tinker Dalton, a down-and-out, gathered watercress and lived in his 'castle', a derelict house where he slept rough on a bed of straw. The town to me is the seventeenth century clock tower; leaning over a five-barred gate patting the muzzle of a horse; gazing at a cow chewing the cud in a paddock; and watching the swallows and martins, after they migrate from Africa, nesting in our outbuildings.

In the 1990s, Watton is no longer just a small town with a market, selling samphire (sea weed) and creamy Cromer crabs, the best in Britain, so they used to say. In addition to servicing the surrounding villages it has become a retirement retreat for pensioners from the Home Counties. Once settled at Watton, life for them consists of shopping, pottering in the garden, observing the approach of the four seasons and waiting to die. Or, as the Chinese phrase it, 'trying to prolong their exhausted panting'.

There is much to be said for the extended family, where children keep the elderly young. In old China it was considered a blessing, and not uncommon, for 'five generations to live together in the same hall'. 'If do not sire children during lean years who will help reap the harvests?'

'A hundred sons and a thousand grandsons!' guests still proclaim at weddings.

But with late marriage, birth control, and the agrarian way of life having disappeared in Hong Kong, large families are now a rarity.

I come from a family of four successive generations of master builders. The business was established in 1853. Looking out of my bedroom casement at Watton, across the flower garden into our adjacent builders yard, I spot where the tallest walnut tree in the district used to tower eighty feet to heaven. As children, when nuts dropped 'bombs' were descending. Mother used to pickle them before the shells had formed.

Under that old tree, before World War I and the introduction of mechanical saws, my family owned a saw pit. Whole tree trunks were cut into planks by Old Fred and Young Fred, a father and son itinerant team, using nothing more than an eight-foot-long hand pitsaw. In 1988 on Hainan Island off the southern coast of Cathay, as China was known in the twelfth century, I witnessed a similar sawing operation. Except it was done horizontally above ground.

China is one of the top ten shipping powers and the eleventh largest trader. Yet in spite of being a major contender on the world stage, and embracing advanced technology in areas such as satellites (like 'Asiasat') and rockets (for example, the 'Long March Rocket'), China is still, largely, a Third World country. Textbooks do not always provide answers. Yet with three million soldiers under arms it is a superpower in military terms. It is a leading arms supplier, a nuclear power and one of the five members of the United Nations Security Council. Although China plays terrific table tennis it has filthy public toilets.

'TAKES me time to get going!' Mother called as I stood by the heavily worn, oak, kitchen-door threshold on which countless family members have trodden.

'Did you hear that dog howling last night? Sign of a death!'

Was it true? I half wondered.

'Dad always enjoyed breakfast. How many eggs?'

'Two please.'

I visualised him in his favourite chair. There was even a whiff of his pipe tobacco!

With western influence the Hong Kong Chinese diet, which used to include little red meat, is changing. Fast foods are now popular. Cancer and cardiovascular diseases have become the main causes of death as in advanced western countries. Life expectancy, in what was the unhealthy, fever-ridden climate of Hong Kong, is now seventy-eight, compared with seventy-six for Britain, the United States and New Zealand.

The traditional, well-balanced, Chinese breakfast, which is low in fat and simple sugar, often consists of *congee*, together with bean curd, *ginko* (white nuts from the maiden-hair fern tree) and sun-dried mandarin-orange peel. This is eaten with Chinese rolls and a few peanuts. All is washed down with Chinese tea to free the system of toxins. Although effects are often exaggerated, many

Asians have an intolerance to dairy produce owing to the lack of an inborn enzyme needed to break down lactose.

'Chinese cook lettuce?'

I nodded.

'Whatever for?'

'Less risk of dysentery and hepatitis in the tropics,' I replied, knowing that we who had suffered such complaints have built up a degree of immunity to bugs, amoeba and other 'spices' that attack the gut.

'Shame to cook lovely, fresh lettuce!'

Basic views of life are formed, they say, before a person reaches the age of ten. Yet the older Mother grows the more she becomes set in her ideas. But I enjoy her cooking!

English fare is not rated as one of the great cuisines, like French. Chinese believe the invention of a dish contributes more to the happiness of mankind than the discovery of a new constellation. Italian cuisine has a great deal to thank Serica for, with Marco Polo taking the recipe for noodles back to Italy in 1295. It was not until the sixteenth century that it was realised that China, Cathay and Serica were the same country.

Yet there are few dishes more appetising than steak and kidney pie, done to a turn, or roast beef with Yorkshire pudding and freshly dug up horse-radish. Then there is Norfolk turkey or pheasant, the latter having been hung for a few days – a process the Chinese describe as barbaric – followed by blackberries straight off the hedge, or newly picked raspberries and clotted cream. Even Norfolk dumplings or a ploughman's lunch take a lot of beating on the right occasion. As the Chinese scholar, the late Lin Yutang, wrote: What is patriotism but the love of food we ate as a child?

Mother interrupted. 'Enjoy your breakfast? We'll go up to the churchyard this morning.'

There was a knock on the ledged door with its worn Norfolk thumb latch.

'Gardener's outside!' I called.

'Mornin' ta yer!'

Old Sid stood next to the trellis adorned with a horseshoe. Mother insists this must be the right way up so the luck does not fall out.

'I'll put up a mawkin (scarecrow) this mornin'.'

With no European proletariat in Hong Kong it is good to hear an old codger like Sid, in his patched Norfolk jacket, again. Yet England is nothing like China, with its multitude of tongues, where Mandarin – now termed *Putonghua* – the lingua franca, sounds quite different to Cantonese. The latter is prevalent in Hong Kong, together with various Cantonese sub-dialects as spoken in the New Territories and by the *Tanka* boat-people. They are as different from the speech of the *Hoklo*, who came to Hong Kong from Fujian and the northeast of Guangdong province, as English is to German. The character for the surname *Ng* in Cantonese is pronounced *Wu* in Mandarin, to give an idea of differences between dialects.

'Fare y'well t'gather, dew yew mind how yew goo!' Sid exclaimed as the tips and clates of his hobnail boots crunched in the gravel.

'Jade is a lucky stone? Many consider green unlucky!' said Mother who was wearing a Chinese, imperial green, jade pendant embodying the Chinese character *shau*, meaning long life.

'Symbolises virtues, such as intellect, purity and sincerity,' I answered.

Indeed Chinese believe jade becomes shinier and 'oilier' when worn close to the body, if a person is healthy. It also provides protection like a lucky charm. The latter applies especially to 'coffin jade' which has been buried with a corpse for centuries and has darkened. It is highly prized.

'Don't care for that,' Mother responded.

Better not mention, I thought, that in mythology jade is sometimes seen as petrified dragon's semen, with the lotus flower representing the vulva!

I gazed at a painting of a smooth-skinned, chubby, Chinese boy, wearing a black waistcoat and a black skull-cap with a striking red tassel. He is calculating on an abacus.

'Exquisite hands!' Mother exclaimed.

Most Chinese have fine hands with long, tapering, delicate fingers.

Mother's house is full of the kind of memorabilia that 'off-shore Brits' bring back on leave. Decade after decade visitors stream into Hong Kong to see the place for themselves. They include British Members of Parliament who pretend to understand the workings of the Territory. Businessmen seem to find an excuse to visit. Hoards of engineers on contract, and others, not to mention servicemen, are posted there. Everyone, on their return, manages to take a few exotic presents back.

I right the brass trivet, in the form of the character *fuk*, meaning 'blessings', which hung upside down. Gracing the white stone mantlepiece is a picture of me, in full Chinese ceremonial dress, with a long blue gown surmounted by a constantly repeated darker blue character, standing for long life, forming the overall pattern. Scrolls with black ideograms painted in squiggly 'grass' or formal 'great seal' styles, or precipitous mountain scenes with tiny inconspicuous figures enveloped by nature in harmony, adorn walls. Coffee-table books with pictures of fascinating Hong Kong, showing the mystique of the Bun Festival, Dragon Boat races and a squirmy-snake shop, are piled on a teapoy.

Also on the mantelpiece are two one-foot high, bulbous blue and white porcelain jars which Mother's eldest sister sent from the Far East when her warrant officer husband served there between the two World Wars. The vessels used to contain sticky, sweet ginger in syrup.

The preserved ginger trade claims to be Hong Kong's oldest export industry. It started in Canton at the beginning of the nineteenth century when a poor hawker, Li Chy, noticed Westerners had a sweet tooth. Business went so well he opened a factory in 1846, when Hong Kong was the first 'notch' in the tree and Englishmen expected China would be 'felled' automatically. Later, the business moved to the Crown Colony.

Queen Victoria was, on one occasion, given a piece of sweet ginger which she liked so much that, thereafter, it appeared among desserts at all royal banquets. It was registered in London in 1851, and Her Majesty herself suggested the trademark, 'Cock Brand'. By then, any party of standing in Europe served sweet ginger. The late U Tat Chee, the 'Ginger King', maintained it was introduced into England in the fifteenth century for making gingerbread. 'Cures coughs, diarrhoea, flatulence, giddiness, headaches and vomiting,' he used to proclaim proudly.

In the days of Empire men from all over Britain served in the armed forces in the colonies. One of Watton district's most famous sons was Company Sergeant Major John Osborn, born to a Romany family in a colourful, horse-drawn caravan in the tiny, out-of-the-way village of Foulden, ten miles west of my hometown.

As a boy sailor he served, in 1916, at the Battle of Jutland, and later on the Western Front with the Naval Brigade. He emigrated to Canada in 1920. In 1941 the CSM was posted with his unit, the Winnipeg Grenadiers, and on 19 December it met the might of the Imperial Japanese Army.

The bitter battle took place in the centre of Hong Kong island, on Mount Butler. By late morning, forty-one-year-old Osborn had taken over command of what remained of his Company after its senior officers had been killed or wounded. Constantly he displayed great courage, led a bayonet charge and covered the withdrawal single-handedly. The end came on what is today a peaceful spur, off Jardine's Lookout, where he threw his body over a grenade to save his comrades because there was insufficient time to hurl it back at the Japanese. The CSM has no known grave and he is Hong Kong's only Victoria Cross awardee. Osborn Barracks, in Kowloon, are named after him.

My mind constantly flits between Watton and Hong Kong. Suddenly, I remember Mother beavering away. At over ninety, garlands of skin cover bones and little flesh. If you want to tell a European's age look at the neck or the back of the hands. Chinese, those with the means to look after themselves, tend to be firmer of flesh and smoother of skin in advancing age. Some develop a special serenity, becoming more graceful and dignified, making them not old but ageless. Hong Kong's damp climate helps to ward off wrinkles and crows' feet, compared to the bracing and less humid air of Norfolk, although parts of the county are noted for longevity.

Accepting that I come from a middle-class, respected family of almost pure Norfolk stock I sometimes wonder how Mother feels, inwardly, about my not marrying a European? Even cosmopolitan Singapore's Lee Kuan Yew, reportedly, does not favour racial intermarriage. 'The elderly prefer to see grandchildren in their own likeness,' he is said to have intimated. There will always be the few who rebel against tradition.

'Can't stand skirts with slits up the thighs,' Mother suddenly exclaimed!

'Oh *cheung saams*! You know old-fashioned Chinese object to off-the-shoulder dresses,' I responded, 'especially for elderly, obese, western women, with shapeless, "plates-of-meat", upper arms.'

'Fancy!' Mother mused.

Although there are looks and stares, and misunderstandings, I have never found race relations in rural England a real problem, although I could have sworn, on the odd occasion when entering a store with my wife, that the assistant's lip curled a fraction. But you do not meet outright hostility in Norfolk. Chinese are not addressed as 'Chinks'. Most immigrants, however, have encountered racism in some form, either open aggression or the institutionalised, subtle variety. The latter is difficult to confront.

'People should marry their own kind and not "mix the breed",' one of our tenants once let slip. Mother was upset!

But in a country where, as soon as one Englishman opens his mouth another Englishman hates him, you have to learn to stick up for yourself. After all, the weaker of pure British stock are often teased unmercifully at school.

'Depends on what kind of a wog you are!' said Timothy Mo, the well-known novelist, himself the offspring of a Norwich mother and a Chinese father, in 1991 in an interview in *The Independent* newspaper.

'If you're a foreign swot, who always gets questions right in class, life can be hell. But if you are a good googly bowler, wear fashionable clothes, hip hair and act tough, you can be popular.'

'Paki bashing' is often exaggerated. People who dwell on race are often psychologically maladjusted, although many Third World nationals with United Kingdom passports barrack lustily for the West Indies cricketers when they play against a British team.

And yet, although there is now a Chinese restaurant at Watton, the handful of Chinese there seem as out of place as I appear to locals, with my ungainly western frame, when I travel to Inner Mongolia or the remote north-west province of Xinjiang (meaning 'new frontier') in China. It used to be easier for an Anglo-Chinese to blend in in England, than in Hong Kong where Eurasians were not always accepted. My wife is pure Cantonese, and the fact that she has done well in business, gives Mother something to brag about.

W HEN I am at Watton we make pilgrimages to the churchyard. The Chinese have three main festivals for the dead. The first is *Ching Ming* (meaning 'clear and bright'), Chinese Easter, when graves are swept, incense burned and sacrifices offered. Preferably, on that day 'teardrops' fall from heaven.

Second is the ninth day of the Ninth Moon, or *Chung Yeung*, when Chinese traditionally climb hills to avoid imaginary flooding and calamities. They visit family graves at the same time.

The third occasion, *Yu Lan*, is similar to All Souls' Day on 2 November, in the Roman Catholic calendar, when prayers are said for the dead in Purgatory. At this 'Hungry Ghosts Festival' offerings are made to unfortunate, wandering spirits. Appeasement is necessary. They may cause mischief. During the Japanese occupation many people did not receive proper burials. Chinese abhor the thought that, when they die, no one will pray and burn joss sticks for their souls.

Peace of mind prevails after visiting Watton graveyard where remains of the Waters' family, including three Daniels and forebears with Victorian names like Charlotte, Mary Ann and Harriet, lie. Few alive today knew them. Relatives and friends who gathered then to bid them farewell are forgotten. At Watton, the flint church tower dates back to about 1100. The ceiling of the chancel was painted by my great-uncle, more than a century ago, to represent the star-studded, blue heavens. He lay on his back, like Michelangelo in the Sistine Chapel in the sixteenth century. The ceiling at Watton is also still resplendent testifying to Thomas's workmanship.

Today in this unstable world more Westerners are trying to trace their roots, although not to the extent of the Chinese whose culture is bound up with ancestor worship. Nevertheless, most people have the urge to learn about great-grandfather. 'When you drink the water remember the mountain spring.'

The heavy, rusty churchyard gate has uttered a drawn-out, high-pitched screech for as long as anyone can remember. The poisonous yew trees, which were used to keep cattle out of graveyards and were known to pagan man as the tree of life, take 200 years to reach maturity. Today, a substance called taxol from their bark shows promise in fighting ovarian cancer. Some yews at Watton could be almost as old as the church itself. They are synonymous with graveyards in England, like the cypress in Italy; or the low-branching, spreading frangipani, with long, glossy leaves tapering at both ends which are common in cemeteries in the tropical Far East.

Frangipani trees flower in the tranquil, well-wooded *Chiu Yuen* (bright and faraway) Eurasian Cemetery on Hong Kong island. Many graves there are large and elaborate, some omega shaped, with photographs on tombs of wealthy personages in Chinese ceremonial dress. Sir M.K. Lo, who died of a heart attack in 1959 as he was preparing to attend a reception in honour of Britain's Prince Philip, lies there. Sir M.K. was a member of one of the great Eurasian families. Fresh flowers have been placed on his grave daily since he died. A magpie's nest – a good omen – in a bombax tree overlooks the serene scene.

Although most tombs at *Chiu Yuen* are in Chinese style, some have western characteristics. Graves at Watton are different. Once inside Watton churchyard the ritual begins and Mother and I wash the Aberdeen granite headstone and cut the grass on Dad's grave. A Chinese family at *Ching Ming* tidies a tomb in a similar way although they possibly touch up the letters using vermillion paint, a propitious colour.

'This is where my ashes will lie, next to Dad's,' exclaims Mother as she pats the grass. 'I want to be cremated.'

It was 1952, February, 'full-dyke month', when he left us. That meant bailing out until the last minute before the coffin was lowered.

'Beautiful spot,' I answered belatedly.

'Don't like the idea of my eyes being burned.'

Inwardly, I winced.

'But God is good.'

I knew what she meant about the eyes. I always wanted to donate mine on death, together with other vital organs.

'Chinese have deep-rooted beliefs a body should be complete when entering the next world,' my wife insists, 'even if it is worn out and is to be replaced for the next life.'

Imperial eunuchs used to preserve their shrivelled up, dun-coloured, castrated private parts in jars of alcohol, up to the start of this century, so these could be placed in their coffins. Even if some superstitions need to be overlooked, with mixed marriages you have to respect each other's culture.

In England, grave spaces are bought in perpetuity. In Hong Kong, land is in short supply. Seven years after the death of my wife's father, in 1966, we trudged up the earth steps of the terraced hills of the sprawling Wo Hop Shek Cemetery. On that damp, chilly morning Father-in-law's remains were exhumed. Two coolies dug them up so the plot could be reused. Hong Kong is not yet like parts of China where coffins are also recycled.

At Wo Hop Shek, I recall one of the labourers muttering that the flesh had not completely decayed and the bones were difficult to clean.

'He's after more *cumshaw*,' Vera's mother mumbled.

The tip was presented later, in a lucky envelope, after the bones had been cleansed in water mixed with rice wine. It is important all flesh and hair are removed as these are harmful and affect a person's *yang*. Bones are revered, although the handling of dead bodies and their remains is not a salubrious occupation. Yet washing the bones of one's ancestors provides a special feeling.

Villagers, whose ancestors lived in the New Territories before the British came, have the traditional right to position earthenware urns auspiciously on hillsides. Bones are arranged in anatomical order inside, in the shape of a foetus ready to 'return to the womb' for rebirth at reincarnation.

The remains of Father-in-law were cremated and the ashes sifted into an urn during a service officiated over by a Buddhist priest. After purification with incense they were placed in a niche at the Taoist columbarium in *Ching Chung Koon*, translated as 'green pine' temple complex. Pine is an emblem of longevity. It can frighten away ghouls that pray on corpses.

The remains of my own father lie, in perpetuity, in a tranquil Norfolk churchyard. Digging up the dead sounds morbid to inhibited Westerners. But with a culture based on ancestor worship and an affinity with the spirit world the expression 'earthy' is more appropriate. Even as an Englishman I do not recall anything particularly gruesome about the exhumation of my father-in-law. His bones were inert. There was no smell of death – the kind of stench that gets in your clothes and stays on your skin no matter how often you wash.

Both my father and father-in-law discarded their worn out bodies like a person sheds soiled garments. Each returned to nature as God and Buddha intended. The process of decay holds a grisly fascination, yet, with one heaven and different approaches the afterlife is infinitely more intriguing.

'Performing good deeds brings not only good fortune to oneself, one's relatives and future generations in this life, but also in the next world,' a Chinese colleague once remarked after a wealthy businessman had donated a large sum for a school.

There is a time to live, a time to die biologically, and a time to be born again. Death is really a form of 'posting' between this life and the next one on earth. With reincarnation, my wife's father may already have reappeared as an officious Communist Party cadre, a scrawny coolie, or even as an animal – one of the twelve creatures that constitute the Chinese Zodiac perhaps? How does release finally come about from the endless, sorrowful cycle of lives, one wonders?

Meanwhile, my own father is in peaceful bliss in heaven – so I like to think.

In death, as in life, worlds apart are the destinies of my two relatives, perched firmly on disparate stems of my genealogical tree. They can be compared to the English oak and the bodhi tree under whose heart-shaped, pointed leaves Buddha sat, cross-legged, for enlightenment when he was tempted by three goddesses.

'What are you thinking?' Mother exclaimed in a school-ma'amish voice, and I was transported firmly back to Watton churchyard. 'See that aeroplane?' She pointed skyward.

'That's where you'll be in a couple of days. Won't get me up there!'

I have met several Britons who were not keen on flying, even my forty-year-old tutor at Manchester University, I recalled as I nodded. You never seem to meet a Chinese who is scared to fly.

'Why don't you stay in England?' She dropped similar hints every now and again.

Although I wrench myself away from Asia at intervals, to seek 'restitution' in Europe, I always return. The pendulum is swinging back east for the Pacific Century. One day, China could again be the 'Middle Kingdom', the 'centre of the earth', as, when written in Chinese (中國), the first character depicts it with a single, vertical line cutting through the middle of a square. 'I'll be all right, Mother!' I insisted.

'Touch wood!' she replied, and I pictured her fingering the timber of the Cross.

I do not suppose she knows some etymologists believe that is how the saying originated, in Germany, with their 'three taps on wood', I thought.

Europeans laugh at the Chinese, but it is surprising how superstitious elderly British country folk can be. Crossed knives at table are a sign of a quarrel. Cross your fingers to prevent bad luck. Although Mother is not so superstitious as her mother, to open an umbrella inside a house is fatal. This, the Chinese think, is ridiculous! If you forget something, and have to return home to retrieve it, it is important, Mother believes, to sit down and put your feet up!

There are countless unwritten 'rules' which we were brought up on as children. To see a black cat is lucky, unlike in Italy where it is unlucky. Yet all these pale in comparison with the web of complex Chinese superstitions which can vary from province to province. Trapped by the elements and material, worldly things over which we lack control, superstitions have provided release since the dawn of mankind.

A TAXI picked me up from Mother's house as she stood by the heavy iron gate that swings to and fro scraping the concrete path. 'I'll be here when you come back!' she shouted, with her thick, white hair glistening and blowing in the wind.

Babies are attached by umbilical cords at birth and intellectual and social bonding does not start to loosen, between mother and child, until it reaches about seven. Most men remain close to their mums all their lives.

I hate farewells! Having been an 'off-shore Brit' for approaching half a century, and, like the overseas Chinese, torn between two cultures, I have had more than my share. Partings are better taken like bitter, Chinese herbal medicine, gulped down as quickly as possible.

'Did you notice?' the taxi driver remarked two minutes later as we drove to the railway station. 'There were tears in the old lady's eyes.'

CHAPTER TWO

LONDON

MY dear chap, our old Empire is often denigrated,' a spare, elderly gentleman exclaimed, stooping suddenly as his monocle dropped.

One could picture him in tropical gear complete with solar topee. He could well have served as one of the 'Heaven-born' (Administrative Officers) in the British India Raj.

'Haven't we given the world the nearest it has to an international language?' he continued.

'How many countries base their legal and judicial systems on our model which concentrates on fairness and impartiality?' a little old lady with a dowager's hump piped up in a hoity-toity voice. She promptly put down her scone and wiped a spot of tea from her *batik* dress.

It is rude to eavesdrop I realised. Britain certainly posted devoted engineers, policemen, soldiers, doctors and nurses to the far corners of the globe. Order was often created out of chaos. Deadly, endemic diseases were combatted. Nevertheless, in spite of colonialism equating in some minds to racist yokes, we were never as harsh or as successful as the French in exploiting our overseas possessions.

British colonialism has, I pondered, been a force for good, in spite of tragedies like the Sino-British Opium Wars, in the mid nineteenth century, which some historians maintain were basically concerned with free trade and not just narcotics. As a result Hong Kong Island, created out of the opium trade, was occupied following gunboat diplomacy in 1841. The three-and-a-half-square-mile tip of the Kowloon Peninsula was also ceded in perpetuity, in 1860, again by what the People's Republic of China describes as an 'unequal treaty'. 'Born in infamy' the United States President, Franklin D. Roosevelt, used to insist about Hong Kong, although we must not forget American colonialism in places like the Philippines.

China could be the only country that has an annual 'National Humiliation Day', on 29 August, when events such as the Opium Wars are remembered. The only demonstrations allowed in Beijing are against foreign embassies.

Hong Kong, together with other British occupied territories worldwide, was later introduced to the cut and thrust of capitalism. Many old colonies like Singapore and Hong Kong, as parts of the greatest empire the modern world has seen, learned their lessons well. A few 'students' now perform better than the 'teacher'. But I have been asked by a few elderly, nostalgic Indians, partly because they surmise that is what one wants them to say, 'Why don't the British come back, sahib? Life was better in India in those days.'

With all these memories occupying my mind I am sitting in the sedate, Royal Over-seas [sic] League Headquarters, with its decorative plaster cornices and ornate, ceiling centre-pieces. Emblems of Britain's past dependencies, from the prancing red lion of Kenya to the leaping tiger of Malaya, adorn walls. By the twenty-first century there will be little more than tiny, lonely Pitcairn Island left, home to eighty descendants of the Bounty mutineers. The wrought-iron scroll staircase balustrade, together with other architectural features, provides an ambience of gracious, slightly behind-the-times, old-world living. Here in the League I shall spend three enjoyable nights.

This is where squirrels perch on window sills of the buttery and sparrows fly in in search of bread crumbs; persons of all colours go out of their way to be nice to each other; and elderly gentlefolk wander amiably around recalling when approaching one-quarter of the world's map was coloured pink. The English in those stirring days felt they had a mission to rule the darker-skinned races even if much of the Empire was run by Scotsmen. One recalls the words of the missionary and traveller, David Livingstone (1813–73), who made the clarion call to save Africa from slavery and poverty, 'to heal this open sore of the world'.

The small garden at Over-Seas House, adjoining (Royal) Green Park, is a picture in the spring, with rhododendrons, azaleas and pink camellia. Clusters of flowers and shrubs provide a haven for birds; from tits and wrens to robins and magpies. Here, in the heart of London, a sparrow hawk has been spotted close by.

Although the Chinese have no precise equivalent to the

English word for 'privacy', and solitude is often interpreted as loneliness, solitude is important to me. Consequently, I spent the evening wandering through well-wooded Green Park, near Buckingham Palace, and across to Saint James's Park with its plane trees partly bare of bark. Pink-footed and white-fronted geese, black swans and shovelers swim on the lake. A pair of mandarin ducks, which mate for life and Chinese consider symbolic of true love and marital faith, cruise together nearby.

'Four sparrows at once!' an Indian shouted with glee as he tried to tempt other birds to perch back on, and eat bread-crumbs from his outstretched hand.

Hundreds of pigeons waddled haughtily around the edge of the lake, like gregarious middle-aged men with beer-barrel tummies, searching for titbits. Meanwhile spirited military bandsmen, in scarlet tunics with gold braid and piping, inflated themselves and played 'Land of Hope and Glory': older, often shapeless, bodies lazed in deck chairs: young courting couples in various states of dishevelment cuddled on the grass. Feeling much like a tourist, I sat in the sun, smelt the flowers and tried to forget about Hong Kong.

From the upper floors of the Royal Commonwealth Society, on the River Thames side of Saint James's Park, where I had dinner, one can spot for the umpteenth time the dome of Sir Christopher Wren's Saint Paul's Cathedral – dubbed the 'parish church' of the Commonwealth. An expatriate on furlough can derive considerable pleasure from wandering around the back streets of London where sedan chairs were used until as late as 1821.

A half-dozen still plied their trade in Hong Kong up to the late 1950s. Their route was up the 1,817-foot-high Victoria Peak where parts of Old Peak Road have a gradient of one-in-two. Little wonder that, on a meagre diet, the working life of a chair coolie was said to be eight years.

BACK at Over-Seas House I stripped and looked at myself in the full-length mirror before taking a bath. Many Europeans have blue eyes and are, incorrectly of course, described by Chinese as being 'double boned' because they have heavier frames. A Westerner, although he may be reasonably muscular, often has flab and a paunch.

Madame Wei Tao-ming wrote in her autobiography, about a well-bred Chinese woman coming to Hong Kong:

I saw my first white man. I was agape. The men seemed very strange, with their light hair and their loud, free mannerisms. But the women, walking arm-in-arm with them, on their big feet, talking and laughing with an equal lack of shyness, stupefied me. On the whole, I thought they were incredibly odd but still something about their bodily freedom stirred responsive chords in me.

Unlike most Chinese, Westerners have a liberal covering of hair, 'like a monkey'. This used to intrigue my young, Chinese niece as she pulled it and stroked my forearm. Many 'clean-shaven' Europeans, in fact, have traces of blue stubble. Others delight in sporting bristling, handle-bar moustaches or bushy beards. Eyelashes that are long and curly are the envy of Chinese women.

Foreigners are often seen by Chinese as sloppy and possessing feelings unlike their own, together with a big nose – which means a big you-know-what – and large sweaty hands. Even today many Westerners are still considered by Chinese as awkward, and gauche, with loud, harsh voices. Having lived among Chinese for so long I have to admit, sometimes, I can see why some Europeans are viewed as ugly with their perspiring faces and sweat-clammy suits. We blow our noses in pieces of cloth and carry 'it' around in our pockets.

In earlier times especially we were said, by the Chinese, to stink, largely because the western diet is rich in meat and other protein. Like the French who speak of l'odeur de male or parfum de femme, the Chinese, with their men's smell and women's fragrance, pay regard to flesh odour. Their language in some ways is more descriptive than English, not only of aromas. For example, different characters are used to describe how objects are carried: including on a pole by one man, on a pole by two men, on the back, cradled in the arms, or at arms length by the side.

Beings alighting on earth from another planet would probably first conclude all humans were much alike. After all, everyone has two eyes, a nose and a mouth. Chinese too, are often seen by Europeans as stereotypes. The lovely oriental siren Anna May Wong, and the evil, slit-eyed Oriental, Fu Man Chu, were both Hollywood celebrities between the two World Wars.

I was still in the buff and staring in the mirror. On my right stood an imaginary, dark-eyed Cantonese. He was naked too. The ivory skin of his chest had tufts of hair on it resembling sparse, pampas grass. But as fascinating as generalisations are China is a large country and its people diverse. Yet it is from the south of

China that most overseas Chinese originate. Any self-respecting person of Chinese descent should, in theory, be able to trace his family back to the dawn of history, to the mythical Yellow Emperor, Huang Ti, the progenitor of the nation, who, legend has it, lived in a small town alongside 'China's Sorrow', the muddy Yellow River, the country's second longest after the Yangtze.

But China is the country with the world's longest frontier, and covers nine-tenths the area of Europe. Hence the bigger, fairer skinned, humorous northern Chinese can differ as much from the often swarthy Southerner as the Italian contrasts to the Scandinavian. Indeed with cultural intermixing over centuries a Cantonese is often more akin to a Vietnamese or a Thai than to a Pekingese. The snake-eating, spendthrift Cantonese are vigorous, enterprising, adventurous, carefree and quick-tempered. Yet to many Westerners the Chinese all look alike. Of course, this is partly due to their physical shape, but it may also be because of their innate 'Chineseness' and their so called inscrutable appearance.

However psychologists stress that, in many ways all men are the same; in other respects some are the same; yet all persons are still unique. The southern Chinese are proud and they believe that they are intellectually superior, even if because of size they are physically inferior to Westerners.

Compared to a European the coarser black haired, dark eyed, smaller framed southern Chinese differs as noticeably as the lilac from the lotus. A Cantonese often has prominent cheek bones with a low bridge to his negrito nose which has broad open nostrils. These, some critical Westerners will tell you, do not enhance the appearance of what can otherwise be a pretty, female, 'goose-egged shaped' face with 'skin as clear as jade and body slim like a willow tree'. Most Chinese lack prominent laughter-lines and wrinkles, largely because they keep a straighter countenance and do not grimace so much as the average Caucasian. Nostrils represent ponds and hair in them correspond to leaves and trees and should not droop into them and obstruct the flow of water, signifying money. Although hair should be pruned in the nostrils it should not be cut on the ears where it connotes long life.

Also the skin of an average (described as 'with round skull and square toes') middle-aged Chinese is often yellowish and creaseless, and even working-class women have soft, silky, unblemished, almost polished, nether parts. There is little body hair and a hairless mons veneris is by no means unknown.

'Daughters of the Yellow Emperor' also have mouths like cherries, thin curved moth-like eyebrows and single eyelids with an epicanthic fold. At least that is what the poets tell us. For attributes like bound feet, beauty depends a great deal, we accept, on cultural background. Nevertheless the desire to conform to western ideals, with a bridge to the nose and deep-set, big round eyes – although the sleek 'phoenix eyes', with over-arched, feathery eyebrows of traditional Chinese beauties are famous – has meant a boom for plastic surgeons. Their task is to create double eyelids from lidless eyes. Double eyelids give a sense of bigness, high spirits, feeling and affection.

Young, delicate, sylph-like girls coyly cover their mouths with their hands when they laugh, and the Chinese exclaim, 'See teeth don't see eyes,' when someone guffaws. Meanwhile, in my room I push my skin with thumbs and forefingers so my eyes appear like two slashes made with a sharp knife in a taut tilt. Childishly I mumble to myself, 'This is my Chinese face ... and this is my Caucasian face!'

Half way between my own reflection and that of the imaginary, naked Chinese is a third figure, a Eurasian. He is the kind of offspring I would have sired if my second marriage had been so blessed. It is easy to discern features in this illusory Anglo-Chinese which originated across the 'four seas', from another soil in sub-tropical China. There are those eyes my wife would have given him, that black, thick head of hair, and the smooth, shave every other day, skin and a body genetically built to excel.

Generally, too, most Chinese believe Asians are more open-minded, patient, self-disciplined, ambitious, fatalistic and that they adopt a more philosophical approach to life, compared to Europeans. Chinese are also less in need of psychiatry. It would also appear that their incidence of left-handedness is lower than ours in the West although this could be partly because they are corrected as children.

Now, with the Chinese and his high 'quaintness quotient' (as defined by a 'barbarian' Westerner), compared to my own image, with the Eurasian coming halfway between, our three physiques in the mirror are worlds apart. But with Eurasians, who sometimes appear European when they are with Chinese and Chinese when they are mixing with Europeans, it is not always so.

'I'm really Eurasian,' a well adjusted, personable, young man, with no apparent identity crisis, once remarked at a United States, Asia Society luncheon.

I had taken him to be pure Chinese. 'I reckon my chances, with an English mother and a Chinese father, of looking Chinese, were about 25 per cent.'

Likewise, he calculated the odds on appearing more or less like a European are the same, with a 50 per cent gamble on being born somewhere between, with the looks of a true Eurasian. In Hong Kong, in line with *Qing Dynasty* law, a man could take any number of concubines or secondary wives. A wealthy Chinese in the 1930s was welcomed to the United States with the newspaper headlines: 'Here comes the man with twenty wives!' Another wealthy Chinese businessman and tin merchant, at about the same time, had ten wives, including one Italian, one French, one English and one German.

There is much to be said for many Chinese customs. Instead of the 'old gentleman' gallivanting around at night, and the wife not knowing where he is, with a young concubine he is ready to come home in the evening. When number one wife is barren, or only able to bear daughters, or no longer interested in sex, concubinage is a solution. As principal wife her position within the family is safeguarded. With that well-known Eurasian the late Sir Robert Ho Tung, his first wife had the final say in choosing the second wife. The two were considered 'equal wives', although, legally, this was not strictly so.

But although taking concubines was not declared illegal in Hong Kong until 1971, it is so entrenched in history that tacit acceptance is often given to affairs which somehow seem less shocking over there. With older Chinese often saying that they had two (or more) 'mothers', it is not surprising many offspring, who are all entitled to the same inheritance rights from their father, do not resemble one another. But with Eurasians, even with the same father and mother, some siblings can still look quite European and others Chinese.

One lighthouse keeper, who appeared almost a pure Westerner, used to surprise strangers by singing stylised, Cantonese songs with perfect tonal accent and Chinese expressions. He was, in fact, a Hong Kong-born Eurasian.

But it is not all in the genes. By living in a changed environment, especially during the formative years, one's old self fades and a different being gradually emerges. Founding father Lee Kuan Yew, past Prime Minister of Singapore, raised the poser of nature versus nurture. In a speech to mark his sixtieth birthday he hypothesised what might have happened if he had had an identical twin who had been raised in Hong Kong. Lee asked whether his 'sib' would have applied himself steadfastly to the pursuit of wealth, Hong Kong style, or if he would have set similar altruistic aims as he, Kuan Yew, has. 'Would my "twin" have rebelled against the British?' Lee questions.

Not only a person's intellect, emotions, sociability, activity level, and even aspects of morality, are affected by genes and environment, we are told. Race plays a part. The brain is composed of two hemispheres and psychologists have hypothesised that Westerners, left-handers excepted, are mainly left-lobe thinkers. This means they tend to think by employing a sequential, systematic, thought pattern, step by step, using a more scientific and logical approach. According to the theory of Chinese cosmic forces mentioned earlier, this is the outer-oriented, *yang*, male principle.

Contrastingly some researchers, such as neurologist Huang Chen-ya and other Hong Kong University academics, believe Chinese use the right lobe of the brain cortex to receive signals to process their complicated, ideographic, tonal language. Those of us who were reared on the phonetic alphabet of the West largely use the left temporal lobe to learn our mother tongue, Dr Wilder Penfield, a Canadian neuro-surgeon tells us. The right lobe is used for learning foreign languages. Such factors affecting the two races have other, overall, effects.

Consequently, the Chinese are mainly right-hemisphere thinkers. With this *yin*, female, approach, they tend to view problems in wholes, rather than in parts, with simultaneous thought processing. They synthesise rather than analyse and believe you cannot comprehend totality properly by becoming absorbed in detail.

If all this is true how does the Chinese fit in who is brought up in a western environment, in California or Cardiff, with a different set of experiences? Has the Eurasian a dual or split personality? The fact that women are said to have more fibres connecting the two hemispheres of their brains so that they, too, see problems from all angles giving rise to, so-called, women's intuition complicates the issue further. As a result of these physiological variations women tend to have greater social skills and select different roles to men. The latter make better chess players and possess stronger spatial and three-dimensional perception.

With this weighty subject on my mind I switched off the light and went to sleep.

WITH warm sunshine streaming through the curtains and the 'chirp, chirp' of sparrows I lay in bed looking forward to my visit to the British Museum.

In spite of a turbulent history China can trace its continuous civilisation back to the Hsia Dynasty, from 2205 to 1766 BC, although these dates are not confirmed by archaeology. The Chinese civilisation was not the first to grace the earth but it has been the most enduring, although it can be argued that, during the Mongol Conquest (1279–1368), it ceased, as such, to exist. Even if the Middle Kingdom developed a culture that has never really been exported to the West it was probably the greatest pre-industrial society the world has ever seen. 'Its literature goes back 3,000 years!' a huge headmaster friend of mine never tired of telling his western pupils.

In fact, work on the most ancient surviving classic, the *Book of Changes* or *I Ching*, dates from about 2800 BC, although the oldest extant commentaries were written nearer to 1300 BC. This book, dealing with prognostication, fortune telling and philosophy, has been banned by the People's Republic: in order not to 'harm society and poison people's thoughts'. This contrasts with the views of James Legge (1815–97), the Oxford scholar who translated it in 1882. He admired its wisdom and suspected the authors had used divination as a pretext for teaching their philosophy. In turn the Nobel Prize-winning Danish physicist, Niels Bohr (1885–1962), recognised parallels between the concepts of the *I Ching* and those of modern atomic science.

The Chinese anticipated the 'invention' of printing by Gutenberg and Caxton by five centuries. They invented paper – including perfumed toilet paper for the Imperial family in the fourteenth century – the compass, the making of steel and drilling for natural gas. They invented gunpowder, concocted mistakenly while looking for the elixir of life, which has since placed the world in a frightful mess. They developed intensive agriculture.

Other firsts include the use of coal, mechanical clocks, suspension bridges and lock gates. They also invented deep-drilling techniques, flame throwers, church bells and fishing reels, efficient horse harnesses which did not choke the poor beasts, porcelain and map grids, paddle-wheel boats, watertight compartments and rudders; just to relate a few. The first toothbrush was made in China in the year 959 and 'reinvented' in Italy in the seventeenth century. Even the gondolas of Venice are, some believe, copies of China's Dragon Boats the design of which was brought back by Marco Polo.

The Chinese observed Halley's Comet as early as 467 BC. It is believed Jin De discovered Jupiter had satellites nearly 2,000 years before Galileo was given the credit, and Chinese Buddhists, led by Fa-Xien (337–422), arrived in the Americas 1,000 years in advance of Columbus. It is likely they landed between today's Los Angeles and Acapulco, in AD 412. Rockets were invented in China about 1150, and, later, astronaut Wan Hu attempted to fly to the moon in a chair propelled by rockets and was killed in the attempt. Joseph

Needham, the Cambridge sinologist who has spent half a century piecing together the history of science and technology in China, believes the rocket was probably China's most important technological contribution.

Discoveries and inventions by China, some listed above, had time lags of hundreds or even thousands of years before they were 'reinvented' or adopted by the West. Steel, for example, was manufactured from cast iron, and row cultivation of crops and intensive hoeing were both, it is estimated, carried out in China 2,000 years before they were introduced in the West.

One of the biggest attractions for the sinologue at the British Museum is the Stein collection. Depending upon one's views, Sir Aurel Stein (1862–1943), the explorer, either ruthlessly plundered the Silk Road or saved invaluable artefacts from total decay. He brought back to England 14,000 Chinese documents dating from the fifth to the tenth century. These included pieces of the world's oldest newspaper, a recipe for hair tonic and the diary of a veterinary who was in charge of horses on the Great Wall.

However the *Diamond Sutra*, one of the five most valuable possessions of the British Museum, is the main attraction. A scroll, the colophon of which bears the date 11 May 868, is believed to be the world's oldest printed 'book'. It was rescued from the sandstone Cave of the Thousand Buddhas, in Dunhuang, Gansu Province, and presented to the British Museum in 1907 by Sir Aurel. This priceless ninth century scroll, measuring 5.1 metres by 25.6 centimetres, with an elaborate frontispiece which is the earliest known woodcut in a printed work, contains a Chinese text translated from Sanskrit. The bound *Book of Psalms* discovered in Egypt dates back 1,600 years, but this, sometimes called the *Book of King David*, is handwritten.

Art, where colours were used 1,000 years before Christ, has been the soul of China. It is beautiful, dignified and stately. The Chinese delighted countless people with some of the most beautiful pottery ever made. However for literature, philosophy and culture, partly because the language is not easy to translate, beauty and meaning are often lost and they have not always been judged fairly in the West. Although China has a contribution to make in the modern world there have been few Chinese Nobel Prize winners.

With the glory of China's past also comprising important crafts and inventions, why then did the Industrial Revolution commence in the eighteenth century in Britain and not in the thirteenth or fourteenth century in the Middle Kingdom when she was well ahead of Europe? Then, it would have been possible, although since, China has made few technological contributions to the world.

Some researchers believe the Industrial Revolution did not materialise in China because there was abundant, cheap, efficient labour, and, although there was rapid technological development from the eighth to the twelfth centuries, this then slowed. There was limited demand for industrialisation and change. The profit motive which forms the basis for capitalism was more firmly established in China than in Europe before the Protestant work ethic became accepted. Joseph Needham has blamed state policies and the bureaucratic system for China's failure to achieve a breakthrough. The Middle Kingdom once led the world. Although she has still not come entirely to terms with the modern age she could do so again. The saying attributed to Napoleon Bonaparte: 'China? There lies a sleeping giant. Let him sleep! For when he wakes he will move the world,' may well come true.

Because the country failed to develop technologically many Chinese found conditions better overseas and some travelled or emigrated illegally, although this was a capital offence in China until 1893. But this law, like many others, was not properly enforced. Consequently, one reads of 'Chinamen' residing in England in the late eighteenth and early nineteenth century. However, it was not until the 1850s that numbers really increased.

Most were seamen, between nineteen and fifty years old, who had jumped ship or been paid off in Britain. In 1901 there were said to be 545, nothing like the numbers that settled in the United States. Figures vary. Other records quote that in England and Wales, in 1901, there were 387 Chinamen, not including ships' crews. This increased to 1,319 in 1911. By then, they could be found in every county except Hereford, Rutland and Westmorland. The 302 who lived in London were mainly government officials from China, domestic servants or students.

There were said to be 100,000 Chinese in France during World War II, digging trenches for Allied troops. Of the 2,000 or so of these who died in Western Europe only six were buried in Britain. These lie, with both English and Chinese inscriptions on their gravestones, in the Shorncliffe Military Cemetery near the former military hospital above the Channel port of Folkestone. All Chinese who served with the Allies were awarded a War Medal although these have become rare and collectors' items.

Looking at individual Chinese who made their homes in Britain: Mak Kam-tong was born in Hong Kong in 1899, when the Manchus ruled his homeland and men wore pigtails. At sixteen, he took part in an uprising in southern China calling for the overthrow of the first President, General Yuan Shih-kai, who sought to make himself a dictator. But the rebels were forced to flee and Mak arrived in Plymouth in April 1915. 'I expected to return home in a year or so,' he said.

Little did he realise then, that he would eventually marry a British girl and have three children. Uncle Mak, as he was affectionately called, opened a restaurant in Londonderry, Northern Ireland, in 1961.

In the 1920s the main Chinese settlements were at Bristol, Liverpool, Cardiff and Limehouse, all ports. But though the last survived the World War II Blitz, that part of London's East End Dockland has since been partially redeveloped. There are now modern buildings and bright red and blue carriages on its light-rail system. Yet parts of the district, along Commercial Road, are still derelict and dirty.

Although signs are not in Chinese, Canton Road, Ming Street and Amoy Place, among others, may still be seen, together with Chinese restaurants, like 'The Taipan'. Coloured people, children of a defunct empire, wander the streets.

After an unsuccessful search in Limehouse for Chinese names on gravestones, I sidled up to a Chinese shuffling past the church. 'Lived in England long?' I asked.

This took him aback when I repeated my question in Cantonese. The old chap, who had dark, bewildered eyes and wore a shabby, heavy overcoat, had come from Hong Kong. He worked as a cook in a Chinese restaurant. He had never heard of Ming Street or Canton Road and spoke little English. 'Live here twenty years,' he told me in staccato barks.

Looking at him, a 'marginal man' if ever there was one, it was not difficult to see why Chinese are considered more mysterious and exotic than Arabs or Africans. He did not belong, even in this old Chinese haunt of Limehouse. I could imagine him in a paddy field in subtropical Guangdong, where the Chinese cosmic cycle keeps everything in tune.

By 1951, Ng Kwee-choo writes in his thesis, *The Chinese in London*, there were 1,763 China-born Chinese, 4,046 Malaya-born and 3,459 Hong Kong-born Chinese in the United Kingdom. Many ran small businesses like laundries. The establishing of restaurants commenced in a bigger way after 1950 when the British eating public became more venturesome. One thing foreigners have done is diversify the food.

The first big wave of Chinese immigrants, seeking a better life after the collapse of farming in the New Territories, came from Hong Kong between 1958 and 1962, to work in restaurants. A second big wave got underway, to the New World and Europe, as a result of the riots in Hong Kong in 1967. Although these were masterminded from within the Colony, these 'Disturbances', as the Government euphemistically called them, were a spillover from the Great Proletarian Cultural Revolution in China. Hong Kong life was frequently brought to a standstill by cropped-haired militants, wearing white, cotton shirts, sensible sneakers and brandishing clenched fists.

You can argue of course that, on occasion, radicalism is required. Society has to be shaken and changed. We need to embrace new ways. The Margaret Thatcher years in Britain, in the 1980s, was an example, albeit in a very mild form.

Certainly revolutions in China are nothing new. There was the coup d'etat by the Dowager Empress following the Hundred Days Reforms of 1898, the decisive rising by the Nationalists in 1911, and the May 4th Movement in 1919. Nevertheless in 1967, during a 'high tide' of Maoism, people left Hong Kong to avoid violence – and the drought, with water on tap during July and August for only four hours once every four days. The 1967 riots claimed 51 lives and left nearly 1,000 injured. There were 8,000 suspected and 1,000 genuine bombs. But although many emigrated, the masses remained in Hong Kong.

'If the Chinese marched past four abreast, with babies being born, the spectacle would never end,' my teacher staggered me by saying in the 1920s.

By the mid 1950s, there were supposed to be 8.5 million wives in China whose husbands were working overseas. Like the British, whose empire fanned out across the globe, the Chinese diaspora reaches all corners of the world. The total number resident outside China proper, including in Taiwan and Hong Kong, approaches 50 million; almost equal to the population of Britain. The population of China now stands at 1.2 billion, in excess of 21 per cent of mankind.

Today, the number of Chinese living in the United Kingdom is somewhere between 100,000 and 200,000 and numerous towns, with populations of 5,000 or less, have Chinese restaurants, Chinese-run fish and chip shops, or takeaways. A commonly quoted figure is 140,000. It depends who you count. Is a person who is one-quarter Chinese included? 'Anybody with a drop of Chinese blood is coloured,' an elderly American lady told us, in 1959.

'That's our interpretation too,' a Chinese in our group, shipbound for the United States, laughed and shot back.

'Anyone with a little white blood in his veins is white!' About one-third of the Chinese in the United Kingdom today reside in London, but Manchester, with 40,000, now rivals the capital and has overtaken Liverpool as the North's biggest and fastest growing Chinese centre. It boasts an authentic Chinese arch, costing

£350,000, and some of the best restaurants outside East Asia. Other important centres are Glasgow, Edinburgh, Bristol and Sheffield.

The Chinese population in the United Kingdom consists of about 70 per cent Cantonese and 25 per cent Hakka. The remaining 5 per cent hail from, or their families originated from, further north – from places like Shanghai. The Hakka, meaning 'guest family', formed the last big wave of migration from the north, inside China. They arrived in Canton Province about the beginning of the Ming Dynasty (AD 1368). Overseas Chinese usually group by dialects. Many Hakka live in Manchester. A large proportion of Chinese in Britain come from Hong Kong's New Territories.

This rapid build-up has taken place with limited conflict or ill feeling, which says much for the Chinese character. It has not always been easy.

A journalist on the *Morning Chronicle* reported on 27 July 1782, that one Sunday he saw a 'genteel dressed' man in a public house in Stepney rile a Chinese who was sitting quietly on a bench:

> '... he strove to provoke him by the most insulting language, which he bore with surprising patience; he then made remarks on his dress, at which the people, who were collecting very fast, imprudently laughed, and encouraged him to proceed; he next took hold of the Chinese man by the hair, though repeatedly requested by the genteeler part of the spectators to desist; deaf to reason, he imprudently continued to aggravate him by pulling his hair ...'

After being incensed, according to the article, the Chinaman ran indoors to summon help whereupon a dozen or so of his compatriots rallied around. The writer continued:

> '... in an instant [they] armed themselves with short bludgeons, kept by them seemingly for the purpose, for they had a large knob at one end, which they held in their right hand; the other end was up the sleeve that you could scarce perceive them armed; their hair they tied round their heads, in an instant, and rushed out in a body, but did not attempt to molest anyone, only formed a ring for the two combatants ...'

Thanks largely to Confucius (551–479 BC), the Socrates of the East, who would not have been out of place in an English public school, there are many 'rules for living', which, although not enforced like traffic regulations, act as guidelines for behaviour in ordered society. They cover conduct, from the 'Five Personal Relationships' (ruler and subject, husband and wife, father and son, elder and younger brother, friend and friend – the last is the only one between equals) to worshipping one's ancestors.

Children are taught self control. 'If a person spits in your face let it dry itself.' If you give someone a tongue-lashing not only do you lose face, but also, stung by your remarks, your victim may react in anger at you or other people. Nevertheless, the Chinese have been described as thermos flasks; cool on the outside and hot within. This was demonstrated in Hong Kong in the 1956, 1966 and 1967 riots.

Nonetheless most Chinese believe, inwardly, in facing up to things calmly. Time does not tick by in a straight line but in a spiral. If something is not completed today, or a deadline is missed, then later, on the helical of time, a similar opportunity will come within reach again. There is a period to live, and a moment to die, and, with the cycle of reincarnation, a time to be born again. What cannot be finished by a man and his sons will be completed by his grandsons. The secret of contentment is self-respect. To achieve that, self-control is necessary, even when horse dung was thrown at the Chinese in England in the post-World War II years.

To be fair, it is not entirely one-sided. Some Hong Kong Chinese are not backward in exploiting the underdog and giving other Asians a rough deal. A handful, which give the rest a bad name, have frequently been criticised for impoliteness and for overcharging tourists. Of course, cases are often exaggerated. Overseas, westernised Chinese are not spared when visiting Hong Kong, and to be told in Cantonese *mong boon*, 'forgotten your roots', is a big insult.

The Chinese, in some ways, are something like us English. They have a reputation for disliking foreigners and can be insular and condescending. As Lee Kuan Yew told the Singapore Parliament: 'I understand the Englishman. He knows deep in his heart that he is superior to the Welshman and the Scotsman. Deep here, I am a Chinaman. Yes, an uprooted Chinaman, transformed into a Singaporean.'

The Chinese knew throughout their long, continuous civilisation that their country was the centre of the universe. Others inhabited by 'barbarians' were inherently inferior.

Unfortunately, as we well know, differences between races and nationalities, which begin as 'tribal' loyalties and patriotism, can degenerate into chauvinism, and, later, into institutionalised racism. They breed hatred as in Northern Ireland; create 'ethnic cleansing' in what was once Yugoslavia and produce the anti-foreigner German People's Union.

'It's the uneducated who discriminate,' the aged restaurateur in Ulster, Mak Kam-tong, believed. Yet even when he first came to England, in 1915, in spite of fear of the 'Yellow Peril', most Britons were friendly towards Chinese, Mak insisted.

'We did not face the degree of discrimination often levelled against Pakistanis and West Indians.'

If a girl is small and cute, of any race, she can usually get away with it, even if there is the odd bawdy joke behind the back of the 'slant-eyed female', such as, 'Which way do the "tramlines" run?' But this is often 'dropped out', intentionally, within earshot of Chinese males to make them feel 'littler and yellower'.

In class-bound Britain dispersal and assimilation of minorities, although not always successful, have been aims; whereas in that huge melting pot of 'permissive differentiation', in the United States, large ghettos, namely Chinatowns, sprang up. That is, in spite of the infamous Oriental Exclusion Act of 1882 which banned immigration of unskilled Chinese workers. Only diplomats, merchants, teachers and students were allowed in. This was not repealed until 1943, when China and America were allies in World War II. Then, at last, Chinese living in the United States could become naturalised citizens. 'In 1940s, for the first time, Chinese were accepted by Americans as friends,' Harold Liu, long-time resident of the United States, was reported as saying.

Nevertheless, in the mosaic of the United States in the 1990s, it is still easier for Chinese to be 'invisible' and to retain their ethnicity than for those living in smaller countries, like Britain, with fewer non-Whites and with policies of integration. In England, there is a tendency to be offended by foreigners who do not wish to adapt and integrate.

Even British Columbians, in 1907, formed their 'Asiatics Exclusion League', although Canada today, like the United States, has striven to attract qualified and prosperous Chinese who can inject something into the economy. This policy, by a process of 'trickle-down economics', creates jobs and benefits the community. Uncle Sam, with approaching two million Chinese residents, has attracted more high-fliers than Britain, many of whom have made inroads into preserves traditionally occupied by European stock.

Chinese to reckon with in the New World include I.M. Pei, architect of the controversial Louvre glass pyramid in Paris, the John F. Kennedy Library in Boston, and the Bank of China, Hong Kong's landmark and one of the tallest buildings outside the United States. There are also a handful of American-Chinese Nobel Prize winners. They include Samual C.C. Ting, who received his award for physics in 1976, and Yuan T. Lee, who left Taiwan to work on his doctorate. He never returned and was awarded the 1986 Nobel

Prize for chemistry.

Every nation assimilates newcomers differently, but the eagerness of Chinese in the New World to take the oath, salute the flag and express American sentiments never ceases to surprise British sinologists.

The Chinese belong to the smallest of the principal minority groups in the United Kingdom. On arrival most are not Anglicised, and, because many have been brought up in a colonial environment the older ones, especially the majority of whom have received limited education, feel insecure and inferior in a white man's world.

Because 65 to 75 per cent of first generation Chinese in Britain are unable to speak passable English, and some who have lived there for thirty or more years have acquired only a smattering of the language, they are the least understood of the minorities. But still they remain proudly independent overseas. There they know, in alien surroundings, the British have the upper hand. Therefore, in a spirit of Confucian propriety with accent on deference, they attempt to avoid confrontation by adopting the 'no cause trouble' principle. To do this, many try to stay apart from the white man and isolate themselves from the unfamiliar language and customs.

In Chinese the family name, of which there are only said to be 438 – including 30 (figures quoted vary) consisting of two characters – is written first: for example Man Fong-yan. The most common name among Cantonese is Chan. But the most common 'under heaven' is Lee. The surname, Mr Man, is often followed by the generation name (all brothers or sisters have the same) and then the personal name. Occasionally, the order of the last two names is reversed. But because, when babies have been born overseas, personal names have sometimes been registered on birth certificates as family names, many Chinese have altered their name order, western fashion, so that 'ignorant' foreigners understand.

When abroad Chinese often work long hours, sleep in their restaurants or shops, have little entertainment and remit sizeable sums back to their families in Asia. Most try to keep problems within the family. Interference from the state is avoided as far as possible. 'When alive, don't enter the door of the judge: when dead, don't enter the gates of hell.' The Chinese are accustomed to their own informal system of welfare, based upon 'kinship networking'. There is an unwritten obligation to help one's extended family, clan or native village members. This avoidance of government assistance saves the state money with less social insurance payable.

Chinese societies have been described as 'shame oriented' (as opposed to 'guilt societies' as found in the West), largely because of the influence of Confucianism and humanism, where considerable import is placed on harmonious, interpersonal relationships. Confucius wrote that by 'disciplined guidance and regulations' people will be law abiding. But they will have no sense of shame. By setting virtuous examples, and teaching persons to conform, a sense of propriety will develop together with personality.

Although differences are not clear cut, shame can be defined as reprehensible behaviour and the transgression of social norms. Disgrace is suffered and face is lost by the entire family, especially the head. Conversely, in a European 'guilt society', a great deal depends upon one's own behaviour, failures, achievements, the preservation of personal standards and the infringement of moral principles.

When fraternising, a brash, outspoken Westerner needs to learn that giving a reticent, non-Anglicised Chinese a hearty slap on the back and enquiring, 'How's it going mate?', is not the way to win friends.

When a Chinese wants someone to do him a favour he is likely to arrange for a friend, as middleman, to intercede. Then, if the offer is refused, nobody loses face. A Westerner approached indirectly, under such circumstances, would likely ask, 'He's lost his tongue?'

Surprisingly, a Chinese sees nothing wrong in enquiring from a casual acquaintance, 'How much do you earn?' Such interest is appreciated. All cultures have a 'comfort level', and, to the average Englishman, such a question transgresses the acceptance line.

As customs go Asians are by nature 'sitters', and still largely work on the floor. Caucasians tend to be 'standers', for instance at a workbench, in a bar, or at a cocktail party. Asians prefer, sensibly, to drink sitting down. It is thus not surprising that an FOB, a 'fresh off the boat' Hong Kong New Territories' villager sometimes feels overwhelmed.

Because he knows more about the sage Mencius, than the English working man does about Chaucer, with uprooting and cultural disorientation, the overseas Chinese often looks to his past with nostalgia. He retreats into himself. With a husband at work, women are particularly vulnerable to, using sociologists' jargon, 'dislocation tribulations'. After a time depression and even insanity (disturbance of *chi*) have been known to develop and ailing relatives have sometimes been manhandled on to a Hong Kong bound flight.

Although a major attribute of immigrants is the will to succeed, a few are overcome by a sense of worthlessness. Years ago especially, many turned to gambling, opium and prostitutes for consolation. In an alien western society some Chinese live for a decade and never speak to a native. It is understandable, therefore, that the wish for one's remains to be buried in one's native soil and to have the characters for one's native district carved on one's tombstone are more important than the desire to learn an alien tongue. Adjustments in a foreign land can be painful. Not everyone yearns to become a pale imitation of a demure Englishman.

Even though stereotyping can be misleading and prejudicial, Chinese living on the fringes of society, often enduring injustices in silence, are frequently seen by Westerners as complex, diffident, unknowable, sly and even dangerous. But acceptance is a two-way process. A Chinese may not find it easy to 'belong' where little interest is shown in the Lion Dance or birds' nest soup.

Notwithstanding, some maintain discrimination varies with the darkness of the skin; others believe inscrutable Chinese are the least assimilable of the ethnic minorities. There are no Chinese Members of Parliament to represent them and only four Black and Asian MPs. Proportionally, around thirty would be needed to match the 4.7 per cent share of the total coloured population.

David Nam, a Welsh-born Carmarthen Rural District Councillor, in the mid 1980s was the first ethnic Chinese politician in Britain. He was elected by an all-white electorate who, interestingly, said they saw him as a Welshman. More Nams are needed.

Surveys have revealed that administrations have failed to impart information to minority groups on subjects such as welfare, including health and unemployment benefits, taxation, housing and immigration. The Chinese themselves are also to blame because of the low profile they adopt. Thus, in addition to their inability to communicate in English and their ignorance of simple law, they do not understand what their rights are. One elderly Chinese, who was disabled in a car crash fourteen years earlier, had been living a hand-to-mouth existence simply because nobody had brought the case to the authorities attention.

The Chinese community in Britain is still relatively small, at approximately 0.25 per cent. 'Once a minority exceeds about 3 per cent of the total population cases of destitution can begin to appear,' stated Wang Gungwu, Vice Chancellor of the University of Hong Kong.

Minorities are the first to suffer in a recession. Not complaining and providing self-help are commendable. Most Chinese are a credit to themselves and the community. However, 'They have yet to learn', a social worker admonished, 'it's not shameful to seek assistance outside their own, comparatively well-off, group.'

Employing 'networks' among themselves, the business-oriented Chinese often try to be self-sufficient and not to compete against Britons. With such restrictions together with their own, often limited, qualifications, running a small business is sometimes the only employment option. Almost 90 per cent still work in restaurants, in special groceries, food distribution and allied trades. Undoubtedly, catering still serves a useful avenue. The trade has also shifted up-market. Other Chinese run travel companies, car-hire firms, gambling dens and insurance agencies. Some are able to bridge the divide and more Chinese are now moving outside their own circle and are employed by Whites. In 1984, Peter Wong was judged the most successful insurance salesman in Britain.

A few Chinese textile entrepreneurs in the United Kingdom employ white workers. But they soon learn that the work culture and philosophy of unions, including demarcation, longer holidays and shorter hours, are different to those in the East.

Although few originated from the New Territories, there are of course, among others, Chinese doctors, dentists, lawyers, architects, surveyors, bankers, teachers and managers in Britain. Yet they, too, often prefer not to compete with natives, and Chinese employed in western firms are more likely to be found in functional posts, such as accounts or work study, rather than in line management.

But even for a professional who displays high standards of education, training and diligence, to win respect and become accepted by neighbours in a select white district is not always easy. Similarly, it is by no means simple for an ordinary Chinese to find suitable lodgings.

BESIDES employees, businessmen, managers and professionals, there have been Chinese students in Britain for many years. Ku Hung-ming, who died in South-west China in 1928, was one of the earliest. As narrated in *On a Chinese Screen*, he was visited in retirement by Somerset Maugham, near the Upper Yangtze River with no railway within 1,000 miles, and from where you could see 'the snowy mountains of Tibet'.

Ku was born in 1857, and was taken at the age of about ten to Edinburgh by a Scottish friend of the family. He obtained his Master of Arts degree there in 1877, after having studied Latin, Greek, mathematics, philosophy and English literature. Later, he studied in Leipzig and Paris. Maugham, whose details of Ku do not always reconcile with those given in Howard Boorman's *Biographical Dictionary of Republican China*, recounts that the tall old man with a pigtail spoke English and German with facility.

Ku was appointed Secretary at the Ministry of Foreign Affairs in Peking in 1905 (the year Imperial Examinations were abolished in

China), and he served in Shanghai in 1908. Afterwards, Ku lived for a time in Hong Kong. Much of his later life was spent writing and lecturing. One of the greatest authorities on Confucian learning, he advocated Confucianism for Europe in 1915, as a substitute for Christianity, to cure British 'mob-worship' and German 'might-worship'. Ku, who some accused of occasionally lacking common sense, was a trenchant critic of the westernisation of China in spite of his own international background. His first wife was Japanese. He had several disputes with European and American missionaries and maintained that Chinese intellectuals despised foreigners. There was, Ku said, no middle class, and thus, democracy was not desirable for China.

According to Maugham, 'he [Ku] was not displeased to say a slightly disagreeable thing'. 'Your countrymen deal only with coolies and compradores,' Ku once told him. 'They think every Chinese must be one or the other ... when you lived in caves and clothed yourselves with skins we were a cultured people.'

Although Ku himself was largely European-educated he was highly critical. He maintained that Chinese students come back from the West and try to destroy overnight the world's oldest civilisation.

Certainly democracy means different things to different people. 'Our views on "freedom" are quite different to those advocated by persons educated in Hong Kong,' a seventy-year-old friend, who went to school and college in China, explained to me in 1992. But even if western education is popular, because 'a monk from afar can pray better', not all Chinese parents are in favour because of 'lack of discipline overseas'.

In turn, university students question their lecturers about Magna Carta and ask why the British fought the 1982 Falklands War to give freedom to 2,000 white farmers. The young, yellow skinned idealists know, in spite of all they learn in the West about the merits of the Westminister system of government, that for British-born, Hong Kong Chinese to obtain a full British passport is difficult. Although the majority believe most things depend on the size of one's bank account, most are clannish and still proud to be Chinese.

When I was doing post-graduate work at Manchester University in 1971–72, a bunch of Hongkongers, the 'material for making rafters and beams' after their return to the Territory, used to occupy a table in the refectory. But because I can speak Cantonese I was 'accepted' by the group. There we discussed world problems and how storms with winds of 100 miles an hour cause havoc in Britain.

'Typhoon Wanda struck Hong Kong head-on, in 1962,' one

commented. 'Gusts of over 160 miles an hour.'

'*Typhoon Rose* scored a direct hit in 1972 with similar speeds and broke an anemometer,' chipped in another.

Notwithstanding, transportation and communications return almost to normal within a few hours of the passing of the eye of a tropical cyclone.

Conversations among my Hong Kong group at Manchester frequently centred on China. We discussed patients who had had their penises sewn back on, or 'reconstructed' after accidents. New 'bazookas' are assembled from flesh, tissue and skin cut from parts of their own bodies. Later, most of the patients are able to father children.

At Manchester, I became friendly with one Chinese who seldom wrote home. 'My father's a coolie' (*foo lik*, meaning 'bitter strength'), he told me frankly. 'Both my parents are illiterate. Very inconvenient; they have to pay a professional writer to respond to me.'

My friend had almost completed his doctorate.

'What we Chinese lack in language ability we make up in diligence,' he insisted. 'The average Britisher studies five days a week. We work seven.'

Although Asians are seen as 'nerds' and inferior by some Europeans, by others they are viewed as bookworms and superior, with higher intelligence quotients, and thus threatening. With their concept of shame it is a big loss of face if a Chinese student, most of whom are good at abstract reasoning, mathematics and science, fails his examinations.

Their weakness in English often means they concentrate more on imitation rather than creativity. And such factors coupled with reticence has often led to them being labelled invisible. This is compounded by the fact that Chinese students present fewer discipline problems. Because they keep quiet teachers often assume they understand. Whereas, in fact, they may lack the verbal skills and be too shy to ask questions.

With Confucian emphasis on intellect and learning, and Cantonese believing 'local ginger is not hot', many Hong Kong students go overseas to further their studies. In 1991, there were about 11,000 in Britain. Parents are prepared to struggle, borrow and 'invest' large sums to educate their brighter offspring. For the less fortunate family they expect this will allow them to break out of their social class, as with the coolie's son studying at Manchester, and they will attain wealth and prestige. Some Hong Kong pupils go to British preparatory schools and then on to famous public schools. There they learn to speak with 'plums in their mouths' and to use four-letter words, which, to an Old China Hand who has been exposed to 'Chinglish', sounds, to say the least, unnatural.

'Gentlemen' in England study 'ideas', preferably antiquated ones. 'Players' study 'things', like engineering. Similarly, Chinese believe, it should be 'Chinese learning for the essentials; western learning for practical application'. A study in Hong Kong revealed that the rate of return on investment in tertiary education is greater there than in any other place, with the possible exception of Singapore. Chinese parents often hedge their bets. One son in Hong Kong may join a well-paid profession which has status, such as law; another studies medicine in Britain; a third reads business administration in the United States, and so on.

Chinese culture basically teaches the acceptance of adversity, and, if necessary, pain. Perhaps that is why their reaction to suffering is said to be different to Westerners and their threshold of pain higher. Chinese culture emphasizes stoicism. Work is not an unmentionable word. 'Only permit success!', the Chinese teacher's voice shrills. Even primary schools are strict about homework which is usually excessive by western standards. Children are told the ageless tale of the tired student who wanted to study. 'He placed a spike under his chin to prevent himself from nodding off.'

With time, a student may find the quest for knowledge becoming an addiction or a perversion. 'Almost like a sexual passion,' one of my own tutors once insisted. But after a while Chinese pupils abroad learn that education in the West means less homework. Rote learning is spoken disparagingly of by most European teachers. However the late F.S. Drake, past Professor of Chinese at Hong Kong University, explained in the mid 1950s that, in addition to being good memory training for some subjects such as Chinese language, rote learning is useful.

The average university graduate can write about 7,000 characters the most complicated of which, 龥 (pronounced *yuh*, meaning request or implore), has thirty-two strokes. These are written, traditionally, using a brush and black ink, in the correct order. Although there are in the region of 50,000 pictograms or ideograms many are no longer or seldom, used. The world's oldest writing is said to have been found in an excavation in Henan Province, in the form of 8,000-year-old inscriptions on animal bones and tortoise shells.

After Chinese students become accustomed to western life, and they see Coca-Cola and American fast foods are the same the 'civilised' world over, most settle down. They consistently do better than most minority groups. In a test conducted jointly by the *South China Morning Post* and the London *Sunday Times* in 1991, Hong

Kong's seven-year-olds out-performed pupils from England and Wales, France, the Netherlands, Trinidad, and Tobago in arithmetic. Francis Leung of the Department of Curriculum Studies, at Hong Kong University, put the success down to stress on memorisation and the importance placed on formal education in Chinese culture.

'Standards in countries such as Hong Kong and Japan are way ahead of those in (British) classrooms,' Senior Research Fellow Professor Sig Prais, at the National Institute of Economic and Social Research, was reported as saying. Although inevitably a few Chinese take drugs and become problem students while abroad there are countless outstanding examples. Wong Ka-lok topped her class in physics at Imperial College in 1991.

Born in 1968, Tse Yuen-har has been almost totally blind since infancy. Nevertheless, she managed to pass ten O-levels and three A-levels in which she scored two 'A's and a 'B'. At Exeter she was top of her year, with first-class honours, and managed to tuck away two extra awards for achievement. Today, she sits at her work-station at Rolls-Royce's factory, near Watford, with her face almost touching her computer screen. Her aids include a talking calculator, a braille printer and a machine for drawing diagrams which she can trace with her fingers.

Yuen-har's parents run a Chinese takeaway in Crawley, Sussex. They speak little English. As a blind woman aero-engineer, Hong Kong-born Yuen-har was presented with the Frink Award by the Princess of Wales in 1990, 'in recognition of what she has done to improve the quality of life for the blind by achievement and example'.

By creating a 'learning culture' and encouraging children to study hard 'Hong Kong fathers have a lesson for us all,' a London head teacher was reported as saying. Like many Hong Kong Chinese they see the need to strive constantly if one wants to enjoy the 'Three Plenties' (sons, money and longevity) and relax among the 'Nine Heaven's Blessings' (high hills, mountain masses, topmost ridges, huge rocks, streams, the moon, the age of the southern hills, the sun, and the luxuriance of fir and cypress) in retirement.

CHAPTER THREE

CHINATOWN

A FTER another sound night's sleep, enjoying absolute peace in the middle of London, I strolled down to Piccadilly Circus where the statue of Eros, complete with wings and bow, balances precariously on the toes of one foot. Within a couple of days I shall be 'up-up-and-away' back to Hong Kong.

The Circus is small, compared with the almost 100-acre Tiananmen (Gate of Heavenly Peace) Square in Peking, believed by the Chinese in the old days to be the navel of the globe. There, well over one million people can assemble. That, to me, is the most impressive *piazza* in the world. It is also where, on 1 October 1949, delirious, acclaiming multitudes milled around to hear 'Great Helmsman' Mao proclaim in *Putonghua*, overlaid with an almost unintelligible Hunan accent: 'Chinese people have stood up ... nobody insult us again!'

In spite of its diminutiveness, and at times shambolic state, Piccadilly Circus has been termed the 'spiritual hub' of the Commonwealth. From Eros, numerous, imaginary spokes radiate to the far corners of what was the old Empire, of which all that remain are a few, small, dependencies like Bermuda, Gibraltar, the Cayman Islands and British Indian Ocean Territory.

Many of Her Majesty's subjects were taught that England was a land of daffodils and men in bowler hats, and that everyone was fair and honest even if it has become a land of impoverished gentry. Consequently, a Hong Kong Chinese friend of mine was shocked when he was conned by a couple of smart alecks in a confidence trick not far from Piccadilly.

Most London Chinese reside in districts like Bloomsbury, Camden or Islington. But the 1980s saw an upgrading of status, and a number of Chinese professionals and businessmen moved to up-market addresses like Hampstead, Saint John's Wood and Maida Vale.

There are no real 'Chinatowns' in Britain, like *Tong Yan Kaai* (Tang People Street) in San Francisco or Chicago which date back to the nineteenth century. But one of the 'spokes' from Piccadilly Circus radiates 300-odd yards to Gerrard Street, and, within this area, 'things Chinese' become evident. There are petite southern Chinese on the streets, the dots, hooks and variant brush strokes of artistic calligraphy adorn fasciae.

On the Soho side of Leicester Square are the *Man Fu* and a variety of other restaurants, and roads off Piccadilly Circus house Chinese shops. These businesses compete for attention with the theatres, cinemas and night clubs of the West End. The Chinese district covers about seven acres. Establishments include Chinese solicitors, and a school for mother-tongue teaching which imparts Chinese values and cultural identity to the second generation. Classes are held in the evenings and at weekends. There are also the Chinatown Youth Club, other community centres, printers and the offices of a Chinese newspaper.

Down the narrow side streets off Shaftesbury Avenue one can discern Chinese taxi companies, tailors and accountants. Most Chinese are hypochondriacs, and, to the delight of 'alternative medicine' buffs, there are herbalists, like *Hong Yuen* which opens seven days a week and provides herbs from China and includes medical advice. There are pharmacists, health food stores and acupuncturists – who treat complaints like eczema, allergies and motion sickness – as well as massage parlours and maso-therapy surgeries. Bonesetters, whom Europeans consult as a last resort, compete with Chinese western-trained doctors.

Alongside these practices Chinese cinemas show 'blue' ('yellow' in Chinese) movies. All Chinese establishments vie for space with western strip joints, sex shops and the sleaze of Soho. To Chinese, 'eating a plucked chicken' means having sex with a beautiful woman and the 'green spring' is a young girl who has strong sexual desires. A westernised, Chinese teenager in tights, with heavy makeup and puffing a cigarette, strides past. She would look absolutely out of place in Hong Kong.

'Ai...yaah!' a little girl with a melon slice of a grin exclaimed, followed by a few words of good English to her squat, presumably Cantonese parents. With two well rugged-up toddlers, the couple of adults wandered slowly past posters displaying bare bosoms and bottoms, together with an advertisement for Chinese recruits for the police force and another poster for a Chinese, knight errant, *kung fu* movie. This chivalric popular culture, with dextrous sword play, acrobatics and feats of strength, swept the Chinese world in the 1970s popularised by stars like Bruce Lee, born of a Eurasian mother and a Chinese opera-singer father.

If Vera had married her own kind instead of me she would have been less Anglicised, and she could have been strolling along in similar fashion to this family. But with Chinese believing 'all marriages are made in heaven' perhaps our espousal was inevitable. If my wife and I were to retire in England, with people joking and telling me, 'Of course you're half Chinese!', I could see us making regular visits to the nearest Britain has to a Chinatown. But the England I departed in 1954, when you left your shoes outside the hotel bedroom door to be cleaned by 'boots' before daybreak, was quite different to the England to which I would return.

You do not have to be a sinologist to know that the umbilicus of Chinese life, and the most popular meeting place and entertainment district in Britain, has to be blue Staffordshire brick-paved Gerrard Street, with its decorative lamp-posts. Here, English children marvel at the thirty-foot high, colourful, illuminated Chinese arches, incorporating green, skeleton roofs at each end, together with gold-knobbed, burgundy-coloured bollards. There is a third arch in Macclesfield Street. These markers contain the area as a pedestrian precinct. A telephone kiosk shaped like a pagoda has operating instructions in both Chinese and English. Here one can 'boil telephone *congee*', as long conversations are dubbed.

Although most Chinese in Britain wear western dress, children with red, padded jackets scampered around a Chinese-style, vermillion pavilion. Colour carries meaning. Red chases away evil and is worn much like an amulet. It is a *yang* colour and not a sign of danger. It not only looks good but 'protects' the wearer and 'attracts' good fortune. According to Chinese belief another lucky colour for me is yellow, based on the 'Five Elements' (fire, water, wood, metal and earth) and the fact that my date of birth coincides with 'earth'.

Neighbourhoods like the Borough of Westminster (translated as *Wong Sing* meaning 'Imperial City'), and Wardour, Lisle and Gerrard Streets, display names both in English and Chinese. These are translated either phonetically or etymologically. Originally,

Gerrard Street was to have been called *Tsui Wah* (Chinese Gathering Together) Street, or *Chek Lok* (Prosperity In Officialdom) street. Eventually, 'Noble Street' was decided upon. In Chinese, this sounds remotely like 'Gerrard'.

Edmund Burke (1729–97) the Whig statesman, and John Dryden (1631–1700) the poet and dramatist, once resided in stately homes in this thoroughfare. Hilaire Belloc (1870–1953) the poet, essayist and historian and G.K. Chesterton (1874–1936), the essayist, novelist and critic, used to meet nearby. Paul De Lamerie (1688–1751), the King's silversmith, lived and worked here from 1738 to 1751. What would these gentlemen's comments be if they could see Gerrard Street now?

Although the skyline here does not change as rapidly as that in Hong Kong, in pre-war London, not a city noted for speedy innovation, buildings were modernised on average every thirty years and replaced after sixty. However, in the early 1960s much of Gerrard Street, with its facades of yellowish, London-stock bricks or peeling paintwork were shabby and dilapidated. There were threats of demolition. From a few Chinese businesses paying low rents then, this main artery of Chinatown has gradually become classier and kept pace with the lifestyle of the more sophisticated, Chinese population. The Chinese Chamber of Commerce played its part.

Rents for many of the refurbished eighteenth and nineteenth century structures, which like old wives can be expensive to maintain, now approach those in districts like Regent Street. 'Mellowed' buildings like those in Gerrard Street belonged to our forefathers, and some will be handed down to our descendants unless we play them false. Most Chinese tend to argue, however, that a modern development can be used more efficiently.

At weekends in Chinatown, besides Europeans, Indian and other tourists, crowds of Chinese, some originally from Vietnam, congregate. They come from London suburbs and other parts of the country. There are many 'cross-cultural couples'. With safety in numbers a festival, almost carnival-like atmosphere prevails with spontaneous shouting and gaiety. Gerrard Street is a crowded focal point, a driving force in the community, undeterred by recession with a zip in the air something like Hong Kong.

A rubbish collection vehicle stands by. In the old China, because of respect for the written word, paper with characters on it was collected and incinerated separately. The ashes were disposed of reverently, in a 'respect for words pavilion'. No such treatment is accorded in Gerrard Street.

In Britain there are a limited number of expensive, northern

Chinese (Pekingese) restaurants, as well as Hong Kong and Singaporean establishments. In addition to the 'Chinatown' and 'Dragon Gate' there are names like *Tai Ka Lok*, meaning 'Big Happy Family', and 'Kowloon' and 'Garden', copied from Hong Kong. Both Cantonese and Vietnamese cuisines are available. In their windows three restaurants display Chinese-style roast pork and flattened, salty, preserved ducks that look as if they have been run over by a steamroller before being dried in the sun in a cool wind. There is also steamed goose and two kinds of spotted, spicy, preserved sausages. They are definitely an acquired taste.

Dim sum, meaning literally 'touch the heart', consisting of both savoury and sweet pastries with a variety of fillings, from prawns to sweet roast pork, and other delicacies, are also obtainable, usually for lunch. Just as a Briton often prefers an English to an Indian curry, so a variety of Hong Kong style buns and confectionery are obtainable around Gerrard Street district – like chewy 'old wives cakes'.

There is also a wet-fish shop, but with fish packed in ice and not swimming in tanks, Hong Kong style. A sign reads, 'No photos'. Why anyone would want to take photographs beats me. The Chinatown Fish and Meat Market, the 'Golden Gate Grocery' and the *Lung Fung* (Dragon and Phoenix) Supermarket all offer wide selections. These include staples like rice and less common items such as salt fish, bean jelly, bean curd, seasame oil and 'Iron Goddess of Mercy' tea that keeps you awake at night. Products arrive from Hong Kong, Taiwan, China and elsewhere in containers of all types, shapes and sizes. Many Chinese who swank around can afford the best. Items like fresh lychees and longans (literally 'dragons' eyes'), and stinky durians from Thailand, are expensive fruits. Tasting them brings back memories of native lands.

A large shop sells Mainland Chinese as well as Taiwanese books and magazines in addition to a variety of English publications, and one can browse to the strains of what has been described by Westerners as 'charmingly horrible' Chinese opera. Music is not always an international language. Some publications employ abbreviated Chinese characters which were introduced by the Communists, while Taiwan, like Hong Kong, still uses traditional ideograms which, although harder to learn, are more 'decorative' and preferred for calligraphy. The Chinese assistant in the bookshop spoke beautiful English. The *Sing Tao Daily News*, printed in the United Kingdom, *Hong Kong Playboy* with international nudes, and the *Peking Review* are all available, as well as treatises on out-of-fashion socialism produced on poor quality paper with inferior printing.

Free copies of Britain's bilingual Chinese magazine, *Si Yu*, which has a readership of about 100,000 are available. This is edited by a thirty-odd-year-old Briton, Simon Jones, and the copy I read contained articles like, 'One Life to Lead, Two Cultures to Live in', and a poem, 'Life as a Banana' (yellow outside white inside). Copies also contain advice, listings and advertisements.

Like the United Kingdom Government the Chinese in Britain, since 1949, have had little contact with the *Kuomintang* (Nationalists) in Taiwan. By contrast, the United States almost pretended the People's Republic did not exist, until the then President, Richard Nixon, sworn enemy of communism, met Chairman Mao, in 1972, in what Americans always described as 'Red China'.

Britain recognised the People's Republic as early as January 1950, just over three months after the veterans of the 3,000-mile Long March (1934/35) came to power. Diplomatic relations commenced between Britain and the People's Republic in 1954, although in the 1950s and 60s, little or no business was conducted and communications were largely the preserve of diplomats.

Ties between Britain and China were largely endorsed by United Kingdom Chinese. There were regular showings of People's Republic films in a theatre in Wardour Street even during the second half of the 1960s, the most hectic years of the Great Proletarian Cultural Revolution. After a film ended the audience would stand to pay its respects as the Communist National Anthem, *The Volunteers' March* or *The East is Red*, was played. Most, who are Chinese first, and whether Communists or Nationalists second, would not have readily done the same, either in Hong Kong or Britain, for *The Queen*.

Those with a limited command of English, rather than attending a local show or watching television (both useful as socialising agents for new immigrants), often prefer, within the bounds of Hong Kong 'packaged culture', to hire videos from a Chinese emporium. Such stores, with notices written in squiggly Chinese characters, do a roaring trade in 'ethnic TV'.

They also carry a variety of goods like Chinese records, cassettes, paintings, lanterns, paper umbrellas, chopsticks, effigies of Chinese gods, joss sticks, lucky, red paper stickers, antiques and kites shaped like brightly coloured dragonflies, eagles and butterflies. There are pairs of shiny 'Iron Balls', 'one of the three treasures from Baoding, China' which are manipulated around in one's hand so vital energy circulates along 'a network of passages' to cure a multitude of bodily complaints. 'Strengthen the ball players and make our country powerful,' instructions state.

Within the Gerrard Street environs one finds 'Tang's Salon Hair and Beauty', a bridal-gown centre Chinese-style, jewellers, fortune-tellers, Chinese arts and crafts shops, money changers, a branch of the Hongkong and Shanghai Bank (unlike most establishments in the district closed on Saturdays and Sundays), and a Chinatown Tourist Information Centre and travel agencies. There is also 'Eupo Air', run by William Man a member of Hong Kong's Man clan. He provides Chinese-speaking guides, if needed. The helpful young lady in the tourist information centre told me she had been educated in an English convent school and had never worn a *cheung saam*. My mother, who detests 'slit skirts', would be relieved.

On a day like that Sunday when I visited, street stalls, some selling fruit, had been set up. 'Give a free one to the first person to swim the Atlantic!' shouted a white Londoner, who, with common patter, was peddling yo-yos. A one-man band struck up an unholy din employing an unusual variety of percussion instruments, an accordion and a mouth organ.

I recalled on my previous visit to Gerrard Street the sweet aroma of burning sandalwood, from joss sticks with three-inch-long red ends, wafted across from a tiny earth-god shrine tucked away in a doorway. For some reason, this time the shrine had disappeared. Such deities formed part of folk religion among the Chinese, including sacrificial activities to door, kitchen and well gods, long before Buddhism was introduced from India on the traditional date of AD 67. Some insist it came to China up to 200 years earlier.

Yet even here in Westminister the 'Happiness and Virtue Loyal God', or 'Great Paternal Uncle', had been on duty protecting buildings and their inhabitants. One of the worst calamities that can happen is to be banished beyond range of communication with one's local guardian spirit. I wondered how inhabitants felt without the gods' protection. Instantly, I was transplanted to the temples of Hong Kong where the potent smell of joss sticks in an enclosed space can make you retreat and gulp down fresh air.

Not far from where this solitary earth-god shrine, in Gerrard Street, used to stand are two marble lions, with bells on their fronts and smirking faces. One, a male, plays with a ball under its paw. The other, a female, has a cub. Plaques in English and Chinese state they were donated by China Travel Service. There have never been lions in the wild in China. Consequently, Chinese lions do not always resemble closely the king of beasts. Many Americans, in fact, describe them as 'foo dogs'.

Close by a man wore a, 'I survived China Airlines!' T-shirt. I recalled my 1987 flight from Chengdu to Chongqing when one quarter of the seatbelts would not buckle and two dark-veined tiger butterflies flew around in the cabin. There were no life jackets under the seats and the crew member sitting on a folding stool appeared uninterested in safety. A government which metes out brutal treatment to its citizens is not so concerned about the odd air disaster. How will such attitudes affect Hong Kong?

'I work for Reuters,' a second young, urbane Chinese informed me. He carried a portable telephone and lolled against the female lion. He held several *Free China* booklets and had helped, so he claimed, to organise demonstrations in London on anniversaries of the Tiananmen Massacre. 'The world wants to forget those who died,' he lamented.

Such repression was inexcusable, although no government would have tolerated indefinitely having its main square occupied by belligerent students upset about price reforms, inflation and privileges handed out to Party leaders and their families. An army crackdown was inevitable. If the Chinese Administration could not control the Square it had lost the ability to govern. But it was the shocking brutality, the way the massacre was put down.

There are similarities between that paroxysm of violence and the Jallianwalah Bagh Massacre, at Amritsar in British India, when troops fired on unarmed Indians in 1919. Over 300 were killed and more than 1,000 injured, including women and children. There was, nonetheless, considerable support among the British at the time, both in India and England, for Brigadier-General Dyer who ordered the shooting.

In the case of the Peking Massacre there was a happier note. At the height of the protest student leaders Li Liu and Zhao Ming, holding copies of *Das Kapital*, were married in the Square. There was also a roaring trade in joss sticks and paper effigies. Had the uprising been successful the birth control programme would probably have been overturned.

Chinese minorities living overseas have a reputation for constituting separate societies largely because of cultural and language differences. Most Chinese are law abiding, often, to some extent, governing themselves and concealing impropriety. Inevitably, under such circumstances, criminal elements, including triads (secret societies or fraternal organisations), flourish. The ornate tong halls in American cities, like Chicago, where the Chinese years ago tried their own cases and disciplined offenders, are still there.

In earlier days, Chinese settlements in Asia and the West acquired reputations as places where the addicted, or the odd, curious Englishman, could smoke opium ('bite cloud' in triad jargon). That, together with tax evasion, gambling and protection rackets, was often looked upon as traditionally Chinese. The police often turned a blind eye to such delinquencies in what was, otherwise, a relatively peaceful society. Charles Dickens wrote about opium dens in East London and it is only comparatively recently that addiction has been accepted as an illness rather than weakness of will.

It would, after all, have been unusual if the Chinese had not smoked it as Britain went to war more than once, in the mid nineteenth century, to ensure it was allowed to sell opium in China. Not until the Communists came to power and campaigned fiercely against the 'seven evils' (drugs, prostitution, pornography, the kidnapping and sale of women and children, gambling, swindling through superstitions and triads) was the opium menace brought under control.

In spite of increasing crime rates in Britain as a whole, law and order are still better maintained there than in the United States where Chinese triads are more firmly entrenched. In cities like San Francisco and New York, for example, they are as grave a threat as the Italian 'Cosa Nostra'. The first triads, the *Wo On Lok*, came to England in the 1930s.

Although most Chinese in Britain, it is stressed, uphold the law, triad gangs, like the 14K which specialises in narcotics, the *Sun Yee On*, and the *Wo Sing Wo* which is the most powerful, make their evil presence felt in cities like London, Manchester, Birmingham, Glasgow, Cardiff, and Liverpool. It was estimated in 1988 that there were about 1,200 full-time triad members in Britain. In the days of the Empire being a member of a triad was not illegal, nor were such societies secret until the final decade of the last century. Even in Britain today, unlike in Hong Kong of course where there are approximately fifty large, active triad societies with their culture of violence, they are not illegal.

All operate in a sub-culture shrouded in mysticism, and over 500 expressions, such as 'crab' meaning wallet and 'hit raw pork' signifying a frame up, are used by members. Elaborately organised hierarchical initiation rites are performed in lodges which are festooned with banners and ancestral signs. Blood from the left index finger of each inductee used to be mixed with rice wine. Now, instead of sipping blood taken from up to thirty initiates in a communal bowl, to symbolise unswerving loyalty, because of the threat of AIDS each is allowed to suck blood from his own finger. A thirty-six-chapter oath, pledging both personal and family loyalty, and vowing not to seduce womenfolk belonging to another triad member, is sworn. The traditional penalty for contravening this pledge is death by a thousand cuts.

Members recognise one another by a variety of signs. With the 'Four Seas' surrounding the world, number 'four' is especially salient. The lodge leader is known as 489, the incense master as 438, while 'White Paper Fan', Number 45, is in charge of administration. 'Straw Sandal' liaises between lodges and 'Red Pole' organises fighting. Gang members, 'soldiers', are ruthless young thugs who have emigrated from Hong Kong and elsewhere in the East and terrorise Chinese shopkeepers and wealthy businessmen overseas. Some prey on their own clients.

This frequently means extortion, blackmail, loan sharking, credit-card fraud, syndicated protection and even kidnapping. Triads can demand to be placed on payrolls. They are also involved in illegal gambling, video pirating of Chinese 'soaps' and *kung fu* films, and drug running, not only in Britain but also on the Continent. Prostitutes are brought in, sometimes from Thailand and Malaysia, exclusively for Chinese clients so there is less risk of contracting AIDS.

Chinese victims, in the main, are terrified of the sinister triads and usually do not report cases or refuse to give evidence. 'Arson or accidents could befall,' a close Chinese friend may whisper.

Consequently, few culprits have been brought to book. There has been a great deal of sensationalism and prejudicial coverage by the mass media although the police were not prepared up to comparatively recently to recognise a problem existed. But triads are now better understood in Britain. A special anti-triad squad has been established headed by a former Hong Kong detective. This helps to combat the increase in Chinese gangsters, who, after 1997, are no keener to live under communist rule, which stifles enterprise, than most other citizens.

Many Hong Kong triad members intend to emigrate. They know dealers are exporting antiques and cultural relics in large quantities out of the Territory in advance of the handover to China when export restrictions similar to those in force in the People's Republic may be introduced.

A few ordinary businessmen do, nonetheless, turn to triads for debt collecting. Mr Wong was owed one million dollars which he had tried to re-coup through legal channels. Eventually, a friend advised him to put it in the 'safe' hands of the 14K.

'Was early hours', Wong said, 'when phone rang.'

The debtor, on the other end of the line, was sobbing that he did not have that amount of ready money and was pleading for the creditor to call the triads off who stood menacingly around his bed.

'I gave him forty-eight hours,' Wong boasted, sticking his chest out.

There was no need for a return visit by the 14K who received 30 per cent of the sum recovered. The small businessman insisted it saved him from bankruptcy.

A stairway next to a conspicuous Chinese sign on an old building, with the odd person shuffling in and out, caught my eye. Unsurprisingly, there are a number of gambling dens, both legal and illegal, as well as several licensed bookmakers within a short radius of Gerrard Street. Names in Chinese include 'Always Win', 'Of the Same Village' and 'Happy Together'. Some gambling is done in, so called, entertainment or leisure clubs. There are, of course, a Ladbrokes and 'one-arm bandits' in the district, too.

Some Chinese have moved away from old haunts where, rumour has it, graft is paid to police and protection money is collected by triads. Although probably exaggerated, some go as far as to say 99 per cent of Chinese establishments pay 'squeeze'. Gamblers have transferred, in some cases to western-style casinos which usually have more pleasant environments, like the 'Golden Coin' and the 'Golden Nugget'. Such places are believed 'safer' than Chinese gambling dens.

Although many consider the four main vices are women, gambling, drinking and smoking, in that order, several Chinese are compulsive gamblers who will bet on how many pips there are in an orange or the number of immigrants coming over the border. To some everything, whether it be working high on bamboo scaffolding without a safety belt, jay walking to destroy a ghost hot on one's heels, or setting up a business, is a gamble. After all the New Territories villager, who speaks relatively no English and leaves Hong Kong to seek his fortune, must be a bit of a gambler at heart. And when he arrives, in his few leisure hours it is not surprising if he has the odd flutter.

As I stood by a dingy stairway a voice called, 'Going down?' There was the chap in the 'I survived China Airlines!' T-shirt. Although Westerners are not specially welcome, there appeared to be no bouncers with expertise in Chinese martial arts. As we descended I could hear Cantonese talking excitedly. 'He's with me,' my companion called in answer to a questioning glance from a well-built Chinese standing at the foot of the stairs. He had 'balcony-style' hair projecting over his forehead and the dragon tattooed on his forearm was impressive.

In the basement the glaring electric light shone on a sunken-cheeked, yellowish-skinned croupier perched on a high, wobbly stool. Behind him was a small shrine in which red-faced *Kwan Kung*, the God of War, sat amidst a bunch of white, mauve and yellow chrysanthemums and two small stacks of mandarin oranges. Spindly joss sticks smouldered in front of two red stickers, near the entrance, on which gold Chinese characters proclaimed, 'In or out go in peace' and 'Wish your business prospers'.

Occasionally sipping Chinese tea, rather than alcohol, most gamblers appeared in their element at this crowded evening session which added excitement to their monotonous lives. My 'T-shirt friend' squeezed forward against the table. A good cross section struck one as being present, including, one imagined, shop assistants, professionals and waiters. The place seemed safe enough with, what appeared to be, housewives and grandmothers. I was the only Westerner. In addition to card games like poker, and the incessant clicking and banging down of mahjong tiles on Chinese blackwood table tops, other games were in progress. There was *pai kau* (Chinese dominoes) which is something like Russian poker, *fan tan*, amounting to guessing the number of plastic beads, and Chinese bingo, known as *paak kop piu* or 'pigeon picking'.

'I've cleansed my hands in pomelo (a citrus fruit) leaf water,' a woman mumbled. 'The force is with me!'

Nearby a middle-aged man, possibly a cook, rubbed a piece of freshly sliced ginger between his fingers to keep adverse influences at bay. Someone else struggled with pencil and paper to work out a system.

'Won so far. See if luck follows through,' an elderly man exclaimed as he threw down a wad of ten-pound notes, dreaming of sudden wealth.

After the dealer called he screwed up his face and displeased several players by muttering, in Cantonese, '**** your old mother!'

Most Chinese are not sore losers. It must have meant quite a bit to him, but after a grin and a word to a friend he disappeared up the steps, with, it appeared, the same 'personality'. Although not riding on easy street, winning would have meant respect, admiration and ego gratification.

If contained, gambling is no more alarming than excesses of food, television or sex. But social workers appreciate the situation is often serious. Compulsive gamblers, whose childhoods were filled with turmoil and rejection, sometimes go straight to the betting shop after drawing their dole money. Family break-ups are not uncommon. For the wealthy amounts wagered can be large, and occasionally, as a last resort, property changes hands. Some are successful. In those establishments linked to triads 'loan sharks' are on hand to provide money without collateral. Physical harm to oneself or one's family can result if, after due warning, one fails to pay the exorbitant interest or repay the loan on time.

With my T-shirt friend concentrating on his chips and me feeling hungry I went back up to street level.

THE Cantonese restaurant I decided to dine in was of medium size. A big Chinese checked in hats and coats. He was probably of Shandong stock, from a coastal province north of Shanghai whose inhabitants sometimes work as policemen in Hong Kong. Qualifications and experience obtained in China are often not recognised overseas and many immigrants take jobs beneath them.

An attempt had been made in the restaurant to blend Chinese culture with western decor so the appearance does not jar. A conservative Englishman, who imagines *chow mein* is a kind of dog, would not have felt too out of place. There were paintings of the 'Four Seasons', common scenes throughout China in various forms, and three landscapes with white cranes and red temples partly enveloped in wisps of cloud.

An aquarium contained 'black molly', 'angel' and goldfish, and one supposes, as in Hong Kong, they were here for superstitious reasons. There were also a large paper fan hanging on the wall and a 'running horse lantern', suspended from a beam, which revolves because of the heat from its electric light bulb on catgut. Down the far side ran a miniature, green ceramic, Chinese-tile roof projecting about two feet.

'Change knife and fork, please,' I motioned.

Waiters have higher prestige and earn more than cooks who usually have little or no command of English. As the young man brought the chopsticks he fingered his western-style pony tail. Several staff gossiped near the kitchen. Fingers then signalled, waved and gestured in the air as a talkative young lady, with a trim oriental figure, took my order. Although Anglicised, she possessed those graceful, Chinese, 'butterfly', fluttering, hand movements.

As she did up a 'flower' button made from brocade, on her imperial-yellow jacket I noticed knife-edge creases on the outside and inside of her trouser legs. Her well-cut trouser-suit was a modification of the type Chinese women have worn through the ages. No such thing as fashion ever really developed in China. Notwithstanding, Hong Kong tends to be the fashion mecca of overseas, popular, Chinese culture. Girls like Hilda Man – 'Call me Hilda' – are frequently influenced more by the Territory than by Paris or London styles. Hong Kong – not Peking – where China meets 'Greater China', is the bridge to the West and the 'capital' of the Chinese-speaking world. 'Came to England when I was two,' she beamed. 'I'm a banana really. My brother's a BBC (British-born Chinese). My cousin's an ABC (American born).'

Females, sometimes English women, are frequently employed in Chinese restaurants. They have a calming effect when skinheads cause trouble. And although older Chinese women keep quiet, younger ones who have been brought up in England soon tell the miscreants where to get off.

Although some 'cultural Eurasians' have difficulty in blending two disparate backgrounds, Hilda, a pure Chinese, seemed relaxed. English came naturally from her lips without measured thought or national sentiment. I doubted if it was true, as a psychologist professor friend of mine once postulated, that bilingual people are less creative.

A plain, middle-aged woman stood at the rear of the restaurant, with poker-straight hair, pointing to her own nose, gesturing that she meant herself. This was coupled with a few words of broken English to a waiter. Oscar Wilde put it succinctly: 'All women become like their mothers. That is their tragedy.'

I tried to imagine Hilda in twenty-five years' time.

Although 'Mum' has lived in England for twenty years she is still not a 'belonger'. Genetic influences limit to what degree a person can be shaped. 'Ma was born and raised in a traditional household in Hong Kong,' Hilda told me. 'She still dreams in Chinese! Cantonese background takes precedence.'

It is not easy to be entirely Chinese in a western society. The mother ambled across to my table. Whereas younger Chinese prefer to speak English the 'foreignness' of the language meant it was not a major part of her life. She was tickled to speak Cantonese with a 'foreign devil'.

'Hong Kong now less fear China takeover,' she insisted.

By this time Hilda returned with that Chinese overseas perennial, sweet-and-sour-pork and my *mooi kwai loo* rice wine. 'Off down the "frog and toad" this evening,' she mimicked in Cockney rhyming slang.

'Only help out in father's restaurant. I'm an accountant really.'

She then continued about how, when she went back to the family native village in Guangdong Province, in China, she got into hot water. Being brought up in the West she just tucked in and did not offer the tastiest morsels to male family members.

'When Daddy first came to England he worked from seven in the morning till midnight in a small noodle shop.'

That was just as the middle classes were earning more and

eating out became fashionable.

'Now,' she continued, 'he says he works "part-time", from eight in the morning to eight at night!'

In 1974, £9.00 of every £100.00 spent eating out was said by William Cheung, in his thesis *The Chinese Way*, to be spent on Chinese food, almost ten times more than on Indian or Pakistani, and almost three times that spent on Italian cuisine. Many small Chinese businessmen work a seventy-hour week, depending, too, on help from the family. 'Small profits, quick returns' is the watchword. There is stiff competition, often with price slashing, from not only Chinese but other nationalities.

High rents are charged, blocks of buildings are taken over. Some undertakings go under. Of course there are success stories. The owner of one of the largest restaurant chains at present, arrived in England as a cook in 1961. Within fifteen years he owned four eating houses and was main partner in seven others.

The clientele in Hilda's father's restaurant, which is run as a partnership, provides contrasts. On my right sat a warm, working class, direct of speech, north-country group. Where they come from snootiness is frowned upon. Among the eight affable men was a Chinese who appeared to be fully accepted. 'I know "nowt" about new player,' he insisted.

I assumed they were soccer supporters. Football acts as a catalyst and changes the way people behave and interact.

The key is pronunciation. He who speaks with a foreign accent is a foreigner. The group did not care what colour their peer was, the important point being that he spoke broad Yorkshire. A dialect is only a dialect if you do not speak it yourself. Accent conveys status, and, to most people, the status accorded to Yorkshire is not high. One of the ham-fisted members of the group was holding a pair of chopsticks coupled together with rubber bands at the top end, Heath Robinson fashion, with a small piece of wood wedged between as a fulcrum.

At a nearby table sat two prim supercilious Englishmen. Their momentary derision could have been directed at one of the north country group who started off a sentence, oh horror of horrors, with, 'Between you and I ...', a mistake that Hilda would never make. 'Dropped "H"s, that accent my dear, how could they!' you could imagine them saying.

Such language contrasted with the way the two Englishmen used words. 'Do you understand?' the one with the spotty face demanded of the waiter.

Even though, assisted by radio and television 'new London

English' is gaining strength, only in class-ridden England can tone of voice convey so much. To that couple, words are a means of control. They have to be weighed carefully, parted with sparingly and always with that clipped accent. The devilish politeness and superiority of English English, and the culture that spawned it, came through clearly. So, too, did their language facility and implied disregard for trade. British culture and upper-class sneers for the 'genteel' middle classes are as complicated as its people. You cannot understand anyone who is more complicated than you think you yourself are. How can most Chinese, who cannot stand the smell of cheese, be expected to comprehend Englishmen? And, even if they do learn to understand, Britain so seldom captures their souls.

'Not frightfully good,' the Briton who had eaten the least ventured to suggest as the two left. The remark came over as self-congratulatory. One's own system is usually best. It was obvious they had not acquired the taste. Goodness knows what they would have said if they been served chicken's claws! As Chinese food abroad goes, that evening's was not bad. Some believe the best French cuisine is found in Rome and the finest, painfully spicy Indian curries in London. During the Vietnam War, the most delicious American steaks were found in Saigon.

To me eating Chinese food overseas, like in London where a New Territories villager becomes a *chop suey* chef overnight, cannot be compared with Hong Kong. Many ingredients are not available. The additive monosodium glutamate is, however, obtainable around the world. Some Westerners are allergic to it. Away from native soil even Chinese teas, let alone dishes which have been blended to suit British palates, just taste different.

During those spartan years of communism in China much of the art of preparing banquets, for which the Chinese were famous throughout history, was lost. When the country opened up, starting in late 1978, cooks had to be sent from Hong Kong to teach those in the People's Republic.

Hong Kong takes a lot of beating for both western and eastern food. For northern Chinese fare possibly Taiwan is slightly better. Singapore also has good variety as has Macau, less than a one-hour jet-foil ride away to the west of Hong Kong, with its Macanese food which is basically Portuguese cuisine crossed with Chinese.

Now that the north-country crowd had left I was able to observe the convivial group of twelve sitting by the wall. One, I noticed, extended his little finger and thumb and clenched the middle three fingers on one hand to signify number six, by sign language.

Another member of the group had a mole on his cheek with long hairs growing from it which he was in the habit of fingering. It takes a Hongkonger to know a swanky Hongkonger and, by their dress, expensive baubles and mannerisms, they did not have to say that property prices were going up to the heavens to make it clear they were not United Kingdom Chinese.

We ostentatious Hongkongers love showing off. But there is no point unless we have an open-mouthed audience. A girl whose name appeared to be Fanny Pong was talking 'Chinglish' to a boy who compressed the clenched back of one hand in the palm of the other in order to make his knuckles crack.

'When speaking English use teeth and jaw muscles. Most Chinese tend to use just mouth,' insists Hongkonger, *bon vivant* David Tang, with his fruity, British public school accent.

Listening to this Chinese group speaking Chinglish I could see what he meant. In addition to using words like 'godown' (warehouse), every now and then a member of the group interlarded English expressions such as, 'yellow colour pullover' (direct Cantonese translation) into their conversation. A certain store was 'on cheap sale'. The bastardised Anglicisation of Cantonese causes concern for both English and Chinese purists. However, in an international city like Hong Kong, this, together with stilted English, is part of everyday communication. There are many 'Englishes' around the world. Chinglish serves a purpose. You can make mistakes and still be fluent.

A Mr Houdini Ng (a surname most Westerners have difficulty in pronouncing), who sported a helmet haircut and seemed to have a penchant for smelly shrimp paste, appeared to be the leader of the party. Much of their unabashed discussion centred on business. Had the two upper-crust Englishmen still been here they would, no doubt, have viewed it all very condescendingly. Most of the Chinese, who would not so readily form a disciplined queue as their English counterparts, talked almost entirely in quick-fire Cantonese, one of the seven main dialects, although China has as many sub-dialects as there are days in the year. The group spoke in boisterous voices interspersed with the odd shout when a person wanted to make himself heard above the hubbub. This is not unexpected where some children are brought up doing their homework close to noisy traffic flows.

There was little or no pause, between two people speaking, and conversations were often interrupted. So much depends on what culture demands. Not only communications, but body language and 'vibrations' transmitted by a group of Chinese are quite different to those from a crowd of British people.

Topics ranged from peddling quick-frozen prawns, to canned birds' nest soup, to plastic kitchenware. The Chinese seemed blissfully unaware of the indignity of talking about such subjects, and, if there was money to be made by trading or speculating in real estate, you would expect to find them in the thick of it. Social culture is translated into the world of business and it is mostly commercial culture, not government or the church, that shapes immigrants. In such a setting, with a group of Hongkongers thousands of miles from home, listening to their conversations you can appreciate that bedrock of Chineseness. There was no British reserve, and, like the French, the Chinese saw no need to keep elbows off the table.

As a tonal language – with language strongly linked to culture – one can have great fun with witty, Cantonese homonyms. Now and again jokes crept in, such as 'You like *kwa*?', where *kwa* can mean either melon or death, depending on the tone. Many of these jokes are almost lost in the translation, but after emptying yet another earthenware bottle of *Shaoshing* rice wine, which is not unlike a dry sherry, the group talked even louder. Two of the men, one of whom was red in the face because of the genetic sensitivity of many Chinese to ethylalcohol, and the other who had a toothpick sticking between his white teeth, then started to play boisterous *chai mooi*. Although there are variations, one of the players flung out fingers, and, at the same time shouted a number which was supposed to equal the sum of his extended fingers added to the number of digits flicked out at the same moment by his opponent who also bawled a figure. Thus, when one player threw out two fingers and shouted 'five!', while the other player instantaneously flung out three fingers and called '*taai luk mo!*' meaning 'six', the first player had guessed correctly and won.

Similar to tombola in the West, where 'unlucky for some' indicates the number thirteen, so *taai luk mo*, meaning 'wear green hat', stands for 'cuckold'. '*Luk*' is a homonym and may be taken to denote either 'green' or 'six'. *Chai mooi* is played fast, and the loser had to drink three fingers' deep of wine as a forfeit. The Italians play a similar game called *morra*. 'The national sport of Italy is *far rumore* (making a noise),' wrote Art Buchwald the American columnist. The Italians and the Cantonese have much in common.

The man with the mole then started to tease the English-speaking girl, Fanny, about Ignatius, her boyfriend, and she laughed and resorted to the cute body language of quickly putting her tongue out and back in. It was the kind of laugh that implied she did not think it very funny. At the same time Houdini called, 'Captain!', in a loud voice, and 'scooped' the maitre d' towards him with a downwards beckoning of one hand. After the bill arrived there was a well-intentioned squabble between Houdini and two others, who all brandished thick wallets with impressive displays of colourful credit cards, which could be misconstrued by uninitiated Westerners. Many Europeans, and indeed Japanese too, would fault them for flaunting money. But wealth gives confidence. The average Chinese is more generous than his western counterpart.

'Thank you, never mind!' one of the group uttered as he staggered slightly and bumped into an Englishman as the party left the restaurant. They were in fine spirits, albeit with, I imagined, the feeling, 'Stick together, we depend on each other.' 'But, with good heart, one should not feel ashamed when one's head is lifted towards heaven.'

A sudden stillness descended. I quietly paid my bill and left.

Even for someone who has absorbed Chinese values and mores without always being aware of them there is a 'comfort level' regarding the amount of noise a 'grey' Englishman, who speaks middle-class English, with the odd trace of Norfolk dialect, can stand. Toleration varies. Compared to two Arabs, a couple of Americans stand farther apart to converse. The closer you get to the equator the more hugging people do. How far can the distance between people vary? How much can you transgress accepted practices and cross British with Chinese cultures without persons feeling uneasy?

With jet travel and shrunken cultures the world is changing. In the early 1960s Gerrard Street was a landscape of cracked pavements and decay. What was squalid and ugly has become a European tourist attraction where the Chinese, with their so called 'soulless' faces, have their own little world and the average Briton sometimes feels an interloper.

But although the Gerrard Street district of 'Imperial City' has added variety to what some consider the drab British way of life, have average Englishfolk, who cannot tell two Chinese apart, really taken Chinatown to their hearts? Gathering from the older and more conservative, who will tell you in confidence they sometimes resent so many foreigners walking the streets of London, still one of the truly great metropolitan cities of the world, the answer would appear to be 'no'.

CHAPTER FOUR

ROOTS

'C OME and stay with us and pick guavas,' my wife's late uncle, his furrowed, mahogony-coloured face wreathed in smiles, used to say.

In the 1960s, we would spend the weekend with him and his family (a second wife lived in China) on the edge of Mai Po Marshes, south of the polluted Sham Chun River bordering the People's Republic. These are extensive intertidal mud-flats backed by mangroves, brackish swamps and large dykes, in the northwest of the New Territories. This is close to 'Man country', the clan that has made a name for itself in Europe.

Parts of their district are delightful. Mai Po, not far from Deep Bay, is a vital 'refuelling' point for migrant waterbirds many of which fly between Australia and Siberia twice a year. Among the rare visitors are oriental white storks, dalmatian pelicans and black-faced spoonbills of which one-sixth of the world's population winters at the restricted area of Mai Po. There are also Saunders gulls, numbering only about 2,000 in the entire world. Over 400 different species of birds have been recorded in Hong Kong since records began. Not bad for a concrete jungle. It is not unknown, however, for the odd Mainland Chinese speedboat to arrive, for occupants to take pot shots, and for the poachers to disappear just as suddenly after retrieving their quarry.

My wife's uncle used to breed carp, mullet, 'big head' and bream for the table. Fish farming, practised in China since 2,000 BC, is combined with raising ducks housed in slatted-floor huts built

over extensive ponds. This allows droppings to fertilise animal life
and plankton on which fish feed.

We used to sleep in Uncle's primitive timber hut propped up
on stilts over the murky water. 'Best place to fish is through seat of
toilet,' the young son repeatedly told us. Here the excreta attracted
fish as snarling dogs roamed to deter poachers. We could see San
Tin, home of the Man Clan, in the distance.

'They're different. The Mans are special!' James L. Watson, the
American anthropologist, repeatedly remarks in his lectures. Although San Tin, meaning 'new fields', has traditionally been a
closed Cantonese community, the well-known scholar was allowed
to undertake research there. He lived in the heart of Man Clan country, in Hong Kong, for over one year in the early 1970s.

They have carved a niche for themselves both in the Crown
Colony and in the London area where they are the dominant Chinese clan. Like many first generation overseas Chinese they display
toughness, resilience, business acumen and a frightening capacity
for frugality and hard work, judging by western standards.

They are agnates claiming direct relationship with Man Tin-
shui, brother of Man Tin-cheung born in 1236 in Kiangsi Province.
He served both as minister and as army general and took part in the
final struggle against the Mongols when the Sung Dynasty was
overthrown. The Hong Kong Mans, who are related to their name-
sakes in Po On District on the China side of the border, centuries
ago moved near Castle Peak, which, in 1898, became part of the
New Territories of Hong Kong, on a ninety-nine-year lease. Because
of disputes with the powerful Tang Clan they later transferred to
Ping Shan before finally settling at San Tin in 1279.

Every year on the 'Double Ninth' (ninth day of Ninth Moon)
approaching 1,000 male Mans, with their lengthy motorcade, a band
and enormous quantities of food and drink, gather at the large,
omega-shaped grave. Dictates of good *feng shui* govern its site on
the hill, near Castle Peak Bay. There the Clan pays respects to its
founding ancestor. Residents of the New Territories, with well-kept
clan records, live with history as do few others.

The almost twelve-square-mile zone situated on a plain, which
includes single-lineage San Tin, had a population of 4,268 at the
1991 census, of whom about half bear the surname Man. It consists
of eight sub-villages, two of which are still partially walled, each
inhabited by a branch of the clan. Twenty-seven generations of the
Mans have lived at San Tin. The lineage is partly preserved by
property and landed wealth which is set aside in the name of the
founding father. Money realised from the trust is used for the ben-

efit of villagers, such as to assist the old and the poor and for the financing of ceremonies. Communities are headed by village elders who, in the past, mediated in disputes and had the power to punish and fine members.

In addition to the Mans, a few families who bear the stigma that their forebears were *sai man* (meaning 'small people') also live at San Tin. The Chinese can be hard on their own kind, exploiting the underdog, and with this system, young boys were bought from poor families to become hereditary servants. They lived in mud hovels, were given small plots of land and did routine work for their owners. Later, they were found wives and married off at their masters' expense. Any children born of the unions automatically became bonded servants. Some females were taken advantage of, sexually, by their owners.

In spite of criticism in some western countries *sai man*, also known as *ha fu*, 'menial persons', lived under the Union Jack until World War II. Then public opinion changed. Nevertheless, trading in humans still continues in parts of rural China (in 1990, 10,475 court cases were heard involving women being sold to become wives) in spite of sincere efforts by the Communist government to end the practice.

Slavery has however, traditionally, been more benign in the Far East than in Africa and the West. At San Tin, some *sai man* children became companions for their masters' sons and many were treated comparatively well even though they were in bondage. Others bought their freedom or ran away. Another clan is said to have adopted their *sai man* en bloc. Since the system was discontinued some descendants of these unfortunate people moved away from San Tin.

When the Man Clan first arrived in the New Territories, with their *sai man*, all the fertile land had been occupied. At San Tin, with hills to the south-east and Deep Bay to the west, they had to make do with brackish-water paddy which only yielded one crop of red rice a year. Some of this was used for making wine or for medicinal purposes. It is recommended as a cure for beri beri. But in the 1950s and 1960s, when Hong Kong was described by one Hong Kong government servant of overseas Chinese stock as 'colonial, solid, reliable and comforting', the 'vegetable revolution' was taking place on better land and the Mans began to grow more sweet potatoes and peanuts, as well as brush for fuel.

Quite early, because they were not rich, although they never went hungry, they started travelling. Between 1900 and 1948, one-third of all households at San Tin had at least one family member who was a sailor. 'Paternal elder uncle brought back lavish presents,' remarked one elderly woman. And still, when old folk gather in grubby teahouses, conversations occasionally turn to the sixty Mans who jumped ship and settled in England, a few as early as 1885.

Hong Kong, until more recently, was an unruly place. In some parts of the New Territories there was a village watch system up until the 1960s. This started at 6.00 p.m. and a drum was beaten at hourly intervals throughout the night to signify all was well. As late as 1924 a Cheung Chau Island ferry, on its one-hour journey to Hong Kong Island, was captured by pirates. The following year marauders attacked a ferry in the harbour. Although there was a general decline, until the People's Republic came to power in 1949 bandits and renegade soldiers abounded over the border in China.

The Mans are tough. They sold protection. Some were engaged in smuggling. As recorded in correspondence in 1963 between two Government District Officers, the late Walter Schofield and pensioner James Hayes: according to the former, before World War I, District Officer S.B.C. Ross wrote in a Government minute, 'All Mans are rogues: this is axiomatic.' Some, he said, extorted protection fees even in north Kowloon. During World War II, several Mans were beheaded for fighting with guerrillas against the Japanese.

Some Mans adjust easily and between 1955 and 1963, when travel was normally at a leisurely pace by sea and home leave was taken once every seven or ten years, about 1,000 Chinese moved to Britain from Hong Kong. A large group obtained passports in 1962, just before the revision of the Immigration Act. With nepotistic conventions, only relatives are trusted to keep their fingers out of the till. Consequently Mans employed Mans, just as people in Edinburgh who hailed from Ap Chau engaged relations or friends from that island when they wanted more hands. Because of this importance attached to clan and native-place associations there is only a small range of family names among Chinese resident abroad. Between 1962 and 1966, the number of Chinese dependants in Britain, including wives, children and parents, increased nine-fold.

In 1968, there were between 30,000 and 50,000 Chinese in Britain and the number of Chinese restaurants had risen from 30 to 40 before World War II to about 1,000. Just as the Mans stood out in the New Territories, so today, owning about 500 restaurants, they dominate the trade in England, Holland and Brussels (in France, Chinese from the old Indochina are dominant). As 'citizens of the world', some are fluent in three languages. Many have diversified into property in Canada where the authorities soon singled out the Mans as being more likely to succeed than most other immigrants.

From relative poverty in their home village, going overseas brought separation, hardship, and later for some, affluence. Running Mercedes Benz cars and with about 20 millionaires in Britain, the Mans graduated from the pre-modern to the post-modern world. Still employing Confucian work ethics they transferred from land at San Tin, which they now let to outside farmers, to restaurants in Europe. Capital to establish these enterprises came from ancestral estates. In spite of being taught 'You are a Man, you must succeed!', a few failed and returned to San Tin.

Although in the New Territories there are lesser lineages, the Mans are one of the 'Five Great Clans', all of which are represented in Britain. They include the Pangs, the Haus and the Lius. But the Mans' main rival has always been the powerful and influential Tang Clan, with their walled village at Kam Tin. (One of my old student's son is the fifty-eighth generation of the Tang Clan.) Feuding used to take place, sometimes concerning matters of 'face' (prestige). In one of the Man's ancestral halls stand nine soul tablets in memory of 'heroes who died for the village'. At festivals, paper offerings are burned for them. (Clans, as such, no longer exist in the People's Republic.)

In 'Man Country', raucous calls from an egretry carry afar as the white birds with long legs and necks squabble while going about domestic chores. Swamp-gums with their peeling 'paperbark', which were introduced from Australia by the British, line many roads in the New Territories. Their trunks unfailingly twist anticlockwise and their leaves provide aromatic cajuput oil for treating skin diseases. Large, delicious, yellowish-green papayas, also used for making meat tenderisers, cosmetics and medicines, are common at San Tin, as are banyans with their dangling 'whiskery' aerial roots, sometimes contorted and grotesquely shaped. Under the branches of one fine tree is an earth-god shrine. There is an abundance of these in San Tin. They have served the prospering community well.

'Where's the nearest pub, mate!' interjected a Chinese male, with a broad English Midland accent and a pale, almost northern European, complexion. He was strolling, hand in hand, with a young, alert, 'black currant-eyed' girl sporting a cute pencil-sized topknot of hair, circled with an elastic band, sticking straight up from her crown. I must have looked surprised because he turned towards a poinsettia shrub, with its five-inch-long, bright red leaves, known as the 'Christmas flower', and said, 'Hong Kong

Chinese ask me why I speak like this. I just can't 'elp it!'

Looking like a 'five pints a night man' he stood with folded arms, signifying defensiveness in the West but often taken as a sign of arrogance in the Orient. Back on holiday he admitted, each time he returns, romantic memories of San Tin fade. After thirty years overseas the dingy village does not live up to expectations. On retirement, he intends spending half his time in England and the remainder in Hong Kong.

'Rivers and mountains change but it's hard to alter man's nature. Nevertheless, I've given up gambling!' he told me proudly. 'My daughter's an accountant. Two of my sons married English girls. One's since divorced. Racial intermarriage draws people away from traditions,' the stocky man, who in spite of hardships had been born with a sunny nature, lamented.

My two new acquaintances and I then wandered along to the elegant *Tai Fu Tai* mansion, with its air of solemnity, stability and delicate blending of kaleidoscopic colours. They include blues and greens, which, as the Chinese phrase it, 'grab the eyes'. The frescoes and friezes are gaudy consisting of humans, animals, birds and flowers. A genie strolls among clouds. A moth perches on a peach. The structure has a substantial, granite block plinth and is built of bluish-grey bricks. The Chinese knew of the arch, where all members are in compression, from early times, but seldom used it. Neither did they employ the principle of triangulation for rigidity and their roofs are of simple 'beam and post' construction.

At *Tai Fu Tai* there is a deep, sweeping, boat-shaped ridge, with the 'Valley of Nine Dragons', ceramic, high-gloss figurines on one side and the 'Birthday of Guo Zi Yi', a heroic Tang Dynasty (619–907) general, depicted on the other. The effigies were manufactured at Shiwan, in China's Guangdong Province, and are more relaxed than the generally formal poses of figures fired in northern Chinese kilns. *Tai Fu Tai* has been gazetted as a monument by the Hong Kong Government. As we entered an old roly-poly caretaker, addressed respectfully as elder uncle by two visiting Chinese, sat having a cool smoke of tobacco from a bamboo water pipe the size of your arm.

The house, which has no windows or ceilings, is richly embellished with terracotta, stucco and polychrome plaster mouldings some of which have western influence. In the middle of the last century this was fashionable. Together with motifs, murals and timber carvings, with a lichee orchard at the back, the house was built in 1865 by Man Chung-luen who sat Imperial Civil Service examinations. 'With boughs of gold and leaves of jade', in other words coming from a noble family, he was of the scholar-gentry class. He was also a philanthropist.

Near the kitchen, with its many stoves, lies a hefty, hollowed-out tree trunk originally used for processing peanut oil. Slender columns each topped with a ten-inch-long, mythical carp – a symbol of success through endeavour – with pearls in their mouths, are mounted at upper-floor level at each corner of a small, unroofed courtyard. Known as 'heaven's well', this lets in light and provides ventilation.

Most of the Mans, however, lived for centuries in small adobe block houses, not unlike the clay lump used for building in my Norfolk home town until the turn of the century. As a material, it is warm to live in in the winter and cool in the summer. In spite of the odd, open drain there are a few architectual treasures on these, often ramshackle, buildings at San Tin, with their pitched 'roll and pantile' Chinese roofs. Gems include three-dimensional murals depicting mountain scenes. These old buildings contrast with the new, garish, pseudo-Spanish style villas. They are of two or three storeys and constructed mostly of concrete, brick and ceramic-mosaic tiles. Some are partly covered with Shanghai plaster. With large modern windows, making it easier for evil influences to enter, they defy superstition.

'Protection' is, however, afforded not only by special groves of *feng shui* trees behind villages and by door gods, but by lucky charms. Five pieces of red, speckled paper, representing the 'Five Happinesses', hang at heads of a few door frames. These five comprise long life, wealth, health and peace, love and virtue and natural death after a full span.

San Tin no longer depends on brackish-water rice farming. 'Sterling houses', the sign of an emigrant community, are wedged between old dwellings. These new buildings were largely financed by the restaurant business in Europe. Eighty-five per cent of able-bodied males work abroad. The women and children, the old men and a handful between eighteen and fifty years of age, are almost entirely dependent on remittances from overseas. The Mans are the largest emigrant community in the New Territories. Many deny themselves and save avidly while in Europe. They then return 'in brocade robes in glory', to their spiritual home at San Tin, and throw banquets in ancestral halls.

On special occasions such as weddings, the traditional way is to throw a 'basin feast'. A variety of meat and vegetable dishes are cooked: including mushrooms, onions, lettuce, bean curd, chicken and roast pork. The pork is cut at a special hour after it has been blessed in the temple. The food is then stacked in layers in two-foot-diameter metal wash basins. One of these is then placed in the centre of each circular table. Each diner helps himself with chopsticks, at times digging deeply. The beer and brandy flow. Some returnees from overseas 'scatter gold like dust' and quickly dispose of savings.

There have been significant changes since they last returned. A new, now often congested trunk road has been constructed close by. Another eyesore is a scrapyard given over to dumping worn-out vehicles and ugly, rusty, mechanical appliances like refrigerators and cookers. Monster container trucks park not far away. Yet although progress can be almost frightening for the elderly, parts of what was off-the-beaten-track, conservative San Tin tolerates limited change. Even if, compared to yesteryear, it is now a centre of relative affluence and leisure, there are paradoxical effects to emigration.

Emigrant villages tend to remain tightly knit with communities reinforcing traditional patterns of social organisation and ways of life. Some of these have long disappeared in more progressive parts of what is supposed to be the rural New Territories. Many Mans donate money and support traditional festivities to outdo other villages. The founder of San Tin is alive and well economically if not biologically.

Many of the Mans living overseas return once every three years for the festival of *Ta Tsui*, unlike in some hamlets where it is held every seven, or even every ten, years. Donors are proud to hear their names proclaimed in a loud, gruff voice – together with couplets – after these have been posted up on the 'ritual memorial'. The long red banner, listing all bona fide contributors, is later 'sent by fire to heaven'. The auspicious days for holding *Ta Tsui*, during the cool weather, will have been selected by a soothsayer. Holding it ensures the future prosperity of the district and the wellbeing of its inhabitants. A five-foot-long 'dirt boat' carries 'plague-causing dirt' from each household to heaven.

Temporary bamboo structures are erected to house images of the Jade Emperor, the City God and *Tai Sz Wong*. Taoist priests, 'ritual specialists' in long colourful robes, chant and perform rites as they pray for peace and blessings and lead the 'processions of incense' around the villages. Gongs are struck. Signs proclaim, 'Keep clear; keep quiet!' The parade visits temples, shrines and ancestral halls to worship gods and ancestors. Village elders wear long blue gowns and some have western-style hats. Paper effigies are burned to appease wandering spirits.

A nine-foot-long branch of smouldering sandalwood gives off fragrance, continuously, throughout the four- or five-day festival. There are spirit trees into which wishes, written on pieces of paper attached to stones, are thrown. Sacrifices are made to earth gods and offerings of food in temples. 'Open the temple and the village will bloom,' many believe. Religious activities are followed by all households. Family altars are 'purified'. Villagers forgo sex and meat during the festival and, at the end, the King of Hell is burned.

But, in addition to the religious side, a *Ta Tsui* is also a happy occasion with all the fun of the fair and fairy lights strung up. At times, electrifying enthusiasm permeates the village. One English-woman married to a Chinese wrote to the *South China Morning Post* after her brief visit: 'I have just experienced the most wonderful event of my life here in Hong Kong.'

As one would expect there is also a great deal of feasting, much of which is Buddhist vegetarian fare.

There are puppeteers, lion and unicorn dances and large col-ourful, congratulatory *fa paai* (flower signs) on bamboo skeleton frames. There are dying arts like Chinese opera. Troupes perform to deafening Cantonese music in a sixty-foot-high, bamboo-framed, tent-like structure seating 3,000. Because Chinese make fewer facial expressions, emotions in opera are conveyed more by hand, sleeve, arm and foot movements, rather than by eyebrow or lip gestures. After the festival, the preparations for which started over one year before the event and cost over HK$1 million, the village is peaceful again for another three years. It is time to start saving for the next *Ta Tsui*.

The villages at San Tin have a *T'in Hau* (Goddess of Heaven) Temple with, some would say, an over-ornate altar. On my last visit I found my companion, a member of the Man Clan, trying to shake out a 'fortune stick' from a bamboo canister. Eventually, 'number one' wormed its way up and dropped on the paving. The message read: 'The first Emperor of the Han Dynasty entered the city.' This means little unless one knows the historical reference. After looking this up in a book of predictions in the temple Mr Man learned, 'It is the right time for marriage. Wealth is at hand. A high position can be achieved and the birth of a son can be expected.' The Communist Government in China, which has constantly tried to suppress for-tune telling, would certainly not approve.

However, one British anthropologist living in England is said to run his household using Chinese 'fortune sticks'. He maintains it produced just as good results as praying to a supernatural power or any other method.

Whether achieved by good luck or not, clan influence used to be measured, in part, by its number of imperial scholars. Education has always been highly rated. Some villages in the New Territories still possess their ancient, formal, study halls which were the first schools. A few display academic honours boards. Such a study hall is said to have stood in Kam Tin village four centuries before Eton College was founded in England in 1440.

There are also a number of village ancestral halls, which are the coolest places in the summer heat, housing spirit or soul tablets for members of branches and sub-branches of clans. Two of these at San Tin, including the Man Lun-fung Hall with three halls and open courtyard together with a 'Speaking of Scholarship' entrance chamber, have been declared monuments by the Government. They are among the finest in Hong Kong. Here festivals and major events are held, ancestors are worshipped and village elders meet. There are also 'lesser' ancestral halls, some unfortunately garishly refurbished with mosaic tiles. Occasionally, spirit tablets hang above altars in recently constructed private houses.

Many Chinese believe everyone has three souls. When he or she dies one remains in the grave high on the slopes above the village, another ascends into the next world, and the third occupies the soul tablet. These are small, oblong pieces of plain wood, rounded at the top and slotted into a small transverse base of wood. With Cantonese custom they are 'banked' by generation, starting with the 'Dragon' and the 'Phoenix', the husband and wife founders of the clan or sub-clan at the top, working down to the more recent at the bottom. Namely A begat B, and B begat C, and so on.

The inscription is written on each tablet with an ordinary Chinese brush and ink, and includes name, age, in pre-Republic days the reign, date of death, and three characters for the 'spirit prince'. Those who die before reaching the age of twenty and the unmarried are not accorded soul tablets. The custom of erecting tablets dates from the Chou Dynasty (1100–256 BC). They receive regular offerings including tea and incense. At festivals joss sticks are burned and vast quantities of food, which is later eaten by the living, are displayed before altars. One should not point at an altar for fear of offending the gods. If one does so by mistake one must bow three times to make amends.

At the turn of the present century it was still a capital offence to strike one's father although practices of Confucian filial humility do not rest easily with the communists. Ancestor worship is, however, still an important part of life for New Territories villagers who make up three-quarters of the Chinese population in Britain. At

festivals in Hong Kong, males pay respects by kowtowing or bowing three times while facing the altar on which stand saucers of oil
with burning wicks.

With many men going overseas marriage can present problems.
A large number of overseas Chinese still return to Hong Kong to
find wives, with or without the help of professional or amateur
matchmakers. The latter are sometimes well-meaning relatives or
friends. For 'mail-order brides' employing the 'picture-bride' system, with a traditional Chinese wedding, a live cock is still occasionally substituted for the groom and the bride drinks some of its
blood. But girls are naturally not keen to marry someone who will
return to his native village only once every three or four years.

Most brides now accompany their husbands to Europe, and
two-thirds of the Man Clan babies are born far from San Tin so they
can claim right of abode in their adopted country. Even by 1975, it
was claimed that 30 per cent of the Chinese living in the United
Kingdom had been born there. But most of the first and second
generation residing overseas want their children to be 'proper Chinese' who have mastered their formidable language and can crack
tiny melon seeds with their teeth. If children are left in London,
with peer group-exerted inflences, they will likely reply to a question in Cantonese from their mother in Cockney English. In Cantonese the word *ye*, with slightly different tone, means either 'grandfather' or 'thing'. 'Not once did little Tat-koon address me correctly!'
complained a disappointed Chinese grandparent who had stayed
with his son's family for a fortnight's holiday in England.

In order that children are brought up as 'real Chinese' a
number are handed over to wives or grandparents, who often spoil
them, to be 'educated' in the 'language of the home and the heart',
for a few years, at San Tin. There their hair is cropped short (traditionally done on the twelfth day after birth) so it will grow thicker.
One little boy, on returning to the New Territories, soon learned
from ancient grandfather that at night when he was outside and
wanted to relieve himself, he should call out, 'Spirits, I am going to
urinate!' They would then not get a dousing and bad joss would not
befall him.

By sending children back to Hong Kong the Mans residing
overseas generally manage to retain their Chinese culture longer
than most. They know when children are raised in Britain active
assimilation continuously takes place. A Chinese 'English banana' is
unlikely to be accepted by pure Chinese as one of them, just as he
is not entirely accepted by Britons. Thus, he remains a 'hyphenated
man'.

There is no problem of acceptance at San Tin on purely racial grounds even for Eurasians. If the father is a Man the offspring is a Man. One dark child who had a Jamaican mother mixed with no difficulty. Some European wives, understandably, are not enamoured of living at San Tin and move out in disgust to a Kowloon hotel. They do not appreciate the richness of culture, rituals and clan genealogy. Certainly, it is quite different at San Tin compared to England. But as Chinese become more deeply entrenched in Europe fewer children are sent back to Hong Kong to be brought up.

Many joke about the 'sex-starved women of San Tin' whose husbands are overseas. James Watson points out in his book that this is a myth. Nevertheless, single women and grass widowers are watched carefully. The sexes do not mix freely. Villagers were not keen he should live there to undertake his research until he assured them his wife would accompany him. Although nothing like the Middle East, a set of uncodified rules apply even if there are double standards for men. Precautions are taken to protect a woman's virtue and to prevent extra-marital affairs. This is a place where, although the fair sex do not live in seclusion, villagers tend to be suspicious of newcomers. Females go indoors when a strange man approaches. There has never been a rape at San Tin.

In the 1960s, a man about to go abroad seduced the wife of a friend living overseas. After the woman eventually admitted the indiscretion, in traditional Chinese rural fashion, the man was incarcerated in a bamboo pig-basket and thrown into a pond just as the border police arrived in time to save him. For other offences, a sack is sometimes placed over a culprit's head and men take turns to beat him.

Previously, when males went abroad they normally went alone. This was because few respectable Chinese women lived overseas. So the males often married or had common-law, native second wives. If a couple cohabited for any length of time they were considered man and wife. Even today there is often no wedding ceremony, although at a reception everyone signs his or her name in black ink with a Chinese brush on a large, decorative red cloth as evidence. The couple then live together with the full force of traditional marriage and the woman, it is hoped, bears sons.

Especially in countries like Thailand and the Philippines a great deal of integration has taken place. Elsewhere, in Southeast Asia and to a lesser extent in Europe and America, there has been some assimilation. Generally, Europeans admit Chinese living overseas make good husbands, and offspring are considered Chinese even if the local language is spoken at the dinner table. The youngsters are usually local in hearts and minds and the country where they live is 'home'.

'I'm British!' Liverpudlian actor David Yip, who was born on the edge of Chinatown of an English mother and a Chinese seaman father, quite rightly, reproves his critics when he faces prejudices. 'While father was at sea I had a perfectly normal, British, working-class upbringing.'

William Cheung discusses Eurasians in his thesis and mentions that many Chinese are not keen on the 'international marriage stakes'. They see European ways and attitudes as quite different, especially those concerning the extended family, kinship, the moral code and sexual mores.

In addition to possessing the 'Four Womanly Virtues' (good character, good manners, good appearance and being a good house-keeper), a respectable female is still supposed to be a virgin on her wedding night. The 'blood' is wiped on a special white handker-chief as evidence. According to old customs the groom's family then presents portions of roast pork to relatives and close friends to in-form them the bride did not have to be sent back in disgrace to her parents. She is expected to remain a faithful wife. The Mans still talk about the 'catastrophe' when the English bride of a Chinese hus-band refused to go on her knees and offer tea to her in-laws.

Even though some of the Mans have European working-class wives, and a few Chinese have wed middle-class British girls, these women are sometimes seen as a threat to economic prosperity. Dutch girls are frequently considered more 'compatible' than their sometimes 'extravagant' English counterparts who want to control the purse strings. 'Why should we remit money back to San Tin?'

In the 1950s, I taught two Chinese students in Hong Kong who later worked overseas and wed German girls. One marriage ended in divorce. Nevertheless, of those Chinese that marry foreigners, few openly express regrets. A long-time friend of mine was in many ways an Anglophile yet still remained inwardly, very Chinese. With a large family, two of his daughters married Englishmen, I always suspected he regretted this when he saw his genetically half-Chinese grandchildren.

Although not a criminal offence in Britain, sexual liaisons be-tween 'Chinamen' and white women caused concern. A commis-sion of enquiry, in 1910–11, examined cases in London: 'because it is undesirable from an English point of view'.

Two cases involving teenage English girls were viewed with special revulsion, although with Chinese girls being small and, in those days, marriageable at fifteen or sixteen, probably to the Chinese the relationship seemed perfectly natural. From the enquiry it was clear there was no sexual coercion.

'English girlfriends are fine,' some say, 'but not wives.' Thus, Chinese men who 'go steady' with European girls and contemplate marriage are frequently teased about losing control of their lives, turning their backs on their own culture and becoming 'set in concrete'. Some fear that, with different priorities, the British wife will desire company which a Chinese husband is unable to provide.

Nevertheless, with vast social change and much of the Chinese community becoming more Anglicised, and with traditional values on the decline, international 'marry-go-rounds' are increasing everywhere. With time, there is also less nepotism and the Mans in Europe are beginning, gradually, to trust outsiders more. But the older generation still bemoans the fact that youngsters have not 'suffered enough'. 'They are not as tough as we were,' grandfather complains.

Given the opportunity, the average Asian enjoys similar indulgences to Westerners. Naturally, the younger Chinese who were born in Britain or came when they were young are not so tolerant, submissive and industrious as 'elder uncle' once was. The present Chinese generation wants to strike a balance between a not more than forty-hour working week and leisure. Meanwhile maternal grandpa insists, 'A lazy fellow is seldom lucky.' Old 'white (haired) mother' chides, 'Harder to make child study than get water buffalo to work!'

Many young Chinese believe they belong in Britain. They try to live in the mainstream and intend, so they say, to stay on in Europe. But others, because they have not been brought up speaking English at home and do not mix with indigenous society, are not so fluent as locals. 'Brits have the edge over us,' they admit with stoic acceptance of racial discrimination. Undoubtedly, with colour and language barriers, Chinese are still often seen in practice as second-class citizens and disadvantaged as a minority group with higher unemployment rates. The catering trade cannot absorb all those in the labour market.

A study conducted in 1986, *Employment Prospects of Chinese Youth in Britain*, examined 100 families in the catering industry in Edinburgh and London where many only manage to scrape a living. The majority would like to quit but their success rate in changing jobs is low. Of the 45 boys and 55 girls under twenty-one years of age who were surveyed, there was one sewing-machine mechanic and one delivery boy working for McDonalds. Of the 100, 83 were still in school and almost all had worked, at some stage, either full-time or part-time.

Although those interviewed appreciated that education in Britain is free, only 48 per cent had adequate day-to-day English. Many, even if under fourteen years of age, helped out in their parents' restaurants in which whole families were involved. This left limited time for study and, positioned at the bottom of the hierarchy, they lacked positive attitudes to education. They know that in England, in theory, everything is possible. Many parents had high hopes of their offspring becoming doctors, lawyers or accountants. But, after disappointments and frustrations, only 21 per cent of those in the survey thought they would ever enter university. Although parents would like their children to steer clear of catering, a family restaurant is often kept for children as a 'safety net'.

Many youngsters are confused, speaking neither English nor Chinese properly and worried about the future. As Chinese, they accept they can never be ethnically English. However, if they are poor to boot in conservative Britain, with its stratification of society and skin colour and features militating against them, many feel that assimilation is virtually impossible. Some of the disadvantaged give up trying.

'If England is a dance to which immigrants have to learn the steps, so often they are not even allowed on the floor,' is how one social worker phrased it.

Accepting that they are failures some become 'invisible Brits'. Other Chinese join gangs, a few in the notorious Soho District. Those that cannot use their energy to create use it to destroy and spray graffiti (not a prevalent practice in Hong Kong), although the majority, in Chinese tradition, are obedient to their parents and not prone to violence.

More research is needed into the lives of generally neglected poorer minorities and the study conducted in Edinburgh and London, which is still relevant, recommended that not only are more intensive and effective language learning facilities required, but also an investigation as to how the Chinese catering industry can provide more worthwhile careers.

Even if the Mans do retain their culture longer than most Chinese, when the young return to San Tin they do not understand properly the clan's complicated customs and soon become dissatisfied with village life. Living abroad opens their minds and gives them broader perspectives. But because their elders, few of whom have become United Kingdom citizens, still have deep-seated ties with their homeland and fantasies about their native village, most will nevertheless eventually return to San Tin. They know inwardly that they 'belong' to China. Only work has exiled them to foreign parts. They do not want their bones to lie in cold, alien, English soil.

Nevertheless, opinions are changing. The 1967, so-called Disturbances in Hong Kong, an overspill of the xenophobic, ten-year Cultural Revolution in the People's Republic, the 'greatest' revolt of all times, serve as a warning. Then, Chairman Mao made the barbarous decision for the Red Guards – described as 'born in famine, raised in chaos' – to run amuck and cut Chinese compatriots off from their ancient culture and heritage. Churches were sacked and temples ravaged. Instructions were: 'Destroy vestiges of the "Four Olds" (old customs, old habits, old culture, old thoughts), repudiate bourgeois ideology and revisionism, inject fresh blood into a simplified administration and revolutionise!' Many citizens took the chance to settle old scores. Mao succeeded in shocking and did not know when to stop.

The fact that the People's Republic is taking back the British Territory is having its effects on the Chinese in Britain. With 'seven-year swings' in China, in the past, who is bold enough to dismiss completely the possibility of a recurrence? But the Mans are not secure enough overseas to sever entirely their Hong Kong roots. How many will eventually decide to settle permanently in Britain remains to be seen.

Mr Hum emigrated in 1908, at the age of twelve, from Toi Shan to Canada. He studied and worked hard. He saved and, as a grown-up, returned to China to find a wife. But Canadian immigration laws prohibited his spouse from joining him until after the Second World War. She remained in Guangdong where, like many others, she was known as a 'widow with a living husband'. Bob Hum is pictured here outside his own Saskatoon hotel. (Photograph courtesy of his daughter, Mrs K.H. Chan)

The benevolent dragon, which guards the treasures of the gods, gallivanting around Toronto streets at the 'Hong Kong 92 Festival' with its theme of 'Bridge the Pacific'. (Photograph courtesy of the Hong Kong Government)

To the delight of 'alternative medicine' enthusiasts, with the West having no real answers to complaints such as allergies, a number of acupuncture, acupressure and moxibustion practitioners are to be found in London. Here, an assistant weighs out herbs imported from China. Chinese empirical medicine offers a rich field for western research. (Photograph courtesy of Kit Hayward)

Demonstrating to commemorate the 4 June 1989 Tiananmen Square Massacre. The two Chinese lions, donated by China Travel Service, look on approvingly in London's Chinatown. (Photograph courtesy of Helena Hung)

Marriage Rock symbolises an erect phallus. Here women burn joss sticks, pray they will wed good husbands and give birth to sons. Earlier this century, a Chinese girl and an Englishman committed suicide together, near this 'Boulder of Pre-ordained Marriage', because her parents forbade them to wed. (Reproduced by permission of the Urban Council of Hong Kong from the collection of the Hong Kong Museum of History)

Taoist priests at the Hungry Ghosts Festival, when paper offerings are burned to appease unfortunate, wandering spirits who were deprived of decent burials. Colourful 'flower signs' are displayed in the background. (Photograph courtesy of Rosemary Lee)

Just as the Chartered Bank building constructed in the late 1950s overlooked the Hongkong Bank by ten feet, so, in the late 1980s, history repeated itself. But both the new Standard Chartered Bank and the angular, space-age-like Hongkong Bank today are dwarfed by the Bank of China with its sharp edges which endanger the Territories' *feng shui* (geomancy). (Photograph courtesy of the Hong Kong Government)

Peel Street, looking south from Queen's Road Central in the 1920s. In old Hong Kong, some of the better class brothels for Europeans and mistresses of taipans were located here. (Photograph courtesy of the Hong Kong Government)

A registered West Point bordello for Chinese clients in the 1930s. According to the couplet, 'one is enticed by the enchanting moon, water, flowers, wind and love in an indescribable way'.

Chinese in Hong Kong, with their names displayed on placards, in the custody of Japanese soldiers during World War II prior to summary execution. They were accused of entering houses and stealing.

After fasting unto death, Abbot Yueh Chi's mummified, gilded body sits in a glass case at the Temple of 10,000 Buddhas at Sha Tin. There, he is venerated by his followers. (Photograph courtesy of Kit Hayward)

Soul tablets banked in rows above the altar in the Man Lun-fung Ancestral Hall at San Tin. The couplet on the left reads: 'Sitting on Loh Mountain one discovers the beauty of the universe. Because your ancestors were extremely virtuous you now enjoy such good fortune'. The author of this book stands in the foreground. (Photograph courtesy of Kit Hayward)

One of several rallies, held in Hong Kong in the summer of 1989, supporting the pro-democracy movement in China. The Neo-Classical, colonial Supreme Court, now the Legislative Council Chambers, is shown on the left. Built on reclaimed land and completed in 1911, its foundations consist of China-fir piles. (Photograph courtesy of the Hong Kong Government)

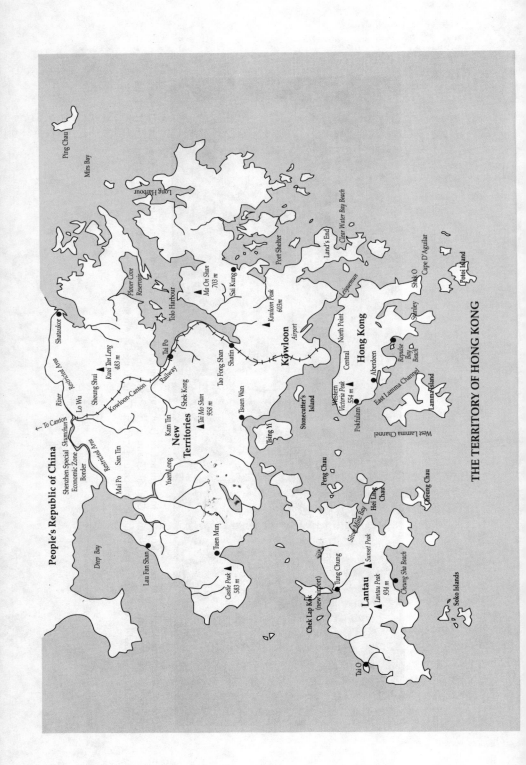

THE TERRITORY OF HONG KONG

Chapter Five

Overseas Chinese

A SEVEN-MONTH-OLD, frail, Chinese girl was abandoned in a squalid doorway in Kowloon. Unwanted babies are usually female. In a land without national social insurance sons can help parents in old age. Daughters are 'lost capital'. They are married off and join their in-laws. Girls feel inferior. In China, with a 'one-child policy' for Han Chinese, infanticide is not uncommon. Many infant daughters are drowned.

'Boys are best!'

'All you need do is stick fake penis on front of baby girl,' the Chinese con man giggled. 'Gullible foster parents take quick glance. By the time it's fallen off you're miles down the road with the cash,' he went on!

The seven-month-old baby girl mentioned above was taken in by a New Territories orphanage and later adopted by an English couple who taught in Hong Kong. Nicole, as they named her, was taken to Britain by her foster parents when she was three; first to live in the South and then in the Midlands. She never really mixed with Chinese and grew up leading the life of a typical English girl. She is a true 'banana'. A 'pure Brit' with Chinese features, albeit with the 'inscrutable' look replaced by English frowns and grins.

Nicole was frequently bullied and ostracised at school which made her ashamed of her ancestry. She reacted by being as English as possible. To closed minds, anything that does not conform is an embarrassment. Like most youngsters she tried to emulate her peers. With a Chinese face, except when on the telephone talking to a stranger, this was not always possible. But, in addition to wearing glasses at an early age and being comfortable on her hunkers, she was content to sit at her desk, with Chinese dedication, studying from morn till night. 'Instead of recommending Nicole to her class mistress, this quality antagonised,' her foster mother glowered. 'She was seen as a kind of freak. The school tried to hold her back.'

There is limited need to describe westernised Chinese to the West. Their predicament should, however, be explained to the Chinese. When Nicole returned to Hong Kong for a holiday, with next to no knowledge of either Chinese culture or language, she encountered some hostility. Taxi drivers and waiters snubbed her. 'Why no speak Cantonese?'

'Sometimes Hong Kong Chinese see you as a threat,' smirked a North-American Chinese who had come to the Territory to work. 'I'm female. I'm young. My western ways, more forceful body language and native command of English allow me to communicate better with Westerners. I'm ethnically Chinese yet culturally Canadian.'

In Nicole's case, however, the reaction was, 'Let's go back home to England, Mummy!' 'Made in Hong Kong, processed in Britain', she is now happily married to a supportive Englishman. She is studying Chinese history. Only as a mature adult did she become inquisitive about her roots. She wears a *cheung saam* on formal occasions encouraged by her husband who finds her Chinese background romantic.

In a similar case, eighteen-month-old Lai Tuen-chuan was transferred, in 1964, from Pinewood Orphanage in Kowloon to English foster parents in rural Berkshire. Living in the mainstream of British life Lucy Sheen believed she was English: until she was a bit older when, with 'slit eyes', she suddenly recognised she did not look like her 'parents'. At one stage she slept with a clothes peg on her nose to force it to grow straight out. Later, she grasped the truth. She was not sad as she wandered with a London accent around Gerrard Street. She realised that, but for a twist of fate, her staple would have been rice instead of bread. Although she had no desire to trace her real parents she bought a wok and started to learn Chinese cooking.

Lucy, long since graduated from drama school, has played Chinese roles where her qualities of 'mystery and toughness' are valued. When she played Portia in *Julius Caesar*, at Bristol Old Vic, she recounted in a *South China Morning Post* interview, '... the dickhead of a critic said it didn't matter if you could speak the language. If you're not white forget it!'

Lucy continued: 'People are blinkered into thinking that to act Shakespeare you have to be blonde-haired and blue-eyed. I'll make some people eat their words if it kills me!'

Timothy Mo the author, mentioned in Chapter 1, is different in that he is not pure Chinese but the son of a Chinese architect and a working-class, English mother. He is not only of two races but also of two classes although, in appearance, his father's Cantonese genes have vanquished those of his mother. His parents separated when he was two, it is recounted in *The Independent* newspaper.

In Hong Kong, he was brought up 'on the back' of a baby *amah*. His mother thought he was too Chinese and his teachers felt he was not Chinese enough, although his spoken Cantonese was better than his English. At age ten he came to England with his mother. 'When the ship reached Suez I'd forgotten all my Chinese,' he grinned.

Mo inherited two, often conflicting, though also mutually enriching cultures. By taking the English path he became a champion boxer rather than an expert in 'open hand' Chinese martial arts. He was short-listed for the Booker Prize, writing books with Chinese backgrounds.

A similar case in reverse is that of Mr Mengxiong Love, born in 1939 at Qingdao, Shandong Province. Before World War I this was German territory famous for its beer. His American father, James Love, worked for British American Tobacco in China and, in 1940, the company sent him on a business trip to the United States. World War II and the Chinese Civil War prevented him from returning to Shandong. After struggling for years the son, Mengxiong, finally had his United States status recognised by both Chinese and Americans. His aim is to go to the States.

He looks Eurasian, understands little English and his way of life, including dress and customs, are entirely Chinese which he speaks with a deep northern accent. A social misfit, criticised because of his father's American blood, chain-smoker Love was branded a spy. He served seventeen months in solitary confinement during the Cultural Revolution with all its class struggles, prejudices and tragedies. His property was confiscated. No friend dared attend his wedding.

Eurasians, of course, have existed since the two races met. The Eaton sisters, Edith (1867–1915) and Winnifred (1877[?]–1954), were daughters of an English father and a Chinese mother. For much of their lives, as writers, they lived in the United States where, in the late nineteenth and early twentieth century, the environment was hostile.

Amy Ling recalls, in *Revelation and Mask: Autobiographies of the Eaton Sisters*, that at a dinner a clerk in a mid-western American town exclaimed, in Edith's presence, 'A Chinaman is, in my eyes, more repulsive than a nigger!' On the same occasion an employer expressed doubts that the Chinese were 'even human', and a landlady affirmed, 'wouldn't have one in my house.'

'But the Japanese are altogether different. There's something bright and likeable about them.'

Until Pearl Harbour, in 1941, the 'samurai tradition' was much respected in America.

Thus, while Edith embraced her Chinese identity writing under the pseudonym of Sui Sin Far, the more prolific Winnifred pretended to be Japanese, using the alias of Onoto Watanna. Late in life she acknowledged she had betrayed her heritage. There were few Japanese in the States at the time and, unlike the Chinese, they posed no economic threat. Conditions for the Chinese living there, with its bigotry which she experienced both from Caucasians as well as from other Asians, was described in her 'sincere and earnest' writing: for example her slim, *Leaves from the Mental Portfolio of a Eurasian*, published in 1909.

'I'd have given anything to look less foreign. My darkness marked and crushed me. I love blondness like the sun,' Winnifred wrote in *Me. A Book of Remembrances*, published in 1915.

Edith Eaton lived in a world where it was taught that 'Whites were superior, strong and beautiful and Asians were inferior, ugly and weak.' When they teased her with 'I'd rather marry a pig than a girl with Chinese blood in her veins', or called her 'a yellow-faced, pig-tail rat eater', Edith shouted back, always trying to right wrongs, 'I'd rather be Chinese than any other nationality.'

According to author Amy Ling, 'Edith's response to racism was a frontal assault, direct and confrontational.'

Edith Eaton sprang to mind when a Chinese lady remarked to a group of Chinese and me at a banquet, 'I'm so glad I'm Chinese! We have everything ... history, art, culture, scenic beauty ... you name it!'

Although taken aback, such an outburst of chauvinism did not altogether surprise me. Countless Chinese feel the same way although they may not normally express it openly to a European.

'Respect for family and elders, the desire for education and self-motivation are Chinese values that I treasure,' my Chinese goddaughter confided in me.

Although ethnically Chinese, she is now a 'cultural Eurasian': a happy blend of two lifestyles. Her two brothers, who also live in the

United States, have never embraced the indigenous culture or acquired an American drawl to the same degree.

A Chinese I met at a wedding in Hong Kong is an extreme example of cultural rejection. He was sent by his father, on the advice of a priest, to a boarding school in rural Ireland.

'Wasn't another Chinese for miles!' the thirty-year old man told me in staccato English.

Yet though he was subjected to 'total immersion treatment', and surrendered a fraction more of his reluctant self every few days, he is, after all he had experienced, still undoubtedly very Chinese. Like many, he is happier among his own kind.

'I'm grateful to my parents for giving me the opportunity to study in the USA,' my god-daughter told me. 'There, I hauled down barriers and accepted new ideas.'

Although at first, with a boyfriend from Vietnam (now her husband), she found difficulty in identifying with American-born Chinese, she admits, after living in the West with its different lifestyle and diversity, she is now 'less narrow-minded'. 'I view many things quite differently.' Christina insists, however, these attributes have not weakened links with her native culture. 'You can take the Chinese out of China but you can't take China out of the Chinese.'

'If I'd stayed in Hong Kong I'd probably have worked in a bank. My main interest would have been money,' Christina exclaimed on a visit to the Territory. 'To think, I'd an identity crisis when I first went to the States! There, Chinese are a minority. In Hong Kong, with us forming 98 per cent of the population, racism is a subtle issue. You know, I sat in front of the TV crying when the Tiananmen Square Massacre was raging?'

In June 1989, all hearts of overseas Chinese beat as one. There was a renewed sense of sinocisation.

'Never felt more Chinese,' my god-daughter continued. 'Yet, contradictorily, we didn't want to be thought of as Chinese. I was so ashamed!'

WHAT is 'Chineseness', which can lead to such extremes of emotion? How Chinese are you? Can you pick up a raw egg in its shell, with the yolk floating around, with chopsticks? Can you write the classical language with fluency or sing stylised Cantonese opera? Do you follow Chinese customs on the three most important occasions in a relative's life – birth, wedding and funeral? To the question, 'How do you know you're Chinese?' a person might answer: 'I was born and brought up as one.' He or she could add, 'I talk the language in my sleep and burn joss sticks.'

But although a female is or is not pregnant, likewise, many believe one either is or is not Chinese. There is no halfway house. There is, however, a range of behavioural patterns. Cantonese have some customs which vary compared to those of the Hakka, Fujian or other Chinese sub-groups.

Although there is no such thing as a 'Chinese race', a term bandied about, incorrectly, at the time of World War II, 'Chineseness', that abstruse, ingrained culture with intimate personal relationships, is not something that is easy to forsake. Such physical and behavioural characteristics, a century ago were described by many Europeans as 'foreign, heathen ways'. This was quite different to the awe-struck days of Marco Polo, leading up to the eighteenth century when the West had a love affair with 'things Chinese'. China was seen, up to then, as an immensely civilised, cultured, peaceful place.

Among first generation Chinese living overseas there is a marked degree of patriotism and secretiveness, coupled with emotional difficulty in adjusting. Similarly, there is a strong desire to retain one's culture although the saying, 'Once a Chinese always a Chinese,' is patently untrue. Wang Gungwu, Vice-Chancellor of Hong Kong University, in *China and the Chinese Overseas*, says: '(Chinese) prefer to keep their own culture but, given the right incentives, would be prepared to give it up gradually. They can assimilate and "de-assimilate" within certain limits.'

Some believe it is easier to jettison being Jewish than to abandon being Chinese, even if there is no real notion of identity but only, rather, a concept of Chineseness. First generation Chinese overseas, where a degree of snobbery often prevails, are not enamoured with 'barbarian directness'. Those piercing eyes gaping rudely, eyeball to eyeball, into talking faces: being 'stared out' as a means of confrontation. Because of insecurity, newcomers feel more comfortable dealing with an overseas branch of 'Honkers and Shankers', the Hongkong and Shanghai Bank, rather than with a local establishment.

The classic pattern is: first generation Chinese living overseas resist change; parents struggle to retain customs. Yet, there is a quest for acceptance locally by both parents and children. When wrestling with identity and discovering what makes them different from Westerners many Chinese perceive responsibilities and do not want to be branded as 'traitors' by their fellow countrymen. 'We are Chinese!', they declare among themselves with obvious pride, in a multi-cultural environment involving cross-cultural misunderstandings.

Native-born, second generation overseas Chinese generally strive to emulate and compete with Westerners. But they are restrained from aping Caucasians and there may be culture clashes with family members. And when children answer their parents' Cantonese questions in English they are quickly admonished: 'Tell me in Chinese!'

This means the second generation of 'culturally displaced' persons is caught in the middle. With both a generation and a racial gap the dilemma is: 'Do I choose my parents' or my peers' ways?'

Meanwhile the third generation, as 'white Chinese', are assimilated. They understand little about Chinese culture. Grandparents, who speak Cantonese when they want to keep something secret from the kids, say, 'Can excuse Chinese being more English than the English, but if really Chinese must understand our ways.'

Simultaneously, children may be ashamed of their parents' 'Asiatic looks' and fractured English. Brought up on a western diet of television, hard-rock and dating, these Chinese youngsters hold the kitchen god, odd-looking cooking pans and back-scratchers in contempt in today's technological world. All 'funny' names are deleted from their vocabulary.

Once parents are westernised and assimilated the chances of their children adopting Chinese ways are remote. Youngsters are less afraid of losing face than their elders who remember the saying, 'You can kill a scholar but you cannot humiliate him.' Although damage to one's ego is important, to a degree in any society, young Chinese brought up in the West are the casualties of transition. But with time, in spite of having lost their 'Chineseness', with a craving to trace their roots, they may come back, full circle, to those previously unwanted *woks* and tongue scrapers. Although not 'born again Chinese', they may feel comfortable wearing a padded Chinese jacket and appreciate the benefit of herbal medicine.

A third generation American-Chinese, whose family, like many early settlers, spoke the Toisan dialect, is an example. He insists that, although ethnic Chinese, he is a patriotic American. He served in the United States Army. Nonetheless, although it is not easy wedged between two cultures developed over centuries, undoubtedly he is still Chinese and proud of it. Suspecting racial slurs, he is ready to engage his antagonist in fisticuffs.

Just as the grandfather of a Chinese friend of mine disowned his sister because she married a Malay, so this American-Chinese had no intention of 'mixing the breed' by marrying a Caucasian. With the help of matchmakers, within a couple of weeks of arriving in Hong Kong, he had wed a 'real' Chinese girl. A month later she followed him to San Francisco. He had 're-established' himself as a Chinese. His wife was expected to sinocise the family. She bore him four boys and a girl. They were made to keep in touch with their roots and learn the language.

After they had grown up, the father, 'with one stroke of the knife', threw the daughter out of the house and forbade the sons to speak to her because she had an English boyfriend. Dad did not want Eurasian grandchildren. He could not bear the thought of his precious daughter sleeping with a 'foreign devil' even within the sanctity of marriage. Although family ties had been strong and supportive he was not prepared to love his daughter uncondition-ally, even if 2 per cent of all marriages in the States are inter-racial and more than half of all Asian-Americans born in the United States intermarry, usually with Whites.

BEFORE 1962, for a person born in the old Empire (later the Com-monwealth), immigration to Britain was comparatively easy. But with the Acts of 1962, 1971 and 1981 new requirements were intro-duced and few Chinese (compared to numbers going to Canada, the United States or Australia) are now entering the United Kingdom. In a city like Vancouver, one of the best examples, in spite of some Chinese upsetting native Canadians by cutting down sequoia trees in their gardens for superstitious reasons and living lavish lifestyles, roughly one-third of all inhabitants are Asian and one-sixth are from Hong Kong. Others choose instead to learn French at Alliance Française, in Hong Kong, and apply to go to Quebec.

Canada imposed a racially biased head tax on Chinese from 1885 to 1923. In 1903, this amounted to C$500 a person. Today, the picture is quite different and, in British Columbia, David Lam, who came to Canada from Hong Kong, is Lieutenant Governor and the Queen's representative. Yet although Chinese have in the past been considered a model minority and praised for their thrift and indus-triousness, now they are frequently blamed for several things, from garbage in the streets to escalating real estate prices. A small insen-sitivity can cause racist emotions just as Chinese grumble about Vietnamese Boat People and Filipina domestic helpers in Hong Kong.

But if, in spite of everything, there is less discrimination against Asians in Canada than in most developed countries, perhaps the creation of a 'cultural mosaic' and general attitudes are responsible. 'The only thing that Canadians probably are offended by', said

Alexander Lukie of the Canadian Commission in Hong Kong, 'are those who don't want to adapt, those who want to ghettoize and don't want to reach out and become Canadians.'

In the United States in 1991, 2.9 per cent of the 248.7 million population were Asian. Of the 1.6 million Chinese Americans (the largest Asian group), over 60 per cent have been born overseas. In some areas, like New York's Chinatown (the largest in the West) it could be approaching 80 per cent. The most dramatic changes have been in California with its colourful mass of humanity. This racial melting pot, with 'permissive differentiation', has been what makes America work. Unity through diversity, as opposed to Canada's colourful, multi-cultural mosaic, has still resulted in the United States and its people, collectively, becoming the most powerful nation in the world.

Certainly, it has not always been easy for Chinese. This is highlighted in a 233-page report, *Civil Rights Issues Facing Asian Americans in the 1990s*, published in 1992 which took two years to compile. It relates how insensitivity can vary from lack of government resources, to police ignorance of Asian cultures, to outright hosility. The report goes on to relate that many, from new arrivals who speak little or no English to wealthy, university-educated businessmen, face widespread racial prejudice at all levels of society. Discrimination, bigotry and threats of violence are facts of life according to the United States Commission on Civil Rights.

Unlike in America, immigration is an issue which lacks romantic resonance in the United Kingdom which has no tradition as a melting pot. Hong Kong's financial investment there pales in comparison with the United States. There has never been a blatant grab for wealthy citizens. Britain, it seems, has never had the foresight to make it easier for businessmen, professionals and people with desirable skills to immigrate on a large scale as have Canada, the United States and Australia. In these countries, Hong Kong 'cash-flow immigrants' boost economies and create extra jobs. Generally, Britain does not relish the idea of linking investment to the issuing of passports.

'We're winners on this one,' exclaimed Al Lukie of the Canadian Commission in Hong Kong. 'We're getting immense benefits from the people who are moving, not just investment but industrious people with skills.'

Around one visa issued in every five is in the business class, and then, if all goes well, within three years immigrants acquire full Canadian citizenship.

A past student from a college where I once taught, suggested

Hong Kong should take over an uninhabited island, say on a ninety-nine-year lease, off the west coast of Scotland. This should then be fashioned into a European replica of 'an Asian Little Dragon' – a 'replacement Jerusalem'. At first, I thought it was a leg-pull. But this old student, now a Hong Kong Legislative Councillor, was deadly serious, although the radical solution was rejected as were similar overtures to Taiwan and Darwin, Australia. In addition, the idea of allowing Hong Kong Chinese to move to the Falklands was also suggested. Imagine dynamic conglomerates like Jardines, Swires, Cheung Kong and Sun Hung Kai setting up branches there.

In 1989, the London-based 'think tank', the Adam Smith Institute, also proposed that a 'replacement Hong Kong' should be established on an island off the coast of Scotland. Islands off West Africa and Mexico were quoted as possible alternatives. After all, there is a precedent for capable and industrious people taking over a 'barren rock' and turning it into a leading business centre. Perhaps these ideas were not so puerile as they sounded at first.

What has been done in Hong Kong – a city-state with comparatively no natural resources apart from purposeful personnel and a deep-water port – can be done elsewhere. We are talking of 'quality people' on whose sturdy backs the Territory has been built. If such folk were to achieve the same results, economicially, for Britain as they have for Hong Kong the English should not complain about handing out additional passports.

The United Kingdom it is true, notwithstanding national sentiment, is issuing passports to 50,000 heads of households who are key personnel in the private and public sectors. Together with dependants, the number provided for was estimated at first to total as many as 225,000. The scheme in some sectors has been under-subscribed. These documents are not intended to provide instant escapes but rather to instill confidence and encourage key Hongkongers only to 'abandon the junk' if stability and conditions seriously deteriorate.

'It's comforting to know I can get out in an emergency,' one university graduate, a public relations specialist, told me. But she also admitted that, at some stage she will emigrate – but not to Britain. She and her husband, who came from the People's Republic, hope to go to Canada.

If the worst happens after 1997 and people avail themselves of this British passport 'insurance policy', with approaching a quarter of a million people haemorrhaging from Hong Kong, travelling by 747 jet, up to 900 flights would be required. To give an idea of the magnitude of the exodus: with, say, one flight arranged for every three days, these would extend over about seven years.

But nationality, which for most of us amounts to accident of birth rather than choice, means more than just a passport. Although Hong Kong has been a British colony for over a century-and-a-half, a limited number of Chinese living in the Territory display overt loyalty to the United Kingdom. Their main reason for applying for foreign passports is fear of living under a communist regime. This aversion was amply demonstrated when in the region of one million demonstrated peacefully in Hong Kong protesting against the 1989 'Beijing Massacre'. But, with time, feelings abated.

Most Westerners see the average Hong Kong Chinese as very pro-China, with its 5,000 years of history, although not necessarily pro-People's Republic. An excerpt from a letter, written by Gabriel O'Hara to the Editor of the *South China Morning Post*, follows. This highlights what was seen as a bad case of 'paradoxaemia', which afflicts some well-off Hong Kong Chinese. It can lead to sufferers making contradictory assertions without their realising, apparently, that there is any real conflict.

> 'I am totally Chinese; I am patriotic towards China. I do not consider myself to be British, and indeed I dislike Britain and the British.' Closely followed by: 'Please give me British nationality.'

Amid the debate there seems to be little nostalgia about cutting ties with Britain. For those emigrating to North America, Australia or elsewhere there are, of course, regrets for friends left behind. But sentiment for the United Kingdom does not seem to be an important factor. Many Chinese members of the Legislative Council, including senior government servants, admit they were never happy swearing allegiance to the Queen and prefer the present oath to serve the Hong Kong people.

But it is untrue that few Hongkongers have anything in common with Britain. Many have studied – a number at post-graduate level – and worked there. David Tang, grandson of the late Sir Tang Shiu-kin (business tycoon and philanthropist who wore long, Chinese gowns, had four wives and lovely twinkling eyes) is an example. David Tang went to public school and worked in a law firm in London. But, as he said in an interview for *Hong Kong inc*: 'If you understand anything about English politics, you're in cuckoo land if you think they will grant six million passports, or three million passports, whether you have the right to it or not.'

Certainly many Hong Kong Chinese today – and it takes all

types to make Hong Kong – value freedom and democracy just like Britons. One Chinese friend, a Rhodes Scholar who married an Englishman half a century ago and has two grown-up Eurasian children, was, I am sure, quite sincere when she told me: 'I love England!' And this is from a Chinese who can trace her pedigree back to a disciple of Confucius.

The British Government at first predicted 300,000 applications for its 'passports of convenience'. But numbers fell well short with greatest interest shown by the business sector. The truth is, the entire Hong Kong population is not itching to live in Britain, which many see as cold, dull, damp, discriminatory and dark at four o'clock on a winter's afternoon, with the economy in the doldrums and high unemployment. 'The English are not nice!' some go as far as to suggest. Certainly it is easier to make money in Hong Kong. Even if a Chinese businessman once accosted me with: 'Why don't you want us to go to Britain? We Chinese could revitalise your economy. Canada welcomes us.'

Wilson Chang, in a letter to the *South China Morning Post*, wrote:

> By birth or by naturalisation (when an oath of allegiance is sworn to the Queen) we are British subjects to start with. Why should we apply for something which is our right? If Britain doesn't want us, why should we go cap in hand?

Some Hongkongers, who are often accused like Britons of being insular, have suggested the whole of the Territory's approaching six million inhabitants should be allowed to enter the United Kingdom in an emergency. Others have said that the three-and-a-quarter million who are British subjects is a more realistic figure. In reality, it would not be easy for even a quarter of a million to integrate. Housing queues are already long and the National Health Service overloaded. Although the British quality newspapers have appeared sympathetic to Hongkongers' plights the tabloids have been singularly unimpressed.

'As an exporter of soccer hooliganism Britain does not want to be leavened by law-abiding talent,' a Chinese civil servant who speaks flawless English and has lived all his life in Hong Kong insists.

There is no doubt John and Joan Bloggs, who live in the conservative heartland of Britain and can be bigoted and prejudiced, have little knowledge of Hong Kong people or their culture. With a domestic backlash unlikely, most citizens and Members of Parliament appear uninterested in Hongkongers' plight, living so far away, even though right of abode in Britain has been given to Gibraltarians and Falklanders. Chinese are sometimes derided for their business mentality and the ability to help themselves. The fact that a person's father fought (and perhaps died) for King and Empire in World War II does not seem important. If they had blond hair, blue eyes and were fond of Yorkshire pudding their chances of acquiring British nationality would be better.

An astute, prosperous, Chinese banker, who has had varied interests in Britain for many years, told me, 'In the UK, now people eye you over and wonder what you're after!'

The last time Britain had a large influx of immigrants was when Idi Amin expelled 40,000 Ugandan Asians in 1972. Then, as now, the average Englishman objected strongly. Today, a large number of those 28,000 independent-minded Indians who came to Britain run small shops. Many have done well. Few are a burden on society. Most have integrated. There have been no 'rivers of blood' as prophesied by Conservative Member of Parliament Enoch Powell.

Another Member, Norman Tebbit, suggested the 'cricket test' in which Hong Kong immigrants should be taken to a match between England and another Commonwealth team to see which side they championed. The trouble is, most Hong Kong Chinese are not interested in cricket!

'If we could import the Chinese work ethic and energy ... that would be an enormous advantage,' he was however quoted as saying. But, Tebbit went on, it was not a question of ability or race. Just a problem of huge numbers of people, particularly as they had greater pride in their 'Chineseness' than they did thirty years ago.

One of the few British Parliamentarians who supported immigration on a large scale was the leader of the Liberal Democrats, Paddy Ashdown, a former Royal Marine who served out East and studied Chinese. He advocated right of abode for all Hong Kong citizens who desired it.

Surprisingly, even Chinese who have lived in Britain for several years do not want a massive influx of elitist Hongkongers. There is rivalry between long-time, Chinese residents born overseas and more recent arrivals, some born with silver chopsticks in their mouths. A working class, New Territories villager knew no English when he arrived thirty years ago with a few pounds in his pocket. Today he owns three restaurants, drives a Mercedes Benz and sends his son to an expensive public school. To him England, where he has carved out a comfortable life for himself, is now home. 'We've little in common with those newcomers,' a long-term Chinese resident remarked. 'They come from modern Hong Kong which we never knew. They're better educated; well qualified; speak good English. We old hands could lose out.'

Many more could, in fact, arrive than the whole of the present Chinese population in Britain. There would be immense friction. Numerous Chinese living there have adopted English ways and many are too unassuming and poorly educated to hold their own in what some see as a comfortable niche. They would rather bring over more of their cronies, via their 'networks', from the New Territories.

Other Chinese in Britain, however, take the view that a large intake would boost the economy. 'They wouldn't take our business,' Peter Chau remarked. 'Most wouldn't run restaurants. They'd be our customers.'

With Canada, the United States and Australia skimming off the brightest and benefiting from about 200,000 Hong Kong immigrants in the 1980s, a new influx to Britain could be the most talented intake of refugees since the Jews fled Europe in the 1930s. A few blue-chip, high-fliers have, of course, invested in the United Kingdom. People like lanky, dapper Dickson Poon, the Hong Kong tycoon who has taken over Harvey Nichols, the 'By Appointment', Knightsbridge store. Other whiz kids, like George and Victor Hwang of the Parkview Group, have bought Battersea Power Station, the London landmark with four prominent chimneys.

When she was Prime Minister, Mrs Thatcher said it was Britain's solemn duty to do the right thing while fully understanding public resistance to mass immigration. The fact is six million people, over half of whom are British subjects, will be handed over to a totalitarian regime on the stroke of midnight at the end of June 1997. Lack of self-determination is 'one of the biggest denials of human rights by Britain this century', Anthony Rogers, Chairman of the Hong Kong Bar Association said in April 1990. The 1992 report by the International Commission of Jurists criticised Britain for failing to provide right of abode for over three million or so British Dependent Territory Citizen passport holders.

It is not easy for someone who has lived most of his life in England and takes a full British passport for granted to appreciate the feelings of a British national in a colony still administered, for foreign policy and defence, from London. Although he was taught as a child to sing 'God save the Queen' with fervour he later found that, because of expediency and through no fault of his own, his birthright has been whittled away.

'It causes me more personal embarrassment than anything I think I knew during my ten years in Hong Kong,' announced Lord

MacLehose in 1986 at the Nationality debate, in the Upper House in London. Sir (as he was then) Murray MacLehose's governorship ended in 1982.

Meanwhile, offspring of professional and business classes who do manage to enter Britain – if the drawbridge allows them – should be watched carefully. In 1993, 77 per cent of Chinese between the ages of sixteen and nineteen are staying on for further education. This is more than Whites (37 per cent), or any other minority living in the United Kingdom. Whether their parents try to prevent it or not these young Chinese will become Anglicised and there will be big influxes to universities, including to Oxbridge. The social structure in the United Kingdom, in one or two generations, will be quite different.

'I doubt if Britain knows how to handle us oriental Jews!' remarked Samson Leung, a Chinese businessman.

CHAPTER SIX

HONG KONG

DURING my three-month stay in Britain, spiritually I journeyed back to Hong Kong many times. But fantasies cannot survive the check-in and bustle of Heathrow, even though, when the time comes to depart, there is that mixed, slightly sad end-of-term feeling.

International airports, with their sameness, are quite unlike exciting, smelly sea ports where we called after completing four-year tours in the 1950s and 1960s. Then, after long leave, one's boat ploughed through the waves and entered the Suez Canal sensing the East, where a whisky soda tastes different, had really begun. Meanwhile aboard, stewards insisted that not all passengers who travelled first class were themselves first class.

On the 8,000-mile journey there were shipboard romances and magnificent sunsets in the Indian Ocean. Occasionally, a green flash could be glimpsed as the swollen, flaming red ball dipped below the horizon. Staring over the side at night, or while flushing the toilet in the darkness of one's cabin, plankton, minute drifting plant and animal life, became luminescent amid the foam after being churned up by the ship.

Now in this post-colonial age, with many expatriates little more than transients on short-term contracts, fewer Europeans dedicate themselves to lifelong careers in the Orient. The first thing one senior contract officer did on arrival, I recall, was to make his will. 'Can't bear the thought of leaving my bones here!'

Now, on a 6,000-mile, twelve-hour direct flight to Hong Kong one is pampered by charming, wrinkle-free, Asian ambassadresses who fill younger sister roles. They also serve as reassuring aunts, playful kittens, and are past mistresses at flashing sultry smiles yet averting glances with Asian humility. In the early 1950s, the same flight would have taken five days by seaplane, with passengers sleeping each night in a hotel. Comparatively recently, Union Jacks have been painted over on tails of Cathay Pacific planes to the mortification of Old Hong Kong Hands. But, by so doing the British Swire Group gives face to China. Cathay, in return, will carry on as Hong Kong's Airline after 1997.

'Always try local beer and local women,' a Birmingham voice piped up a couple of rows back as I relaxed after take-off. 'Little Heat' (seventh day of Seventh Moon) and 'Great Heat' (twenty-third day of Seventh Moon), by the Chinese calendar, had already passed. Autumn weather with static electricity shocks from metal doorhandles, snake soup and Mongolian hotpot will soon be with us.

The first real hint of 'homecoming' was the number of Chinese on the plane, a few with portable telephones. One man, erect and stiff with a protruding Adam's apple, carefully folded his handkerchief everytime after use. Others, not so immaculate, would think twice if they had bad omens before boarding. People searched for locker space, minded their own business and were generally tolerant and relaxed. In English society, so often there are tensions when classes mix.

Not that class distinction does not exist out East. On this flight, half a dozen People's Republic Chinese sat talking in *Putonghua*, chain smoking and taking full advantage of the free drink service.

'Only Mainland Chinese puff away like that today,' a Scot grinned.

Hongkongers tend to deride many from the People's Republic with their hayseed accents. Two decades ago China was remote and impenetrable. When travelling, Mainlanders feel threatened in the West in what must seem like another planet. Unflattering programmes have been run on Hong Kong television about such 'yokels' who again differ, considerably, from the Taiwanese.

One elderly Hong Kong Chinese, with a squashed-in face, kept his cap on in the plane and spoke the odd word of broken English. This reminded me of the China Coast pidgin English my *makee learnee* amah, Ah Hing, parleyed in the 1950s. 'Me go top side,' she would call before climbing the stairs.

Pidgin developed as a 'bridge', so Europeans and Chinese could do business before the First Opium War when anyone who taught foreigners to speak Chinese could be beheaded. It was sophisticated in its way, and, although traces remain, pidgin came to a virtual end in the 1960s.

After what seemed almost like non-stop eating and ritual toilet going, sometimes related in earthy detail, the announcement came that Number-Three Typhoon Signal had been hoisted. I recalled Typhoon Wanda, in September 1962, when our concrete-framed, multi-storied building swayed. It was the last killer-wind, accompanied by severe flooding, from which the Colony learnt bitter lessons on how to batten down.

Looking down now, I saw Hong Kong. It's just over 400 square miles which is that of a good-sized, Texas cattle ranch. I spotted where the burnt-out hulk of the *Queen Elizabeth*, gutted by fire in 1972, had lain. As usual, there would be a number of People's Republic ships in port, none of which ever condescends to fly the British Red Ensign courtesy flag.

There in the clouds nestled 200-acre Stonecutters, with its colonial-style, army buildings, an island no longer. During World War II, it was used by the Japanese to breed snakes for extracting serum to develop antidotes for snake bites. In 1992, the island harboured over seventy species of birds, as well as magnificent butterflies and other insects. There is a significant night heronry. Before reclamation work when the island was joined to Kowloon in the same year, it boasted the world's largest colony of enormous black-eared kites, numbering about 1,200. These are the major cause of bird strikes at Kai Tak airport. Kites were the most common scavengers in London during the Middle Ages.

Kai Tak is the fourth busiest airport in the world for cargo and the fifth for passengers. The final approach to it is one of the most difficult to negotiate. At best it involves tricky curves to avoid hills, coupled with danger of wind shear. Spontaneous applause broke out as we landed. With Number-Three Signal up relief flowed through bodies like electricity.

There was a warm welcome from my wife. 'Chinese girls do kiss,' I was once told enthusiastically by a visiting Dutchman as if it was the most important discovery he made while attending his one-week seminar.

Old-fashioned Chinese, it is true, display less affection and believe smooching spreads germs. The 'seven bodily orifices' (eyes, ears, nostrils and mouth) are closely guarded. Babies are often nuzzled.

From our taxi amid dust and pollution, the curse of Hong Kong, giant wreckers' hammers were busy in Conduit Road. New thirty-floor, concrete box-like structures with multi-storey living long firmly established, now block out the sun. Work progresses at a pace unknown in Europe. Hong Kong hums. Higher and bigger, in a city where every Hongkonger memorises the floor area of his own flat, is the never ending aim. Few gracious, colonial-style, three-storey mansions with balconies and colonnades remain.

Stately granite-block retaining walls, with large banyan trees clinging octopus-like to mortar joints, have survived countless typhoons. Symbols of Buddhism, stability and longevity, with multiple trunk and root systems, these trees resemble webs of extended Chinese families with inter-marriages. Banyan timber has no commercial value, but the bark and milky sap are used to manufacture medicine and lac.

Meanwhile, the search continues for buildings to demolish thereby creating new sites in the race to become rich. As deafening pile drivers boom, drowning cries of an itinerant knife grinder, lumbering lorries clog what, in the 1950s, was peaceful Conduit Road plied by the odd sedan chair. Occasionally, then, there was the call of barking deer. Mid-Levels are now burdened by tremendous strains on infrastructure causing disruption and discomfort in what has been described as the most stressful city in the world.

'Welcome home, Sir!' our Filipina maid exclaimed. Over 90,000 now work as domestics in Hong Kong allowing both Chinese and expatriate wives to earn second incomes for their families. Filipinas replaced Chinese amahs, with plaited pigtails and immaculate black and white trouser-suits. Many came from Sun Tak, in Guangdong Province, and other parts of the rural, Canton Delta. To them, going into service was a calling. Together with their independent 'sisters', while still in their teens, they vowed before a deity to remain single. A banquet followed vows of celibacy and the hairdressing ceremony in the temple where their hair was combed up. If forceably married off by their fathers they resisted consummation. With a distaste for heterosexual relationships and childbirth this included wrapping themselves up, mummy-like, under their bridal gowns, to attempt to maintain purity and chastity. Some drank herbal tea to stop urination. A few employed magical charms.

'If your old man is poor he sends you out to work. Soon as he's better off he takes a concubine,' they used to say.

Women's Liberation commenced in southern China in the early nineteenth century, long before it caught on in the West. There were lesbian relationships. Dildos were made of expandable raw silk or filled with beancurd. The latter gave rise to the term 'grinding the beancurd', in Chinese, for lesbianism. These 'marriage resistance sisterhoods' endured for about a century. Most westernised Chinese women today, however, find it difficult to be Women's Libbers. Their Confucian background prevents them.

Our home in Conduit Road stands on the site of the once imposing Foreign Correspondents Club, where *Love is a Many Splendoured Thing* was filmed in the 1950s. With moderate inflation, our flat appreciated in value forty-five-fold in twenty-one years. The effigy of Chung Kuei, the eighth-century Shanxi physician, clad in maroon and white robes, smiling, stands on a glass ledge by our main door. He is protector against evil and, holding a fan on which a bat perches, expert at catching ghosts.

'Lovely mixture of East and West.'

'Sights and sounds reveal personalities of inhabitants,' is how a visiting English academic described our home. Perhaps it does reflect some of our complexities!

Sterling silver vases and western figurines stand unashamedly alongside ornately carved jade ornaments and delicate Chinese snuff bottles. Double-sided silk embroidery is mounted in slim black-wood frames. Miniature Chinese classics three inches high, like *Red Chamber Dream*, one of the world's masterpieces, are exquisitely carved with minute characters on 'pages' of ivory. The reclining figure of that prince of vagabonds, Li Po (alias Li Tai Paak, born in 701), with an empty wine cask, carved in cow bone, looks down wishfully from a glass shelf. This poet's colourful life ended when, on reaching in a drunken stupor to embrace the reflection of the moon, he fell overboard and drowned.

> With a jar of wine Li makes a hundred poems,
> He sleeps in an inn in Ch'angan city ...

There is also a variety of crystal ornaments in our 'humble abode', including a number of dishes each containing one antique silver and six antique bronze coins. These receptacles are placed in 'strategic' positions. There is one inside the front entrance, where the light is switched on permanently and others on bedside tables. Much like the jars of salt water, one of which is positioned behind the gas cooker, these crystal containers and their coins reflect radiation. They counteract evil influences and harmful elements in the atmosphere, similar to Goddess of Mercy (dwarf) bamboo whose non-calcified stems filter out harmful chemicals in 'sick' buildings and purify the air. These 'fortune plants' also absorb static electricity which causes nervousness and irritability, especially when a typhoon approaches. Two octagonal clocks, roughly resembling the shape of a Chinese *paat kwa* (the 'eight-sided divining diagram'), hang on walls.

Although an 'uneducated' westerner deduces such objects are to allay the jinx there is far more to *feng shui* (meaning 'wind and water') than that. It in effect brings a form of 'cosmology' within the grasp of common man. It is concerned with living in balance with the universe, one's environment and the 'Eight Elements' [heaven, thunder, wind, water (rain), water (the ocean), the earth, hills and fire]. A golden thread of spiritual vitality, *chi*, runs through every form of existence and binds together, as a living body, everything that exists in the heavens above or the earth below. And woe betide anything or anybody that does not conform.

Although the People's Republic has labelled *feng shui* a superstitious practice and one of the 'Seven Evils', living in harmony and at peace with logical rules is really what it is all about. It embraces disciplines like ecology, architecture – including spacial orientation – and ergonomics, similar to western bodies of knowledge. Colours affecting mood and disposition are important. *Feng shui* is, therefore, really a complex web of metaphysical beliefs which affect man's place in the universe, so that you, living or dead, can adapt. So that you are content. One grave in the New Territories is situated in a '*feng shui*-friendly' place, among hills which are said, with the aid of some imagination, to resemble the crotch of a naked woman. 'Returning to the womb' is especially auspicious.

Feng shui masters, in 1992, charged about HK$3 per square foot of floor area and western firms in Hong Kong seek advice regularly. Engaging them helps promote harmony in the workplace and improves personnel relations. It augments everyone's chances not only for conducting business but for everything from avoiding illness to taking a mistress.

'Feels comfortable here,' visitors often remark on entering my flat in Conduit Road.

And, on looking out of our French windows, following the 'language pattern' of *feng shui* and interacting with the environment, one is able to interpret the spiritually based landscape. Following Taoist principles there is rhythm in nature. Modelled on animated ground rules of farming villages in ancient China much is common sense. Nobody, anywhere, chooses to live next to a cemetery. With the setting often more important than the jewel, the aesthetics of Chinese geomancy offer lessons for western planners and environmentalists today.

Victoria Peak, with its spurs behind my flat, symbolises strong backing. Its 'cosmic breath' brings 'blessings' which are just and inevitable rewards for the skilful and diligent. Water courses stream down from this mountain during heavy storms keeping fortunes flowing into our flat and protecting our well-being. The 'cosmic breath' of *feng shui* rides on the wind and is dispersed and checked by water courses. Too much 'energy' drives good influences away. Too little causes stagnation. Like salt in cooking it is to some extent, an individual thing. Too much, and the food is inedible. Too little, and it is tasteless. As our flat has brought us good fortune in the past we would be ill-advised to move.

Water signifies money. That is why an informed friend remarked about the ill-fated, liquidated Bank of Credit and Commerce in Hong Kong, which used to have a water feature cascading away from, and out of, the entrance: 'They were asking for trouble!'

Again, largely because of water, London's Docklands are considered by Chinese to be a propitious district. The River Thames with its constant ebbs and flows, especially during the days of Empire with goods shipped around the world, has played an important part in Britain's prosperity.

Derek Walters, British *feng shui* specialist *extraordinaire*, wearing Chinese ceremonial robes, has built up a lucrative practice in Britain where he advised Prince Andrew and Sarah Ferguson in happier days. Some Europeans appreciate an added concept based on abstract reasoning, with a pragmatic approach rather than just the supernatural element and mumbo-jumbo mystical aspects. This fourth dimension, some believe, can create a new 'soul' to a building.

Feng shui believers maintain that those living in dwellings facing south enjoy better *chi* and are more intelligent and successful than persons in residences facing north who lack vitality. Houses, temples, graves and the emperor on his throne, all should preferably face sunny south. It is warm. It is auspicious. It is pure. It is *yang*. Victoria Peak, one of the most beautiful backdrops in the world, to the south of our flat, is covered with shrubs and trees in various shades of green. A fair amount of wildlife, much nocturnal, remains. I have occasionally sighted ferret-badgers, masked-palm civet cats and porcupines. Snakes, such as hooded king cobras and bright green, poisonous bamboo snakes, abound. They can sometimes be seen sunning themselves. There are squirrels, edible freshwater crabs and skinks with vivid, bright blue tails. There is evidence that elephants and rhinoceroses once roamed the forests of South China.

In the humid spring, beds of cottonwool cloud lie in ravines and gullies to the south of my flat; wisps of mist rise, smoke-like, from craggy haunts of countless creatures giving the impression the slopes are on fire. Looking out from my balcony, where the warm sun shines in winter and the cool south-west monsoon blows in summer, provides a special tranquillity. This counteracts the effects of crowded, frenetic Hong Kong. Towns without trees are dead. Eyes need to rest on greenery and nature's beauty regularly, rather than on hideous concrete. Otherwise, the heart sickens. One has to appreciate one is part of God's awe-inspiring ecosystem. Back to nature, one derives a special satisfaction when one defecates in the bushes. Yet some people never stop and stare over the equivalent of a five-barred gate. Spiritually, perhaps they do not need to. Byron wrote: 'I love not Man the less, but Nature more.'

Thoughts turn to eighty-acre oak and hazel Wayland Wood, one mile up the road from Mother's house in Norfolk, with its seasonal carpet of snowdrops and bluebells. Here the Babes in the Wood were murdered not far from the Wicked Uncle's house. It is probably the oldest wood in England after Sherwood Forest and Selwood. Nightingales sing there in spring.

No *'feng shui* woods', behind Hong Kong villages, date back more than 250 to 300 years, although corridors of primary rain forests, centuries ago, ran continuously from the tropical south of China to the frozen north. We British started planting trees in the Colony, including on Victoria Peak, in the 1870s. Fortunately, there have been no major hill fires on the Peak for the past century. With its luxuriant vegetation and good soil it would make a wonderful final resting place, near a fried-egg-flower tree. My wife objects. 'We couldn't visit you if your ashes were scattered,' she insists.

Gazing out of the French windows, with two courting, black-eared kites wheeling in the sky, I turn towards the image of *Kwan Yin*, the Goddess of Mercy. She sits placidly, in one of her thirty-three different manifestations, with a rosary around her neck alongside a statuette of the Athenian philosopher Socrates, the West's counterpart of Confucius. *Kwan Yin*, born in a blaze of celestial light, the third daughter of a king, originally a hermaphrodite, is often depicted as the Far East's equivalent of the Virgin Mary. *Kwan Yin* is merciful and indiscriminate of status, fame and wealth. She is capable of preventing misfortunes.

Sufferers need only whisper her name to be rescued. And, as I look at the gracious lady revered by Buddhists and Taoists alike, and turn my ear towards Victoria Peak, I heed the music of the breeze in the greenery intermingling with a faint, continuous, distant murmur. It is a not uncommon call. Perhaps the message is what the Virgin Mary and the Goddess of Mercy both hear when they gaze down, listening to the plaintive cries of the world. Will the pleas change after Hong Kong is reunited with the Motherland?

Although a chasm often separates a mélange of Chinese and western attitudes, with conflicts and contradictions between religions, there is at times a fertile combination. British policy in 1834 in India created a class of person who was Indian by blood and colour but English in tastes, opinions, morals and intellect. No such edict was enacted in Hong Kong, where the Chinese were not overly enthusiastic in identifying with Europeans, although there was a great deal of over-idealising British civilisation by Westerners and casting the Chinaman as inferior.

Most Europeans lived and worked in white circles and working-class Chinese had few western contacts. Both races looked down on each other. With the introduction of the 1904 Ordinance, no Chinese were allowed to reside on Victoria Peak and even English governesses required a permit to live there. Similarly, after 1923, the hill, with fifteen boundary stones on the island of Cheung Chau (Long Island), was reserved for Whites. An exclusive 'garden city' was also planned for Europeans in Kowloon Tong. These segregation laws were repealed by the Japanese during the Occupation.

There was, however, no persistent ill-treatment of Chinese in Hong Kong, like the mob violence in California and Australia, where the 'White Australia' policy lasted until as late as 1967. Yet Europeans interned in World War II prison camp, at Stanley, frequently complained about the behaviour of Chinese women married to Britons who were interned with them. Even two or three decades later some Englishmen still spoke down to Chinese in loud, hectoring tones. 'They've got to have a European behind them,' an old colleague of mine always insisted.

But, especially since the late 1960s, a middle class has emerged resulting in more mixing between races and less jaundiced, colonial views being taken. Even though not all Europeans are prepared to acknowledge it, most Chinese do not jump queues, shove and spit, even if a diet of salt fish, and oyster and shrimp sauce is a cause of bronchial complaints. But, in a city-state where many, after washing, dry their faces on wet towels, eat dog meat, take birds in cages for walks and arrange cricket fights, some Old Hong Kong Hands are still sometimes baffled by Chinese culture. 'China is a puzzle to annoy, flabbergast, please or perplex,' they insist.

Lord Northcliffe, British newspaper magnate and politician, took a different view. The Chinese were, in many ways, much like the British, he asserted, and, on a round-the-world trip in 1921, he cited such issues as fair play and one's word is one's bond. Many deals are made in tea houses and contracts are seldom entered into. 'Like the British, Chinese have their own sense of humour and ability to overcome adversity cheerfully,' Northcliffe maintained.

Partly because of possible discord mixed marriages were not common at the time of my 1960 wedding. Even uni-cultural marriages can be a jigsaw and a gamble at the best of times, without having to juggle complications of race, customs and varying perceptions of relationships. If a young mixed couple go back from hectic Hong Kong to England to live, with unrealistic expectations, there are added difficulties. 'He took me back to Sheffield, of all places!' fumed one Chinese girl. 'Beautiful countryside in England. Eat scotch eggs in the pub. But horribly long, dreary winter evenings!'

A tall, Shanghainese wife could only stand five months after she accompanied her husband back to Luxembourg. 'He was a different man to the one I married out East,' she alleged. They returned to the Orient.

Another mixed couple lived together and delayed tying the knot because the Englishman, who at first sought a 'one-night stand', maintained: 'I want my offspring to look English and not shoulder a stigma for the rest of their lives.'

'We have tiffs.'

'Don't understand each other's culture,' countered his chirpy Chinese partner with a 'goldfish mouth', who sought a permanent relationship.

Yet the *yin* and *yang* of a mixed marriage can be more adventurous, with exciting social dynamics, a wider circle of friends, varied travel and additional interests. The girl went on to explain that in spite of a strong sense of loyalty to parents, some Chinese had to defy family in order to marry a foreigner. 'Why don't you wed a nice Cantonese boy!' they exclaimed, insisting opposites attract but not in marriage.

Europeans are usually more straightforward and liberal than Chinese. That means a mixed marriage is often more open, free and egalitarian. However, because European bosses frequently marry secretaries, or women who are junior to themselves, there can be status difficulties in relationships with associates. When inviting friends to dinner care has to be taken that cultures do not separate the two races and they can relate. A modern Chinese is also sometimes torn between matching her career ambitions with being a good, 'subordinate' wife along Confucian lines.

'Mother-in-law wanted to take charge of my baby. Had to put my foot down,' a domineering Scottish girl, married to a Chinese, exclaimed.

Perhaps in a culture where a Chinese does not marry a wife but his parents take a daughter-in-law ('inside the womb of the family you and I are one'), this is not surprising.

'Same bed, two dreams,' another Chinese saying has it. Indeed, a Westerner can still remain outside Chinese society even if he does marry a local girl.

Learning an alien language does not come easily to many. The European husband may struggle with Cantonese but, unless it is 'plugged into the brain' as a child, he usually speaks it with 'flat' tones so that he mispronounces the word for nine (*kau*) and makes it sound like a man's private parts. Yet, if a person develops an interest in Cantonese this so-called barrier can help kindle relationships. He may also be fond of Chinese food, observe the wife's customs and be interested in 'things Chinese', even if he does (so his 'better-half' insists) 'speak sibilant English in parables'.

The Chinese wife, with a good command of English, may have been educated at a convent school in the days of colonial Hong Kong when sums were taught in pounds, shillings and pence. 'Norman Conquest 1066,' her teacher drummed into her; 'lieutenant' was prounounced 'leftenant'; she was not taught Chinese history. Yet, true to Hong Kong style, she writes 'Present' at the top of an envelope, when it is to be delivered by hand, even if she worked in a British firm and is westernised – at least superficially – to a degree.

But occasionally, in spite of the couple ostensibly being of the same religion, even if marriage provides a new dimension to life, they often think quite differently. The gap between the two frequently does not close and they can be way apart in a twilight zone. But, with mutual curiosity, they have much to learn from each other. Diversity and living in two cultures extends one profoundly and adds spice and a new richness. It can also bring misunderstandings and confrontation. Living, breathing and tasting another culture from an inside perspective, is more personal. One picks things up through exposure, sees both sides of racism and appreciates better the strong views Chinese take on special issues.

Why do Chinese, traditionally, avoid open confrontation, just as the English dislike being asked, 'How much you earn?' Are Westerners really more promiscuous? Why do Chinese readily accept they should support parents in old age? Even if two people have a common language they may not understand everything their partner says. 'Enquire how an invalid is,' a Chinese smirked, 'and the English answer, "As well as can be expected". Can mean anything!'

With language closely intertwined with culture, communications are obviously important. 'That pleased you no end!' I once said, with appropriate inflections, to a middle-class, Chinese academic, who, 'corrupted' by western education, I always feel has an excellent command of English. Unfortunately, she took me literally when I meant exactly the opposite. Unless you learn an alien language and the sentiments it transmits as a child from native speakers, it is not easy to acquire absolute proficiency, appreciating fully nuances of mood and character.

Certainly pillow talk helps, even if it is stuffed with chrysanthemum leaves to induce a sound night's sleep. There are many Anglo-Chinese marriages, when at Chinese New Year he goes off on the yacht to avoid mixing with in-laws. So often it would help if he tried to look at things with an Asian approach rather than falling back on, 'We Brits do it this way'; or insisting, 'There is a right way, a wrong way and a Chinese way'. Even those that learn their partner's language may have inadequate mastery for the deep understanding desirable within the intimacy of successful marriage.

Some Old China Hands do not favour learning Chinese. 'Only cranks and policemen bother,' my first Hong Kong boss contemptuously insisted.

Although similar remarks are sometimes made by those who appreciated how difficult Cantonese tones are to master his views were not new. Sir S. George Bonham, popular Governor of Hong Kong from 1848 to 1854 insisted: 'The study of Chinese warps the intellect and undermines judgement.'

He may have been influenced by his unpopular predecessor, Sir John Davis, a notable Chinese scholar. 'There is the danger of "going native" and being mesmerised by Chinese culture,' many insist.

'There's a "Five Elements" beauty dinner tonight,' my wife interrupted. 'Friends want to welcome you back – *Chiu Chau* food.'

After a journey from afar it is common to 'wash off the dust'.

WITH the two sexes frequently preferring to discuss different subjects, the Chinese custom is for men to sit at one table and wives at another. As there were only twelve of us we sat at one circular table next to our own wives, unlike European fashion where a man sits next to someone else's wife. Customs, both Chinese and European, have of course changed in this post-modern, evolving world. A society originally established essentially on Confucian ideology has been torn apart and precepts questioned.

'Chinese don't divorce,' everyone insisted when I first arrived in Hong Kong.

Now, four decades later, one-third of those Chinese present at this 'washing off the dust' dinner were parted from their spouses.

One had been married to a European. 'Till divorce does us separate' would be appropriate wedding vows in Hong Kong these days where one in seven marriages ends in divorce. Chinese career women no longer put up with their husbands' philanderings. Wives know their rights and realise, 'If one woman is not enough, 100 are not too many'. No such word as 'woman-hater' exists in Chinese.

Polygamy has been widespread throughout the history of the human race. Monogamy is a relatively recent introduction. In Hong Kong, only a decade or so ago a *tai kam tse* (a specially loyal, old, female servant who became mistress of ceremonies) would follow the happy couple from table to table at the wedding dinner reciting aloud such lines as, 'Have new baby every year have great fortune!'

But even though the Beatles used to sing 'All you need is love', for some reason, things had just not worked out for many females at our dinner that evening. Divorce is no longer a social stigma, like it was in the old China where a man could divorce a wife for barrenness, lasciviousness, jealousy, talkativeness, thievery, disobedience towards his parents and for leprosy.

About all our group had in common was that most members worked in the professions or in business. The families of three diners originated from Shanghai. Others could trace their 'native villages', for which there is a semblance of a 'pecking order', to somewhere in southern China. When the Shanghainese first moved to Hong Kong, when the People's Republic came into being, they thought Cantonese were 'barbaric and backward'. The latter believed Shanghainese were 'show offs, loud and lacking in dignity'. Now, after working together for over forty years, sometimes intermarrying, with younger Shanghainese speaking 'native Cantonese', the two groups get along fine – something like the Welsh and the English!

Mr Tam, a short, sturdy Hakka Chinese sat at our table. He had swum across Mirs Bay from the People's Republic as an illegal immigrant in the early 1960s using a short ladder as a raft. Outsmarting border guards, he found his way to a relative's home in Hong Kong. Relations still help one another. Two weeks earlier 'freedom swimmers' on inflated pigs' bladders had been mauled by sharks. 'Been lucky,' Mr Tam insisted as he sat pressing two middle fingers on pressure points at the sides of his eyes to relieve a headache. Now, the fact that he runs his own thriving printing business, with branches in Singapore and China, smacks more of hard work than of luck.

'Why is *koro* found in Singapore and not in Hong Kong?' asked Betty, who was wearing a dress with a traditional, high Chinese collar and whose face, with high cheek bones, could be described as pear-shaped. She has varied business interests and gets on and off planes like many get on and off buses. *Koro*, I knew, is when a person panics thinking his penis is retracting into his abdomen.

Fifty years ago researchers maintained that different cultures spawned different emotions. Today, psychologists tell us that happiness, surprise, fear, anger, sadness, disgust and contempt are common to all. With some nationalities, however, emotions are less intense. In spite of all Chinese at our gathering being westernised to a degree and feeling comfortable among Europeans, with their 'fragmented characters' they would, I knew, act differently if a strange Westerner was present.

Gossip and 'soapography' are, as in all cultures, part of Hong Kong life. Many yarns need, somehow, to be spun in the local language if one is to enjoy the full flavour. A tram rumbled past outside our restaurant with an advertisement on the side; 'Sunny Removals: Moving Overseas?' Annie, dying to get a word in as she tugged at her 'mutton-fat' (white) jade earrings, exclaimed: 'Emigration business booming!'

In any crowded, noisy Chinese restaurant there comes a time when your brain switches off. You create an imaginary island of privacy, do not eavesdrop on adjoining tables and have ears only for friends' conversations. Toasting my return consisted of gulping down hot, yellow chrysanthemum tea. This not only improves eyesight but is capable in an emergency of reducing fever.

Certainly this beverage suited me better than *mao tai*, a Chinese spirit made from fermented rice to which a variety of herbs have been added. It is distilled in the village of Mao Tai, in Guizhou Province. 'Spill any, burns a hole in the tablecloth!' they say.

Hong Kong, like most places, has its own gags which visitors may not fully appreciate. The 'Six M's' hardly falls into that category. 'Know what girls expect boyfriends to have?' Angel Wong, addressed as 'four-eyed girl' because she wore a pair of large glasses, asked.

She took a mouthful of tea and let it remain in her mouth about ten seconds before swallowing. 'No suitor,' she went on, 'is worth a second glance unless he is: male, macho, has money, a mansion, a Mercedes and a mobile telephone.'

'And an overseas passport!' cut in Bertha, who ran a booming real estate company and had recently returned from Australia, where, unlike Hong Kong, it is not the done thing to display your wealth.

Rebecca Lee, artist, designer and environmentalist, author of *China with Backpack and Camera*, nodded. As the first Chinese woman to set foot in both polar regions and having been 6,000 metres up Mount Everest and crossed the Taklimakan Desert on foot, she is in many ways typical of the younger, high-flying Chinese of today.

With seven out of ten people in Hong Kong having fled communism in China, or having at least one parent who did, the 'baby boomers', who were born in Hong Kong in the 1950s or 1960s, see things quite differently from their parents. Many, now around forty years old, in the twilight of colonialism went to elitist schools at the time that a cosmopolitan middle class was developing. Although not young enough to think like twenty-year-olds, who do not know enough about communism to be afraid of it and often idealise China, many in their thirties and forties are still deeply committed to Hong Kong and will only leave under compulsion. 'We are Chinese!' sometimes creeps into a conversation. They are ready to work with the Motherland. But, having said that, in spite of countless bright people, no single person really stands out, like Lee Kuan Yew in Singapore, to serve Hong Kong as Chief Executive after 1997.

Looking around the table I had to admit several had admirable qualities. People like Stella, a stock broker for example, who had a mole under one eye and intended having the blemish removed because, in that position, 'tears flow over it'. 'Invites bad luck. I'm very superstitious,' she admitted.

'People superstitious world over. We're being "creolised",' a man who had not spoken before interjected in a muffled voice. Most would not entirely agree. A unified, popular, worldwide culture, which nevertheless respects some diversity, is a long way off, even if American jeans with tight bottoms, western pop music and 'me-ism' have spread rapidly around the globe.

Chinese are good hosts. They made me feel at home. Rich or poor, a great deal of ritual that surrounds eating out is much the same. 'Appetite for food and sex is part of nature,' said Kao Tzu, in conversation with the philosopher Mencius, 2,300 years ago. The food at our restaurant, not far from a McDonald's, favoured by today's youngsters who are fatter than they should be, was nevertheless unusual even for Chinese.

The first dish, with a large carrot carved in the form of a unicorn in the centre, consisted of lily leaves from the People's Republic and de-boned ducks' tongues. A pregnant pause followed ... Everyone was urged to drink tea to welcome me back. Then, after what has been beautifully described as the 'ceremony of the first mouthful', everyone was invited to 'Take up chopsticks' and not to stand on ceremony. If a group of uneducated coolies were eating formalities would be similar.

Do not ask me why, but at that moment I suddenly thought of the E Sing Bakery. There persons unknown, on 15 January 1857, tried to poison the 400 or so strong European population of Hong Kong by lacing dough with arsenic. Fortunately, too much was added which induced vomiting. Baker Cheong Ah Lum was said to have rallied to the anti-European xenophobia sweeping China, but although Europeans were furious because he was acquitted of murder for lack of evidence – saying much for British justice – he was deported. Sir John Bowring, Governor from 1854 to 1859, composed a hymn commemorating the event which was sung in Saint John's Cathedral. A chunk of the bread was kept in the Chief Justice's office until the 1930s.

Chinese believe there are five basic tastes: salty (also slang for sexy), pungent, bitter, sour and sweet. If I were capable of writing lyrics they would be about Chinese food, although not everyone agrees. At one of our 'beauty dinners' a member brought along an Australian friend. But when the ducks' tongues, sea slugs or pigs' uteri were served she politely declined. Food characterises society. You are, after all, what you eat. To study cultures you need to examine eating habits. In Chinese you do not take a head count but a mouth count.

The Chinese invented health foods and, for thousands of years, employed dietary supplements. A harmonious diet does much to balance life's forces of *yin* and *yang*. Disease represents a loss of equilibrium of the humours of the five organs (Chinese have an affinity for the number five) of the body, namely spleen, lungs, heart, liver and stomach. 'To cure emperors' disease it is sometimes necessary to eat beggars' food.'

Certain dishes, like bean curd and honey, or green peas and dog meat, we are told can be dangerous, or even fatal, if they are eaten together at the same meal. If one eats over lengthy periods, especially as children, large quantities of salt fish or 'burnt' roast pork, to which colouring has been added, they are thought to be factors in causing cancer. Even Cantonese who emigrate to the West, research has shown, are more likely to suffer from 'Canton cancer', affecting the nose and throat, than Westerners.

Dishes are grouped and 'heat-giving substances', like beef or dog meat, should be followed by 'cooling' dishes, such as mandarin oranges, watermelon or winter melon. The last, as one of Hong Kong's illogicalities, is only available in the summer. Mouth ulcers signify a person's system is 'overheated' and suffering from, so called, hot air. Children are made to drink special *congee* to rid their systems of 'wetness'. There are countless herbal shops all over Hong

Kong, although patients are warned not to mix western and Chinese medicine. The science of medicine was said to have been started by Emperor Shan Nung, about 2838 BC.

Donkey skin, powdered clam shell and ginseng are among the ten ingredients that make up a concoction to build vitality, even if an elderly, wealthy Eurasian, in the 1950s, slept with a string of virgins in the hope of absorbing some of their *chi*. 'I only want a girl once,' he was quoted as saying. Rare, ground rhinoceros horn and tiger's bone, as well as tiger's penis, all aphrodisiacs, are expensive, although many aficionados consider that mood on the occasion, rather than food, is more important for sexual prowess. Nevertheless, it is believed firms in Hong Kong, producing fake tigers' penises from animal parts, enjoy good business.

Fungus growing on the inside of coffin lids, near the nose and throat, is said to have penicillin qualities. One of the first Chinese medicines to find its way overseas, in the sixteenth century, was the so-called China root, Chinese sarsaparilla, once reputed to cure syphilis.

We enjoyed the sophisticated culinary art that memorable evening at that *Chiu Chau* restaurant. All dishes had been chosen for their health-giving properties. Nevertheless, with Chinese cooking, colour, appearance, sometimes significance (because of homophones many are deemed lucky) and, of course, taste, are all important.

'At Wong Tai Sin Temple I pledged not to eat beef for three years,' a girl next to me said, as she left the lid off the teapot to let the waiter know it needed refilling. 'Ox man's best friend. Helps plough fields.'

> All things bright and beautiful,
> All creatures great and small,
> All things wise and wonderful,
> We like to eat them all!

'Not true,' she giggled.

It is interesting that J. Dyer Ball wrote, in *Things Chinese* (1903), 'The Chinese are not sufficiently civilised to take delight in killing birds and other game for pleasure!' Yet to the average Englishman, while eating dog meat is repulsive, for Buddhists not to eat beef and for Muslims to refrain from eating pork is all slightly illogical. Nobody need have worried at our 'beauty dinner'. No beef was served. Instead, waiters dished up soup made from red ginseng, *kau kei* (matrimony vine) and chickens' feet, to make me, a veteran athlete, run faster! As they say, 'Eat image to strengthen image'.

That evening, we ate green beans and lily petals to calm nerves and induce sound sleep. Two kinds of *beche-de-mer*, commonly called sea cucumber or sea slugs in Britain, followed. These can be precarious to handle with chopsticks, like the slippery abalone, labelled 'rubber soles' by Europeans, with which it was served. Anything a Chinese can eat I can enjoy too.

Chinese food somehow tastes better when eaten with chopsticks rather than with metal knives and forks. However Hu Yaobang, previously Communist Party Secretary in China, once advocated Chinese should use western cutlery because of the danger of passing on germs while eating from a communal dish. Yet 'partaking from the great pot', with shared meals, is always taken to imply bonds of commonalty and social forces.

We were next served frogs' spawn surrounded by protective nutrient jelly. Then came fish stomach and sharks' fin. One of the best dishes was 'gold coin' turtle soup made from a special species from southerly, sub-tropical Guangxi Province, in China. This soup is said to be good for the skin and rids the system of poisons. Some nutritionists even claim it can cure cancer. Turtles are considered to have spirits. An elderly lady, who had seen one standing on its hind legs in a dream, declined to drink the soup. Another diner quietly suggested the master chef looked unwell possibly because he had cooked too many turtles.

All present enjoyed the soup. Two persons made loud, slurping noises. Chinese, as children, are taught to take their soup hot. Sucking in cold air, as one sups a mouthful, helps to cool it. While doing this, lowering one's mouth close to the bowl, to avoid spilling any, is not bad manners in Chinese society even if it is frowned on in the West. 'You English may have good table manners but we Chinese have good food and know how to appreciate it!' was how a Cantonese once explained it to me.

In a country where famine was once endemic the late Lin Yutang, eminent scholar, when characterising China's culinary sophistication, wrote: 'We eat crabs by choice and tree bark by necessity.' They also eat rice worms, bear's paw, fish lips and caribous' nose. All are considered delicacies.

Placenta, which has therapeutic properties and is also available in tablet form, is taken occasionally by a few Chinese at home. Of course it has to be cleaned properly and boiled, together with chicken or lean pork and the herb angelica. It is taken by women to build up hormones. The few that take afterbirth regularly are said to have lovely complexions. The Swiss buy it from China, treat it, and use it for injections or apply it externally, for example to treat burns. The medical history of the donor should preferably be studied and that from the firstborn is said to be the most nutritious. The fact that nature tells animals in the wild to eat their own placenta, which has nourished the fetus, after giving birth, should provide some proof of its properties.

With the four main schools (Peking, Shanghainese, Sichuan and Guangdong) and numerous sub-schools of Chinese cooking, there is immense variety. Many dishes are especially good for some complaint. The actual number of courses served at a banquet is also important. Nine is auspicious. Seven dishes are only eaten at funerals. Should you forget and order seven on some other occasion, the waiter will probably jog your memory.

'Who'll still be here after "dread year" 1997?' Bertha suddenly chipped in.

'In the 1980s, people complained about "China countdown". Now, everyone concentrates on finding a way round it,' Dolly, who was cleaning her glasses, responded.

Hong Kong has changed so much. In the 1970s, all radio announcers had pukka English accents. Now, life is partly Americanised with commercial 'media pollution'. Civic pride and community spirit really started in Hong Kong with the 1966 and 1967 Disturbances. That was the watershed. But social awareness accelerated rapidly in the 1980s. Today, although Hong Kong is shifting into high gear and many are raking in as much profit as they can before leaving, money is not quite so much the be-all and end-all.

The black, glutinous rice arrived followed by dessert. This consisted of birds' nest soup mixed with egg white, milk and finely ground pearl dust. 'Good for complexion,' whispered my wife. If taken regularly it retards ageing. Cooked sweet pomelo skin was then served and a variety of fresh fruit.

'Lived through Cultural Revolution,' said a well-built man who immigrated legally to Hong Hong in the late 1970s after bribing officials. 'Not going through another. With British passports can get out in emergency.'

Under the 'British Nationality Scheme' there are 50,000 like him. But others, with their doomsday utterances, say they will be off to Canada, Australia or the United States before the Union Jack comes down even if Hong Kong's lifestyle still has much to offer. It is easier to achieve here than in most places although Hong Kong is unlikely to accomplish so much under Chinese as under British rule.

'China taking dog in manger stance, endless hassles,' said a pensive chap at our table. 'Everything UK does, it is damned if it does, and damned if it doesn't.'

Others predict China, with its record of lack of personal freedom, xenophobia, authoritarianism, corruption, nepotism, self-sufficiency and pride, will change but little over the next generation. The 'One Country, Two Systems' policy is dead, a few would have you believe. There will be limited autonomy for Hong Kong.

As we said our goodbyes a man with a high forehead, resembling the God of Longevity, arrived to take his wife home. He sported a beard which 'lacked substance' (Cantonese slang).

'Hong Kong jitters blown out of proportion,' he insisted, bowing slightly. It is a pity this dignified gesture has disappeared in Europe, I thought.

I wondered how many of my Chinese friends would continue to live in Hong Kong after the takeover. By the same token, how many Legislative Councillors who speak passionately now about the Territory, many of whom have foreign passports, will remain after 1997? Most will stay only if China shows good faith.

There are worrying incidents like incursions into Hong Kong waters and raids by security vessels, little more than state-sponsored piracy, manned by officers in Chinese uniforms. Houses have been robbed on Hong Kong's outlying islands and Mainlanders squeeze fishermen for protection money by levying tariffs on boats trading within Hong Kong's boundaries. In fact piracy, the second oldest profession, has become rampant.

A huge number of luxury, right-hand drive cars are stolen in Hong Kong, which turn up later in the well-stocked, stolen-car lots in Guangdong, China, where they are as obvious as an African on the streets of Beijing. Vehicles in the People's Republic are left-hand drive. Now that right-hand drive vehicles have been banned in Guangdong they are mainly taken to other provinces. Few are returned to Hong Kong. Obviously, the authorities choose not to look. On one occasion a bulldozer, so new the paint was hardly dry, was nearly smuggled across the Hong Kong-China border. One China official maintained, in an interview, 'Hong Kong should pay the People's Republic for recovering its stolen cars in China!'

In 1992, gunmen sailed into Hong Kong waters, moored alongside a jetty and seized a consignment of luxury cars, including their favourite Mercedes and BMWs, at gun point. These were disposed of to authorities in Guangdong who later dismissed undeniable evidence as lies. Photographs taken of gunmen at the scene of the crime were never published. China is not a disciplined society. All such happenings are signs, one suspects, of things to come in Hong Kong. Lawlessness can be frightening in any form. Yet you can, of course, argue that the crime rate in this part of the world, where in

China capital punishment is meted out even for relatively minor commercial offences, is nothing like so rampant as in the United States.

But when China, which considers true democracy depends on strong leadership, acts, it comes down heavily. It believes in 'slaughtering the chicken to warn the monkey.' Laws so often are not applied properly in China. Mercy is a rare quality in Chinese justice which even today can include torture to extract confessions and months of detention without trial. Perhaps this is not surprising in a country where, traditionally, nine relatives, from various generations, could be executed on account of the wrongdoing of one family member. In Hong Kong today, journalists insist, 'Anyone who writes anything controversial, the "New China News Agency" has a file on them'.

Nien Cheng, who recorded her experiences during the Cultural Revolution in *Life and Death in Shanghai*, in an interview with the *South China Morning Post* said, 'After 1997 Hong Kong will go slowly downhill. One of the first things to fold up will be the "Independent Commission Against Corruption".'

Without the ICAC, and indeed without British rule in Hong Kong, much commerce would have become little more than a casino out of control.

Everybody who has done business in China knows, 'If you don't play the game you don't stand to gain.' 'Tea money' is looked upon as business etiquette which helps to build up good relations. 'Get them on your side and your bed's warm,' the saying goes. In an ICAC survey, out of fifty Hong Kong firms doing business in China, thirty-five admitted they paid bribes. These amounted up to 5 per cent of operating costs. The more senior the official the bigger the favour expected. With syndicated and pernicious corruption long lines of trucks are left standing for hours at the Hong Kong-China border. On and beyond 1997 fraud and theft will increase. If corruption is bad in China it will also be bad in Hong Kong.

According to Taffy Hunt, a bent copper who did time in the 1970s, when the 'corruption bus' came past he had three choices. 'Try to stop it and get run over, jog alongside or jump on.'

The Hongkong and Shanghai Banking Corporation together with the old British *hong* Jardines, and as many as ninety quoted companies, because of future uncertainty, have moved their headquarters from Hong Kong to places like the British Colony of Bermuda, London or elsewhere. However, Sir William Purves, Chairman of the Hongkong Bank, says: 'China manages its affairs far better than many western countries'. Hong Kong, of course, is one of the most stable territories; compared to Italy for example, where, since World War II, the average life of a government has been about the same as the gestation period of a mare.

Although there have been pronounced steps towards representative government in Hong Kong in recent years, entrepreneurs like Sir Gordon Macwhinnie demand business must come first. 'China has offered Hong Kong far more democracy than Britain did in 150 years,' he was quoted as saying.

'It's sad to see exactly the same thing happening as we feared in the 1950s,' said Lord MacLehose, Governor from 1971 to 1982. Political unrest culminated in riots in 1956. With more democracy there was 'polarisation of pro- and anti-Beijing factions'.

Although the rich can always buy a passport, and professionals and businessmen can leave, Hong Kong democracy is not the most important issue for housing estate residents, who, with little command of English and few qualifications, are unlikely to have the prerequisites to be able to emigrate. For them, as a *South China Morning Post* survey revealed in 1992, law and order, housing, the cost of living, juvenile delinquency, Hong Kong's economic future; education, transport, employment, health and social welfare rank far higher on their list of priorities.

In the past, many of the misfortunes which befell China were its own fault. Today, countries ignore the People's Republic at their peril. Besides being the most populous nation on earth it has the tenth biggest economy, a seat on the United Nations Security Council, three million soldiers under arms with an arsenal of nuclear weapons. Since the Open Door Policy was introduced in 1978 its average GDP growth has been 9 per cent a year. If this pattern continues, within one or two generations it could become the most powerful nation on earth and possibly still communist – tempered by neo-Confucianism – to boot. Nevertheless, unlike Eastern Europe, its claim to be following this doctrine has never been taken too seriously.

The Pacific, *feng shui* consultants tell us, is where a great deal of the economic action will happen in the twenty-first century. China, having never known democracy, wants a functional Hong Kong under one-party rule. The city-state will continue to be efficient if China refrains from meddling – either intentionally or unintentionally. If it monkeys about, Hong Kong will 'screw it all up' and no longer be the region's financial centre.

During the last few years of British rule in Hong Kong, China, some will tell you, wishes to agree as little as possible with the United Kingdom so its hands are not tied beyond 1997. All the aces

are, after all, held by the People's Republic. If it can delay the development of democracy and resolving the many problems until it
resumes rule over Hong Kong it will be able to do, more or less, as
it wants. While some insist China must, at some stage, open up and
change for the better, others believe that in the next century, life in
Hong Kong, for the man on a tram in Wan Chai, will be almost as
closely supervised as it is in China.

Many of those emigrating believe the idea that Hongkongers
will be left to govern themselves is nonsense. Why take a chance
when a new life awaits one overseas? Any proposals the Territory
makes will have to meet the sometimes irrational approval of the
sovereign power. Some sectors of Hong Kong's citizenry are impatient and want full democracy now. The danger is that, for the sake
of stability, they will demand too much too soon.

Ever since Britain took possession of this 'barren rock' it housed
a transient society and has been a staging post to something better:
Europeans returned to Europe, Chinese went back to China, students went overseas to study. Many never returned. Hongkongers
have relatives and friends scattered around the globe. Increasing
earning power in recent years has enabled people to travel more
allowing them to see how Westerners live. Even without 1997, the
bright lights of countries like the United States would have continued to beckon. Emigration from Hong Kong, unless China restricts
movement as it does for People's Republic citizens, will continue
unabated after 1997.

At this crucial stage an overseas passport is an insurance policy
in case things do not work out. It is also a status symbol. Many
mothers are emigrating early so babies born overseas have right of
abode. Families moving include members who previously endured
hardships themselves under communism. With a few Hongkongers
a spirit of hopelessness and helplessness prevails with the thought
of living under a totalitarian overlord. It needs pluck to emigrate.

In a survey conducted by the *South China Morning Post* in 1991,
55 per cent of interviewees had little faith in promises made by
China under the Joint Declaration or the 'One Country, Two Systems' concept. Fifty-nine per cent believed Hong Kong people
would enjoy less freedom after 1997. Only 21 per cent said they
wanted to see the Territory return to China. Yet, 58 per cent said
they were (in 1991) more confident about Hong Kong's future than
they had been in the 1980s.

Although the exodus is often exaggerated and figures can be
misleading, as previously stated, the most popular destinations are
Canada, the United States and Australia. Countries like Thailand,

Taiwan and Singapore are also attracting limited numbers of Hong Kong Chinese who prefer to live in a society with closer cultural ties. Even places like Bolivia, Costa Rica and the Dominican Republic are out to lure professionals and the wealthy. Not just Chinese form the 'passport parachute brigade'. There are Indians, Pakistani, Portuguese, Malaysians and Eurasians, many of whom were born in the Colony and some whose families have lived here for three, four or more generations.

With 20 per cent of the population under the age of fifteen, too young to remember, a history lesson about the Cultural Revolution would afford perceptions of Hong Kong's future rulers. They have run a notorious regime in the People's Republic, including in places like Tibet, with a saga of brutality and poverty. After the Tiananmen Square Massacre the People's Republic Government has repeatedly accused Hong Kong of being a base for subversion. Six out of ten of its residents were born in the British Territory, a large number speak English but limited *Putonghua* and some have been to Trafalgar Square but not Tiananmen Square.

'Have you eaten rice yet?' is a common Chinese salutation. Instead, a few now joke that 'Are you emigrating yet?' has replaced it. Certainly Hong Kong cannot afford to lose its best and brightest minds, together with their savings, although the more critical factor is who is leaving rather than actual numbers. There has to be a functional core of accountants, computer analysts, engineers and the like, who understand the growing complexities of technology, in order to keep Hong Kong functioning efficiently. Teachers, policemen, social workers, nurses, civil servants and even secretaries are also eyeing overseas employment opportunities and seeking boltholes. According to a survey conducted in 1988, up to 70 per cent of doctors plan to leave, although they face an over-supply of medics in several developed countries where earnings are lower. Many Hong Kong physicians and surgeons are now having second thoughts about emigration.

The church, which plays a key role in fields like education and social welfare, bemoans the fact that as many as one in five of Hong Kong's Christians, and one in four of clergy and lay workers, could ultimately leave. With a large number of lawyers emigrating, the safeguarding of the British-style judicial and legal systems will be difficult but vital to maintain. In the extreme case, the unthinkable alternative in Hong Kong would be rule largely by individuals and personal relationships, as in China.

There were poses, photographs and friends left behind at the airport, with 66,000 haemorrhaging from the Territory in 1992. It has been estimated approximately 600,000 could leave Hong Kong during the ten years up to 1997 – roughly one-tenth of the population. If people really lose faith in Peking, because of say, riots on the mainland caused by high inflation, disparities in standards of living, corruption, or other factors, then the scramble from Hong Kong could resemble Moses leading the Jews out of Egypt. If conditions seriously deteriorated then the massive outflow would include key personnel receiving passports under the United Kingdom 'insurance' scheme. Even now, a small number abscond leaving income tax, credit card and other bills unpaid.

Hong Kong has always been, using sociological jargon, an upwardly mobile society. There has never been a shortage of talent. But replacements cannot be trained overnight. Ten of the richest families control more than half of the financial market. In fact, most of the Territory's successful businessmen were themselves immigrants from China – people like Li Ka-shing (the world's richest Chinese) and Sir Run Run Shaw, the Movie King.

Owing to excessive unemployment and heavy taxes overseas, however, numbers emigrating from Hong Kong are dropping. 'Leave now, I'd have to start my career all over again,' many say. Re-locating means lower positions and salaries than they would receive in Hong Kong. But once they have right of abode some Chinese males move back to the Territory, to harvest the last conceivable dollar, in this city-state of uncertainty, leaving their families overseas to stake their claims. It has been estimated that 10 to 15 per cent return, wearing the gold watch they were given as a farewell present. This 'reverse braindrain', again, is not new. Many left during the 1967 riots when parts of the Territory were in turmoil, although it was actually a good trading year. Later, many emigrants returned. Returnees today, once back, bury themselves in their work. 'Job opportunities in Hong Kong are amazing,' said one.

'I'd never make a living in Hong Kong now,' insisted another who has remained overseas. 'Not sharp enough! Been away too long!'

Families communicate during their 'long-distance relationships' by correspondence. Some run up high phone bills. 'Extreme space' (astronaut) husbands fly back and forth regularly to relieve long periods of separation. 'If too obvious that we prefer to live in, and return to, Hong Kong, why should foreign country give us passport?' one returnee whispered. He admitted, however, that he found Canada boring. 'Miss the noise.'

'Want to *yam cha* (literally 'drink tea') have to drive for miles.' Many find difficulty in settling and adapting to the new lifestyle.

'Naturally I'd rather live in Hong Kong,' one woman who had come back on holiday retorted.

'Of course I can trust my old man,' another visiting Chinese woman chipped in on being told one in ten marriages involving 'astronauts' had broken up .

With time on their hands, and with a history of Chinese men going overseas for long periods alone and raising a second family there, today too, all sorts of things can, and do, happen. Some lonely Chinese women lacking emotional support are involved in extra-marital affairs. There have been suicides.

One husband in Hong Kong phoned his wife in America to say he had found another woman. Before emigrating, his wife had a loving husband and most things money can buy. 'I thought only other's husbands womanised,' she added.

Another wife, having heard of her husband's infidelity, rang to say she was coming back to join him in Hong Kong. 'Don't ever mention your affair in my presence!' she threatened. Later she told a friend: 'Previously, never believed I would arrive at scene of battle and then retreat! But, I was not happy in Canada away from parents anyway,' she smiled, as she passed it off.

An increasing number of emigrants, who are not taken in by promises of Peking officials, are even taking the remains of their dear departed with them. Those who have died recently are some-times embalmed and air-freighted as special cargo. Those long dead are exhumed and bones cremated so ashes can be transported. 'Do it now,' one husband insisted, 'May not be permitted after People's Republic takes over.'

'Export business booming,' a funeral parlour manager admit-ted.

Traditionally, Chinese preferred to be buried in their homeland where *feng shui* rules apply. The new phenomenon of emigrants taking their dead overseas is contrary to what anthropologists would have expected. It goes against normal Chinese burial cus-toms. But 'long-distance relationships' also apply to the dead. A family must pay respects and tend to their requirements on special days.

'Father hated communists. He'd kick my bottom if I left his remains back in Hong Kong,' a close Chinese friend told me. I knew his old man. I believe him!

Is all this uprooting of the dead and the living worth it? Only well beyond 1997 will we be able to tell.

Chapter Seven

Eurasians

THE dense clumps of bamboo at the university, where gaggles of black-faced laughing thrushes gather in winter, were still there, but one of the Old Halls was in the throes of demolition. There was an unholy clanking. The Territory never ceases to be one gigantic building site.

All notices posted up by students and their Union at this bastion of higher learning were in Chinese, mother tongue of 940 million. Up to the 1970s posters would have been in English, language of power, passport to international trade, everyday speech of a mere 320 million souls. But the vocabulary of the colonialists, which wins an economic argument, was also the language of gunboat diplomacy, opium trading and often the destroyer of native traditions, culture and morality around the world.

After walking down the steep slopes at Hong Kong University, where two old women wearing hot pants built up their *chi* by holding railings and swinging still quite shapely legs like ballerinas at the bar, I approach the site of what was Ball's Court. Named after an occupant in the 1860s and 1870s who served both as Chief Justice and Colonial Secretary, this once four-storey, anchor-shaped dwelling on plan, built about the same time as our house in Norfolk, had recently been torn down. It remained vacant for years largely because it was haunted. One old resident was buried in the garden. On major Chinese festivals, it was claimed, ghosts of people who once lived opposite King's College (built with red facing bricks shipped from England as ballast) in Bonham Road, congregated there.

As early as the Shang Dynasty (1600–1100 BC) the Chinese kept records of the weather on bones and tortoise shells, including details of rainbows, thunder, rainfall and wind. The typhoon that had just passed was not severe, but it brought approaching twenty inches of much needed rain to ease the water storage situation. Now, skies had brightened. I had been looking forward to this stroll while staying in England. The old saying, 'Typhoon come close but "no arrive" brings three days' rain,' is usually true. The storm did not record a 'direct hit'.

My wife used to walk up Western Street past Ball's Court, to Saint Clare's School daily, starting when she was ten years old, in 1946. There, she learned about Sir Walter Raleigh and his cloak, and of buttercups in English meadows. Her education was delayed because of the three-year-eight-month brutal Japanese occupation. My wife, her mother and two sisters lived with her maternal grandfather then, who gave Vera away when we were married.

The old man had five wives and, because he was unable to sire sons, he adopted one for each wife. Sons care for mothers in old age. Grandfather was a gourmet. He wore long *cheung saams* made from fine material and smoked sweet, sickly opium for forty years. Not surprising when a government committee disclosed, in 1924, that up to a quarter of Hong Kong's Chinese adult males 'chased the dragon'. Europeans, too, were not averse to the odd pipe, which provided 'inner peace' when doing business with a Chinese firm.

During the Japanese occupation everything was in short supply. Grass grew in the streets where, in the mornings, bodies could be seen with dismembered arms and legs which had been bitten off by Japanese 'dogs of war'. Shoes and clothing of dead victims, who had broken the curfew, were soon removed by thieves as one man discovered after he placed a notice on the corpse of a relative. This read: 'I will return to collect'. Despite harsh military rule crime was everywhere. Half the working population was unemployed.

Because Grandfather kept a salt-fish shop the family fared better than most. People were often left to fend for themselves, as hunters and gatherers on hillsides and seashore, resorting to boiling leaves and seaweed for survival. Sweet potato mixed with rice was an everyday staple. Although cannibalism was never common in China even when stricken with famine, 1941 to 1945 were difficult years in Hong Kong. Thus the less said the better about enticing, high-priced, dripping cuts in butchers' shops, sometimes suspected of being slices off human buttocks or thighs.

As the Japanese constantly sought out 'flower girls' to 'grind the corn' with, women seldom ventured out alone and never at night. When outside, the young and attractive hunched their backs, wore old, dirty clothes, smeared mud over their faces and put on sanitary pads. Village guards patrolled in the New Territories so, when 'turnip-headed' Japanese approached, women working in fields had time to hide. Some rape victims, an act euphemistically portrayed in Chinese films by rain falling on flowers, maintained Japanese had pointed penises.

Those were frightening, lawless days and slappings and beatings for minor offences were common. About one million people left Hong Kong for neutral Macau, or embarked on the long, hazardous trek west to 'Free China'. For the 600,000 remaining in Hong Kong, ways to survive included smuggling and street peddling. It often meant being a good scavenger.

But survive the war many did and my wife, still a child, was one. Afterwards she trudged daily, up steep Western Street from Sai Ying Pun, to attend school, passing not far from the *Fuk Tak Kung* Earth God Shrine in Sheung Fung Lane. During his time on earth, before he was created a deity, he practised medicine. His lean-to shrine is still there with its large granite, gaudy red and green painted altar, carved with figures at each end and its corners chiselled to represent bamboo. When I visit, groups of elderly gamblers usually sit nearby. Opposite a blind rugged-faced, fortune teller was woken by a woman client. The blind possess the ability to 'see' on a non-material plane, aided by bone fragments taken from dead children which they carry in their pockets.

Nearby were two schools of Chinese dominoes. As I approached one player kicked off a shoe, scratched his itching 'Hong Kong Foot' on winning a round, gave a phlegmy, fruity laugh brought on by years of chain smoking, and hawked. During World War II spitting could result in heads being chopped off, summarily, with one swift slice from a Japanese officer's sword.

An earlier *Fuk Tak Kung* shrine, on the same site, can be traced back to the severe outbreak of bubonic plague in 1894. At its peak, 100 people died daily. The Colony came to a standstill. A 'plague medal' was presented to both military and civilians who helped with relief work. The temple managers arranged for processions of gods through nearby streets whenever there were serious epidemics. Up until 1920, cases of plague occurred almost yearly. There is a splendid photograph hanging in the shrine of one keeper in the 1930s, a determined lady indeed it appears, as many keepers are. She died in her eighties.

Edward Yorke McCauley, an American traveller, wrote in his diary on 27 July 1853:

More was to be learned by a visit to the Chinese Museum I saw in
Boston than could be seen at the expense of leather, to the amount
of a new pair of boots, in trudging around promiscuously in Hong
Kong.

Provided you know where to look, and it is often advantageous to
be alone to capture atmosphere in fascinating back alleys, few
would agree. On one's own one can try to deduce what cultural
logic applies and make sense of often puzzling behaviour.

The kindest time to see decaying buildings is in early morning
sunshine. The Territory has derelict structures but fewer than most
towns, such as in northern England or in squalid parts of New York.
Hong Kong is a vibrant city with an enormous heart.

'Walking the streets was an overwhelming experience,' said
David Yip, a Liverpudlian Eurasian on his first visit to Hong Kong.
He discovered an inner quietness in himself which he believes to be
his Chinese side. For me too, as an Old Hong Kong Hand, walking
the byways is evocative of my arrival. Smells are some of my earliest recollections. Understanding foreign lands is not only absorbing sights, colours and accents.

'The aroma really put me off,' remarked a British army wife
who preferred the 'little piece of England', at Stanley Fort, overlooking the South China Sea. Certainly places like Kenya, Rhodesia and
parts of India were quite unlike the back streets of 'un-British' Hong
Kong, which lacked European settlers and emotional attachment for
most, where language, cultural attributes and ways of thought were
so different.

With a good nose smells, including oil and cordage, can be
legion and varied. Only in recent years has the Hong Kong Government taken industrial pollution seriously. The Territory now gener-
ates three times more plastic waste than comparable cities in Europe
or America. The 'fragrant harbour' today is nothing like as clean as
when I swam in the cross-harbour race in 1955. Low cloud and high
humidity for much of the year helps make the pungent mix different to the cool, dry air of rural Norfolk; even if Hong Kong scores
high marks for public health, including life expectancy. Nevertheless, the number of vehicle exhausts is daunting compared to some
cities in China where compatriots 'pedal to glory'. Posters there
proclaim, 'Drive your bicycle safely, earn eminence for China'.

Continuing my walk in Western I was confronted with spicy,
steamy whiffs issuing from street stalls, including delicious smell-
ing noodles. Persimmon cakes, five-inch, white catherine wheels
with squares of dried fruit in their centres, are on sale. Golden

brown, roasted, whole geese, with curved necks like abbots' cro-
siers, hang in restaurant windows. Stalls display neatly laid out
greens, including Tientsin cabbage, Chinese kale and 'slippery vegetable', as well as bright red and green bell-peppers. Alongside
these are giant green Chinese radishes, water chestnuts and golden-
beige, grotesquely shaped, ginger, with bulges in unlikely places.

Shanghai, another rough, brawling seaport, did not alter for
thirty years. But in Hong Kong, an international city with a Chinese
flavour, many changes emerged rapidly from within to necessitate
survival. Such as establishing manufacturing. Yet timeless structures, like the *Fuk Tak Kung* Shrine, and a few age-old customs still
remain as mini-skirted Chinese girls with lurid lipstick walk by.
These include Chinese facials, performed in the open in side streets,
consisting of scraping a person's face with a long, cotton thread
while applying white powder to remove unwanted hair and dead
skin.

A woman, who must have been in her nineties, hobbled across
the street a block away. She walked hesitatingly, not just because of
age. Having feet bound as a child, the 'fashion of the golden lilies',
restricts movements. Small feet, a 'basinful of tears', the mark of a
well-bred woman, were considered attractive. At the age of five, on
an auspicious day, the process and agony of young, tender bones
slowly breaking, veins collapsing and flesh forming into a gro-
tesque, misshapen hoof began. The process was aided later, if necessary, with a mallet. One can sense the excruciating pain. Girls
were too scared of their parents to cut off the figure-of-eight band-
ages.

With temperature well into the thirties the sun beat down that
morning like fire from heaven. I wore shorts and an open-neck shirt,
as we dressed before airconditioning became popular in the 1960s.
In the 1950s we 'went into whites' on 1 May and changed back to
winter clothes at the start of November. Farther down than Second
Street I approached Possession Point, where we, the British, first
landed on 25 January 1841. The Party returned to ship that evening
landing permanently the following day. 'Three cheers for Her Majesty the Queen!' the group chorused, drinking to Her very good
health.

I walked along and up to the old Tai Ping Shan District, translated as 'Hill of Great Peace' . Not many Europeans ventured there
years ago, apart from a few discharged soldiers, men who had
jumped ship, and beachcombers or adventurers. The well-to-do always feared that such 'riffraff', who were poor, lacked breeding and
hobnobbed with Asians, would lower the prestige of the white man.

Tai Ping Shan was, because of open drains and piles of garbage, the spawning ground of the virulent bacillus plague and, in 1894 the Government put the rat-infested area to the torch. The epidemic was arrested.

A *Kwan Yin* temple stands in Tai Ping Shan Street, crowded to overflowing with supplicants amid clouds of incense on the nineteenth day of the Second Moon, her birthday. She sits there demurely clad in a green and red floral patterned white vestment, rosary around neck, gazing across at the main door. This image dates back to 1840. It was said to be carved from a block of wood found floating in the sea which gave off mysterious, golden rays. Outside under the canopy hangs a gold-coloured carving titled 'Court for Demonstration of Combat Skills'. Two generals, Meng Liang and Chiao Tsan, demonstrate their prowess before Yang Lung Kung, aged marshal of the Sung army, and P'an Kuang Mei, Imperial Commissioner.

Unlike most temples, no part of this building is unroofed. A large vent is usually left so spirits of gods can descend into their images and the fug caused by burning incense can escape.

Chinese and Europeans years ago, with few exceptions, lived in separate districts, although a Chinese elite, consisting of contractors, craftsmen, shopkeepers and traders, started to emerge by the middle of the last century. But segregation was not always the rule. The Portuguese, Europe's colonial pioneers, settled in Macau in 1557. In 1999, they will be the last colonialists to withdraw from Asia. Together with the French, they always mixed more freely with the natives than did the British. In sixteenth-century Goa, for instance, the Portuguese were encouraged to take indigenous wives and to settle the land as farmers, artisans or traders.

Yet even in the British Empire there was a so-called golden era, in India for example before the opening of the Suez Canal in 1869, when members of the 'world's finest race' and Indians mixed freely on relatively equal terms. Sir James Brooke, the first White Rajah of Sarawak, encouraged liaisons between Whites and native women and 90 per cent of planters in Malaya kept local mistresses.

This, together with the invention of the steamship and the fact that in Hong Kong Victoria Peak started to be opened up, when roads were built and wells sunk, meant that British *memsahibs* came east in greater numbers. What had been amiable, inter-racial friendships were then replaced by aloofness and segregation. Some suggest this was a direct ploy by white women, the sharpest in the pecking order, to keep their men's hands off local girls, although there was a purity movement gathering pace back home which aimed to halt the 'decline of the British race'.

The settling of the Peak also divided Hong Kong's white community with its increasing interest in status. There was stuffiness and squabbling over seating in the Established Church, at Saint John's Cathedral. 'Do you reside on the Peak or are you single and live in Kowloon?' was a common, pointed question.

Eventually, in 1909, a Colonial Office circular stated concubinage with native women was a serious offence, although this order appeared to make precious little difference in many parts of the Empire.

The 'kissing and merging' of two great civilisations in Hong Kong did not end with the coming of white females. Many Britons still kept local, 'protected' women, as they were called, who were issued with certificates to prove to the police they were not prostitutes. Because unity is strength many of them, often titled 'spinster' on old documents, which gave a clue to their identity, lived in the district above Queen's Road Central. These include haunts like Staunton, Peel, Elgin, Graham and Gage Streets, and Hollywood Road, home of many fine antique shops today. The European male bought a house for his ladyfriend or paid the rent. Lord Byron wrote:

> What men call gallantry and gods adultery
> Is more common where the climate's sultry.

Unlike Buddhists, Taoists have no interest in eliminating sexual desires and, similarly, Lord Lugard, Governor of Hong Kong from 1907 to 1912, argued that, for good or evil, the sex drive was the most potent influence on his life. Even in starchy Victorian times Englishmen flirted with Chinese women in a way that would not have been accepted had they been Africans or Indians.

The lifestyle of a typical Englishman in Hong Kong was certainly not so spartan as R.C. Hurley's keep-fit formula which he followed for forty-six years until his death in 1925. The routine went as follows. At daybreak salt-water gargle, walk two miles, cold shower using mild carbolic soap followed by rub down with rough towel. At 7.30, breakfast: prunes stewed with oranges followed by a farinaceous dish. There should be no superfluous drinking. Water was the safest lubricant. Tiffin, Hurley believed, should be the 'lighter the better'. A one hour's stroll in the evening preceded a tumbler of warm water before retiring. A small, hard Chinese-style pillow, made of pottery or rattan, ensured a good night's sleep.

Most Westerners ate and drank far too heavily in those days with both diet and clothing more suited to a temperate, European climate rather than the tropics. A three-piece suit with waistcoat, tight-fitting trousers and top hat were *de rigueur* for businessmen. Breakfast often meant fish, rice, fruit and claret; tiffin consisted of eggs, curry and two or three glasses of beer. Dinner was a substantial meal including claret, champagne and port. But a number of men walked to keep fit. A cricket ground and horse racing were provided as early as 1846, soon after Happy Valley was drained. The Victoria Recreation Club held its first meeting in 1849. The Golf Club was established in 1888. This was in an age when Royal Navy seamen were flogged for being last up the rigging.

Although most men were single they were unable to live, or to be seen publicly, with their mistresses because of the social stigma attached to such relationships. Protected women, who kept separate households, were visited in the evenings before their gentlemen returned home. Many of these women were *Tanka*, namely Boat People, some of whom had smuggling or pirate backgrounds and spoke pidgin English.

Often they were aggressive, with shrewd business sense, and in the early days of the Colony, their families provided services to newcomers, such as provisioning, piloting, ferrying and *dhobiing*. The *Tanka* as a whole are still a marginal, depressed, illiterate group, who were not bound by Confucian ethics as were the Cantonese and Hakka with whom they were precluded from marrying. Like the Hakka, the *Tanka* did not bind their women's feet – a practice Europeans found objectionable. Settlement ashore and taking part in imperial examinations were also restricted. They lacked ties with Chinese gentry.

The arrival of Westerners provided opportunities for the struggling, pariah Boat People to break out of their circumscribed social position, something like today's beauty contestant who becomes a wealthy man's mistress for a year and then sets up her own boutique with the proceeds. Those 'salt-water girls', as they were termed in Cantonese, bore Eurasian children or adopted Chinese children. They employed servants and were free of in-law or male control and could thus escape much of the bondage of traditional Chinese life.

The late Barbara Ward, Cambridge anthropologist who lived with the Boat People for various spells, wrote in an unfinished manuscript that she had even heard well-educated Chinese landsmen expatiate upon the non-Han descent of the *Tanka* and their un-Chinese characteristics. According to Ward, critics sometimes accuse them of speaking a non-Chinese language, of not really being human, having utterly alien customs (alleged to include a matrilineal system) and a special biological distinction which gives them six toes to each foot.

'Eyes and ears alone would be enough to inform anyone [that] the Boat People have the usual complement of toes and speak Cantonese, albeit with a broad accent ...' Ward wrote.

Marriages between Europeans and Chinese were soundly condemned by the taipan class, that breed of men who headed *hongs*, large business houses. The rule was even more firmly established after British wives arrived towards the end of the nineteenth century. Those European males that did wed, typically ships' captains, police and overseers, were ostracised by genteel, European society. Neither did Anglo-Chinese marriage mean automatic entrée for Europeans into polite Chinese society. A culture which allowed Westerners to become full members of Pacific island or American Indian communities was not present in Hong Kong. A European marrying a Chinese woman became very much a marginal man. A minority group thus gradually formed consisting mainly of Europeans employed at supervisory level.

Nonetheless love has a universal, human theme which can transcend race. Some of the relationships, including between taipans and Chinese mistresses, were enduring, even if Chinese professed to finding Europeans repulsive in intimacy. The Eurasian children born out of such liaisons were largely cared for by their mother with their father's financial support.

In the tradition which started in Portuguese Macau, where many British merchants lived before Hong Kong was occupied in 1841, these Chinese kept-women were known as 'pensioners'. After their white beaus retired and returned to Europe these 'paramours' were often placed on firms' payrolls. If they did not already own accommodation, property was purchased or rents paid. In other cases, trusts were set up to keep women and offspring in reasonable comfort for the rest of their lives. One doctor, on departing for England in 1832, set aside $4,000 for his Portuguese mistress on which she was allowed to draw up to $420 interest a year. The father's connections also helped the children find employment.

Certainly many set store by such relationships, although it is recorded that David Jardine 'showed disappointingly little spirit when his own Chinese girl, Alloy, left his "protection" (as he put it) for his business rival, John Dent'. Jardine was humiliated rather than enraged and sent protest notes. Nonetheless, he wrote from London in 1856 to Joseph Jardine in Hong Kong: 'As a general rule the system of non-married partners is, I think, a good one.'

Many were steady, permanent, honourable relationships. The system flourished.

To some extent cross-cultural relationships were (and are) a 'macho thing'. They demonstrated not only that a European had control over a woman of another race but also dominance over menfolk by being able to take their women away from them.

The Eurasian children resulting from such relationships were usually educated in missionary schools or in the Government Central British School. A Church of England establishment, the forerunner of the Diocesan Girls School, was almost closed in 1867 when it was revealed that many graduates, with their sound command of English, had become mistresses of Europeans. As few Westerners spoke Chinese they were in demand. Children resulting from such unions, additionally, would more likely be brought up as Christians.

Although centuries after progeny from Marco Polo's expedition had been assimilated into Chinese society, many Eurasian descendants of liaisons between Europeans and Chinese, dating from the last century, live in Hong Kong today. Lady Mak Sau-ying, first wife of Sir Robert Ho Tung, was acknowledged as the daughter of Hector MacLean, who became a partner of Jardine in 1849. He died in the Colony in 1894 after living in Hong Kong for forty years during which he returned to England only once.

The Reverend Carl T. Smith has probably researched cases of 'pensioners' more than anyone. In his paper, 'Ng Akew, One of Hong Kong's "Protected" Women', he wrote that her 'protector' was James Bridges Endicott, captain of a ship of the American firm Russell and Company. Endicott bought the *Tanka* girl, Ng Akew, in Canton and had several children by her. She was described as shrewd and intelligent. She traded in opium, but at one stage her consignment was seized by pirates, whereupon she visited their lair and threatened them with vengeance from her foreign friends. After giving two warnings she was compensated with cargoes of betelnut and ships containing cotton, cloth dye stuffs and victuals. Perhaps this is what the late Australian Richard Hughes, doyen of journalists, meant when he, himself happily wed to one, said, 'Never marry a Chinese! They're steel rods swathed in flowers!'

Later, Smith relates, Endicott decided to end the relationship with the Chinese girl and Ann Russell arrived from London as a 'mail order bride'. The couple were married in 1852. Provision was, however, made for Ng Akew by executing a deed of trust. This included property for her and her ten-year-old son. She continued in business and appeared for some time to be doing well. Unfortunately she over-extended herself financially, living in style, and was later declared bankrupt.

In liaisons with foreigners many protected women soon found opportunities existed, and they engaged in business, such as real estate and money lending. A Hong Kong Eurasian family well-known today, bought and trained girls to serve as mistresses years ago. Other protected women invested in brothels and bought and trained girls for prostitution. Some owned nurseries of purchased (often *Tanka*) children. Others were kidnapped. One occasionally hears tales of how girls were mesmerised or drugged. Today, a number of young girls still go missing.

Prostitution is considered more leniently by Chinese than by Europeans and is seen as a necessary evil. 'How can you blame a man for finding a woman if he has no wife to "serve" him,' is a typical remark. Some believe prostitution is, in fact, a convenient, low-status occupation for 'surplus' females and, as a result, they tend not to be treated as social outcasts or 'fallen women' as in the West. Some prostitutes even became respectable concubines.

Governor Sir John Bowring was, however, concerned because, directly resulting from various types of liaisons, in his words: 'A large population of children by native mothers and foreigners of all classes is beginning to ripen into a dangerous element of the dung-hill of neglect. They seem wholly uncared for.'

Hong Kong always tended to be a man's town and, in 1872, when the first real census was conducted, there were 3,264 European males to 669 European females. Similarly, Chinese men outnumbered Chinese women by a ratio of 7 : 2. Not surprisingly therefore, during the first few years in the life of the Colony, numerous brothels sprang up. By 1857, a system of registration and inspection had been introduced. By 1880, Barrister J.J. Francis estimated there were 4,000–5,000 respectable women to 18,000–20,000 prostitutes, sometimes known as 'Queen's Women' ('chickens' in Cantonese slang). An inspector of brothels was appointed and each bordello keeper had to pay HK$4 a month tax.

As with many things in Hong Kong there were both Chinese prices and European prices. Houses of ill repute for Chinese and Indians, graded first, second and third class, were confined to West Point District, on Hong Kong Island. Europeans, many of whom were newcomers commonly called 'griffins', frequented brothels which were located at the eastern end of the city and sometimes housed Japanese or Chinese girls. Records show a 'foreign brothel' was fined HK$100 for admitting a Chinese. There was once a whorehouse next to the Catholic Cathedral.

In 1851, the following advertisement appeared in the press:

At Mrs Randalls – a small quantity of GOOD HONEY in small

jars; also GIN, PORT, CHAMPAGNE, CLARET, bottled BEER,
PORTER, & &
Lyndhurst Terrace
Victoria, 12th June 1851

All girls were trained in ways to appeal to Britishers: such as
how to light a man's cigar and other social graces. No gentleman
need meet another on the establishment unless he wished. For those
who wanted only to relax there was a lavish drawing room. Merce-
nary aspects were avoided.

Daniel Richard Caldwell, a British government official, was
accused in 1858 of consorting with pirates and owning land in Tai
Ping Shan on which brothels operated. His links with the underworld were well known although a commission of enquiry did not
recommend that Caldwell be dismissed. The property was retained
by his Chinese widow after his death, and, later, by his family until
the 1890s.

The better-class bawdy houses were situated around Peel,
Graham and Gage Streets, Hollywood Road and Lyndhurst Terrace.
European prostitutes were outcasts in Hong Kong and came mainly
from working class origins. Many were seasoned hands, forced into
the profession by poverty, originating from the red-light districts of
Melbourne, Sydney, Continental Europe, Honolulu and San Francisco.

Bridget Montague, a Californian who married a Portuguese in
San Francisco and was abandoned by him after the couple arrived
in Hong Kong, was an example. In 1873, aged twenty-three, she was
accused of running a 'sly' (clandestine) brothel. Montague was fined
HK$50, sentenced to one month in prison and forced to undergo
medical checks. In 1877, there were seventeen European prostitutes
known to the police.

That early September day, as I wandered around this mixed
commercial and residential district in Central, where so much has
happened over the past century and a half, where earth god shrines
and Chinese lucky posters abound, it was a rarity to see a building
which had been constructed before World War II. In a few cases
structures have been demolished only five or so years after con-
struction because a landlord has retrieved his invested capital and
a taller or different type of building offered better returns.

I tried to bring psychic powers to bear in this old district of ill
repute. What did Europeans learn from 'Chinese lady friends' about
'jade stems', 'pleasure pavilions' and the 'thirty Heaven and Earth
Positions'? Of these thirty, how many Europeans practised 'Two
Swallows with a Single Heart' or the 'Leaping White Tiger'?

Male and female energy forces, *yin* and *yang*, complement. If correctly channelled, by absorbing *chi*, both partners can improve sexual energy and health by judicious practise of 'Wind on the Horserider' (intercourse). The woman normally absorbs her partner's ejaculated semen. However older Chinese men, who are not 'half-past-six' (sexual failures), sometimes 'recycle' sperm by exerting digital force on the pressure point situated between anus and scrotum. They thus ingest both the woman's vaginal fluid and their own semen.

As I walked down quiet Peel Street, not far from its junction with Rednaxela Terrace (letters painted in reverse by a signwriter who could not understand English), I spotted a middle-aged couple. Palms together in front of chests, Buddhist fashion, they bowed three times before walking away. Four feet from the pavement, propped against a block of wood to prevent them rolling down the steep slope, lay three oranges. Stuck into each of two oranges were three, smouldering joss sticks. Ashes from burnt paper offerings lay scattered. Only then did I recall how a vehicle had been parked in that road months earlier. The brakes had failed. There were fatalities.

As I wandered downhill searching for more local colour, understandably, I had difficulty imagining where Russian-born Ethel Morrison could have lived. A long-time resident, she was probably Hong Kong's most famous bordello madame. At intervals, she undertook her rounds to posh firms to collect overdue payments. Why should anyone be allowed to get away with bad debts owed to her brothel in Lyndhurst Terrace? If unsuccessful in getting IOUs honoured, which she tried hard to do in a loud, deliberate voice, she would occasionally put the slips in the Sunday collection at Saint John's Cathedral. A memorial service was held there for her, in the 1930s, as she made her way to heaven.

Just as Ethel Morrison ran bordellos so Stella Benson (1892–1933), who had been involved with woman's suffrage in Britain, strove hard to have them shut. Registered brothels started to be closed in the early 1930s, with Chinese establishments being phased out more slowly. The last finally shut in June 1935. The likes of Benson could not claim total credit. With changing public opinions towards protection of women the time had come to draw the curtains.

From the start of war-time occupation, however, the Japanese reintroduced a system of controlled and medically inspected houses in Wan Chai for their service personnel. These were all promptly shut by the British in 1945.

One main purpose of a controlled system of brothels was to keep the town relatively free of streetwalkers. With the mass exodus of refugees, however, after the takeover by the Communists in China in 1949, hookers abounded in Wan Chai and even in Central District. But with rapidly rising standards of living, and better policing, few were left on Hong Kong streets by the 1960s. Yet prostitution is still alive and well. A stroll around places like Kowloon's Sham Shui Po, where signs in Chinese advertising sex and 'one woman brothels' (the latter are not illegal) are common, will confirm that. Over 2,000 housewives are estimated to be engaged part-time. Yet every so often, in letters to the press, someone will suggest licenced brothels should be re-introduced.

Single men have always had problems. In a letter to his sister Joseph Jardine wrote: 'Long residence in the East does not certainly improve a man's chance in the matrimonial line.'

Of five nephews of William Jardine (the founder of the firm), who all followed him out East, only one married. Of the first eleven partners in Jardine Matheson eight died unmarried, two married after they retired, and only one, Alexander Matheson, married while he lived in the Far East. However, all the eleven that followed married, five of them while still in the Orient.

Groups of unmarried girls, known as 'fishing fleets', regularly set out from England looking for eligible husbands. But Hong Kong was the last port of call, in more ways than one. Most men serving here, even if they were senior government officials, merchants or professionals, came from the middle classes or tenant-farmer families in England. Although many Hong Kong white men saw themselves as elite, upper class, in the British sense with status being determined largely by birth, they did not rightly belong there. Hong Kong was unlike India where the British Raj attracted members of the aristocracy.

M Y walk had taken me from Mid-Levels down to Western District, along to Sheung Wan and Central District, to the streets where Europeans kept their 'paramours' and where brothels were situated in earlier times. As in other parts of the Territory many of the buildings, with shiny curtain walling, like the golden 'Amah's Tooth' and 'Jardine's Stilton with 10,000 orifices' (actually there are 1,748 circular windows), have been erected during the past decade or so.

'Hong Kong strikes me as a miniature New York,' an American tourist took pains to point out.

The two are similar in some ways just as parts of Shanghai

resemble Liverpool. New York, however, so often represents the worst and the best: from rape and robbery, to dynamism and excitement. Although Hong Kong has a global flavour and is go-getting, it has a considerably lower crime rate. Before long, no doubt, its 'intelligent' buildings, with the third most expensive office rents in the world after Tokyo and London, will offer piped sunlight and automatic switch-off devices for all services as last employees leave at night.

With China taking over Hong Kong in capitalist style, by buying into foreign companies, the place is no longer a colonial anachronism, the last outpost of the British Empire with the culture of one nation imposed on another. The Bank of China, a People's Republic status symbol, is one of the most modern and the fifth tallest structure in the world. With vaulting and severe black and grey interior, like a last resting place for a Ming emperor, and shortages of grass, trees and shrubs externally, it lacks sensitivity and portrays the traditional, harsh values of Hong Kong's future communist rulers.

With a tall aerial on its roof, which has been likened to either rugby goal posts or bamboo shoots, it is nevertheless a fine, if austere, piece of architecture, and, with such buildings, Hong Kong has acquired a new beauty. The sharp edges of the Bank of China do, nonetheless, affect the neighbourhood's *feng shui*, which depends largely on the vital 'dragon artery' that runs down from the Peak to Government House and on to the Hongkong Bank.

Although the Prince of Wales might evaluate them differently, if one wants to confirm faith in the Territory one need only look at its new buildings. The Hongkong and Shanghai Bank, resembling an oil rig with girders at erratic angles, which under sound British management turns in handsome profits, says everything about efficient Hong Kong.

Close by, where until the mid 1970s the lush-grass cricket ground used to be, before a different age forced it to make way for concrete-paved Chater Garden, a Chinese policeman in immaculate khaki drill directed traffic from a small, white and black 'pagoda' with 'swept' roof. It was simple yet elegant objects like these, all part of British superiority, which made many of us fall in love with Hong Kong. We were one better than American or Continental European tourists who peered perplexed into scurrying Chinese faces for the umpteenth time. We belonged. British colonial rule had been good for Hong Kong in spite of its checkered past. The place was a monument to Imperial enterprise. It was ours – so we liked to believe.

Across the road from Chater Garden, The Mandarin, with starched sheets tightly stretched on beds, welcomed you to its embraces after the room-boy had served tea. It used to be graded the finest hotel in the world by tourist associations. Three decades later with the seduction of mass consumerism, like countless other arcades over much of Hong Kong, the Mandarin's shops still display glittering Canon cameras, Rolex watches, Gucci bags and Dior perfume. No longer are there the bargains of the 1960s, however, when I too gorged myself on items I did not really need. Today as an Old Hong Kong Hand, I sometimes pray that, on rounding the next bend, I can be spared the feeling 'greed is good'.

In the Mandarin's bars young chaps from the *hongs* chat up visiting lassies who form the 1990s 'fishing fleets', whingeing about how tough the going gets here when the Filipina maid is on leave and no help is available to empty dehumidifiers in the sweltering heat. Among other 'imponderables' discussed is, when the People's Liberation Army marches in will an excuse be found – if one is needed – to move the Cenotaph away from the square adjacent to The Mandarin?

Lord MacLehose (Governor from 1971 to 1982) said in a radio interview in 1992, he would be surprised if Hong Kong people, who created this wonderful city with all the wealth that is in it, cannot solve their own political problems. Looking around from the heart of this extraordinary place one can appreciate what he meant.

On the day of my walk, it was then on from Central District to Wan Chai, past 'No-Squeak Wong' the shoe-maker, to where there has been an attempt to 'green' the 'concrete jungle' with trees. 'The Wanche' has altered since the glitter of Suzie Wong days, in the 1950s and 1960s, with American servicemen on 'Rest and Recreation' from the Korean and Vietnam wars. Then, some bars employed up to fifty hostesses who could be 'bought out'. They would accompany a man for a meal and then spend an hour or so with him in a boarding house. Girls carried 'blue cards' revealing results of medical hygiene checks. It was the innocence of an age before AIDS although much further back, in 1897, half the soldiers in the Territory were under treatment for venereal disease.

Wan Chai was Hong Kong's first red-light district. A few Chinese will tell you that although the British propagated their language and systems of administration and law throughout their Empire, they also spread venereal disease – together with race courses, botanical gardens and technology. Many subjugated societies in colonial territories were, in fact, better adjusted sexually before the arrival of the prudish English.

However to intimate, as some Chinese scholars do, that sex is a western invention, and that rape, incest, paedophilia and homosexuality did not exist before the coming of the white man, during the Ming Dynasty, is patently untrue. There has never been a law banning buggery in China although the People's Republic is well known for giving gays a hard time. Just as in Tibet where homosexuality was even encouraged because it helped monks remain celibate, so in old China, love songs were frequently composed for male lovers. sayings to signify homosexuality are well known – such as 'dividing the peach' and 'cutting off the sleeve'. In the latter case an emperor severed his garment rather than disturb his male companion who was sleeping on it.

Other Chinese, while insisting the Portuguese introduced syphilis and gonorrhoea to China in the sixteenth century, will tell you, just as these two complaints are mentioned in the Bible, that *lung yeung tuk* (emperor's poison), a form of venereal disease which some even liken to AIDS, existed in ancient China. If it really did, then sages would probably take the same philosophical view as bar girls in Wan Chai today who put more trust in fate than in condoms.

'If I die then in my next life, maybe, I shall not have to come back as a bar girl.' The old saying has it: 'As soon as you come down to earth you cry three times, and whether you're to have a good life or bad your fate is already fixed.'

For some Chinese women 'starving is a small matter but losing one's chastity is a great calamity'. By contrast, there are the 'Angels of Wan Chai', who, of necessity or for whatever reason, do not remain monogamous.

Whether one looks on multi-faceted bars and the like as tawdry dens of evil, or exciting and serving a purpose, depends largely on the beholder. Many house small Buddhist shrines displaying the sacred lotus, with 1,000 petals representing infinity, the 'wheel-of-life', with everything inter-connected within the universe. It is a beautiful flower, symbolising purity, that springs from a pond of mud and slime.

Walking fast, by this time I had arrived in Ship Street. In earlier days, before land reclamation when the sea front was close to this cul-de-sac, it housed brothels whose purpose was to keep British soldiers out of Victoria – as Central District was then named. Most of the buildings in Ship Street today date from after World World II. There are a couple of old, once gracious edifices, now derelict, at the top of the street, which do not give the impression of having been brothels. There is a children's playground. Do any uneasy souls of pretty prostitutes roam here one wonders? Does anyone buy joss sticks at the little corner shop, to burn in their memory at the Hungry Ghosts' Festival, to assuage their pain and hunger? If not, *Kwan Yin*, to whom numerous miracles are attributed and whose anger can scare away evil, does, I am sure, hear their disconsolate cries.

In spite of what Stella Benson and Lady Astor, the first woman to take a seat in the House of Commons, had to say, some, like Bob Yates, a British soldier, spoke highly of the 'Angels of Wan Chai'. Most servicemen then were single. Sexual problems arose and a 'squaddie', an 'outcast in peacetime' in the 1930s, had little chance of meeting a chaperoned girl from a good-class Chinese family. There were 20,000 prostitutes in Hong Kong. Most were 'on the game' because they needed the money. Their beats stretched along by the bars in Wan Chai and outside establishments like the China Fleet Club. 'Hello Jonnie, you go top side short time?' Pre-war it normally cost HK$2, but during the week, when soldiers and sailors were short of 'lolly', it was HK$1. According to Yates, in *History Notes on Hong Kong 1*, some girls did it on account.

Streetwalkers still patrolled outside the Methodist Church in Wan Chai in the 1950s, when Hong Kong was a poorer place than it is today. By then, the lowest price had increased to HK$10. Up to the 1930s, Yates recalled, licenced brothels were well-run and there was a much greater chance of contracting venereal disease from an enthusiastic amateur.

Some men in the armed forces would take a temporary 'wife' to whom they gave HK$5 a week. She would find a Chinese-style cubicle near her man's barracks. Soldiers were not allowed to sleep out at night but would visit their girls and 'pluck the fragrant buds' during daytime. 'Downhomers' did their men's washing, ironing and 'household' chores. According to Yates the girls were loyal and never complained. A few were prepared to make similar arrangements in the 1950s.

Some British soldiers maintained that, when fighting the Japanese in 1941, their Downhomers brought them food and drink, and sheltered the wounded. As the British were marched off to prison the girls lined the route and cried. After the men were interned in Sham Shui Po camp some, under extremely harsh conditions, took their boyfriends food. This often resulted in ill treatment. One cold day a girl was completely stripped and made to stand by the perimeter, wire fence for five hours to suffer the stares of men and being touched by the Japanese when they came off duty. This included throwing icy water over the pathetic figure. Rather than humiliate the girl, unlike the Japanese who considered they had staged a free strip-tease show, several Tommies refused to look.

A few British soldiers married girlfriends and one Eurasian talks with affection of his 'illiterate Chinese mother'. She and his

soldier father were married in 1935, and, when the Japanese attacked, Dad manned artillery situated on Mount Davis. Through
hard times his mother scraped and saved, and, as a Eurasian child
he used to be sent with food parcels to the fence at Sham Shui Po
prisoner-of-war camp. The Japanese are generally fond of children
and no harm came to him. As the mother was Chinese, with an
English husband she had the choice of going into, or staying out of,
prison camp. By remaining outside she could assist her man more.

After the war the gunner husband was posted back to England
with his battery. For a time he paid marriage allowance. Then, this
ceased. Mother brought up her children alone. The army refused to
help or to trace the husband who had probably been demobilised.
Later, she too sailed for Britain where she married another Englishman after obtaining a divorce. She raised a second family in Liverpool.

As a young man the Eurasian son also visited England. There,
he searched through telephone directories. Letters and question-
naires were sent to try and find his father. Many recipients did not
answer. 'You're wasting your time, son,' his mother insisted. 'Your
father's not worth it.'

'I wanted nothing other than to trace my roots,' he maintained.

In those days all brothers and sisters could have lived in England. After changes to the Immigration Act, which did not apply to
their mother who arrived earlier, they were unable to claim right of
abode. 'There's many of us poorer Eurasians left over from the
British Forces,' the son, now a Hong Kong Government pensioner,
told me.

Eurasians in Hong Kong originated from many different backgrounds. In 1897, the year before the New Territories were taken
over on a ninety-nine-year lease, there were said to be 272 'half-
breeds'. But even before the island was occupied in 1841, and British
merchants lived in Macau but moved up to Canton to trade for
several months of the year, a number kept mistresses. The Portuguese population of Macau, not being so prejudiced as the British,
inter-married and cohabited openly with Chinese producing a middle-class, 'Macanese', community.

Several Macanese threw in their lot with the British when Hong
Kong was founded and came to live and work here. Many fought
against the Japanese in 1941 even though their Macanese and Eurasian womenfolk were refused refuge in Australia during the war
because they were not of 'pure British descent'. 'Hong Kong is our
home,' many Eurasians have told me. Today in the Territory it is the
Eurasians and the so-called Portuguese who have strongest claims
to full British citizenship. In some English schools in Hong Kong

Eurasians, of one blend or another, now make up 20 per cent of student numbers, although if their fathers were born in the United Kingdom they can secure residency there.

During the 1870s, a Chinese student named Ho Kai left the Colony to study in Britain. He returned in 1882 with Bachelor of Medicine, Master of Surgery and Barrister-at-Law degrees, together with other qualifications for good measure. He also brought Alice Whitcombe, his Scottish bride, back with him. Governor Sir John Pope Hennessy, while addressing the Legislative Council, referring to Ho Kai, said: 'If the Chinese could throw off their feudal bonds they would rise to the greatest distinction of a nation dedicated to progress.'

Ho Kai's was one of the Colony's first mixed marriages and Whitcombe was said to be 'one of the most gracious ladies ever to step into Hong Kong'. Sadly, she died a few years after arriving and the Alice Memorial Hospital is named after her. They had no children.

Sir Kai Ho Kai is not only believed to have been the first Chinese in Hong Kong to have worn western dress but he also pursued a distinguished public career. Together with Mr Au Tak he owned the original site on which Kai Tak Airport stands. He was respected both by Europeans and Chinese, and, like Sun Yat Sen, was a Mason. Like Sun too, Ho Kai was active in the Chinese Nationalist Movement.

Other Hong Kong citizens also became involved in politics, not always by choice. The Kotewalls, a well-known Eurasian family, has a road named after it at Mid-Levels. When the Greater East Asian Co-Prosperity Plan was unfolded during World War II respected citizens like Sir Robert Kotewall were invited to sit on the Japanese Co-operative Council and other committees. To refuse would probably have been akin to suicide. After the war Sir Robert was censured, and, together with others, labelled as 'a betrayer for his actions'. Nothing was proven against him. Only people who were living under Japanese rule can, no doubt, appreciate what conditions were really like.

Probably the greatest Eurasian 'dynasty' in Hong Kong is the Ho family who are linked, in a striking genealogical web, not only to the Kotewalls but also to names like Zimmern, Cumine, Lo, Choa, Gittins, Hall, Greaves, Fincher and Fisher. 'I'm related to all of them,' writes Peter Hall, author of *In the Web*.

My long walk that hot day, on my return from England, continued over to Happy Valley, where Sir Robert Ho Tung (1862–1956), the Colony's first millionaire, was interred in 1956 in the, then, Colonial Cemetery (renamed Hong Kong Cemetery). The family is bi-lingual, bi-cultural, mainly Christian and partly Buddhist. Its ancestral tablets and shrine are located at the picturesque Tung Lin Kok Yuen Temple, with curled-up eaves and golden-yellow roof, a colour reserved for the Imperial Family years ago in China. I have recollections of the old man in his nineties, with white, wispy beard and Chinese robes. Sir Robert's father, named Bosman, was British, but of Dutch descent. His mother was Chinese. Ho Tung was content to live the life of a Chinese gentleman.

He was highly respected for his ability and wealth, which, before World War II, was said to be in the Carnegie and Rockefeller bracket. He was decorated twenty-two times and was the first non-European to live on the Peak where the only Chinese to be seen, because of the 1904 Reservation Ordinance, were servants or coolies. According to a daughter of Sir Robert the family had to endure snide remarks from neighbours. 'But in the main, Daddy's influence and wealth kept Europeans at bay.'

Just as working class Chinese had few, if any, European contacts, so most 'foreign devils' as far as they could, kept to themselves, and, if they were anyone, lived on the Peak. In healthy, spacious surroundings, by the mid 1880s, thirty to forty families spent their summers 1,300 or so feet up, where it was three degrees or so cooler than at sea level. There they did their best to retain their English culture. 'I know nobody living below May Road,' one Englishwoman is credited with boasting.

The best-known member of the Ho 'dynasty' living today is Stanley, sometimes known as 'Mr Macau', whose grandfather, Ho Fook, was Sir Robert's younger brother. The two, like other family members, were compradores in their earlier working lives and were as prosperous as the taipans of Jardine and E.D. Sassoon for whom they worked.

Foreign merchants depended on compradores who were proficient in both English and Chinese and understood intimately the cultures and customs of both communities. These go-betweens provided the 'bridge' to straddle two worlds. Compradores engaged local staff for whom they vouched. A great deal of their money was earned through commissions, much of which they invested in real estate – always a money-spinner in Hong Kong.

Hong Kong-born septuagenarian Dr Stanley Ho, a colonial blend of East and West, thinks on his feet. He owns a fortune invested in countries like Portugal, Spain, Australia, the Philippines and, of course, Hong Kong and Macau. His interests include the syndicate which controls the casinos, horse racing (taxes on gambling bring in 40 per cent of Macau's GDP) and the world's largest fleet of jet-powered ferries which take people to Macau from Hong

Kong. The casino mogul has been assured by China that gambling will be able to continue in Macau after 1999. His other interests include hotels, restaurants, transportation, television and property, with a residential complex in Tianjun, in the People's Republic.

Through foolish buying of shares before World War II, Ho's family lost everything – 'including face'. 'I couldn' t even afford to ride on a bus!'

Stanley is a good raconteur. As a young man, he had the job of earning it all back. This he has done many times over. 'You need business in your blood,' he maintains. Although not an outstanding chemistry student at Hong Kong University, by the age of twenty-three he had made his first million in wartime Macau. He learned Japanese.

Since then, with three Rolls Royces, he has never looked back, in spite of more than one death threat. Yet in addition to being a brilliant businessman and an ebullient personality, according to one of his daughters, Angela, Stanley Ho is still, with more than one wife, very Cantonese. 'In some ways he's very reserved,' she insists. Because he enjoys dancing he has, however, been titled 'King of Tango'. At one stage he suggested Hong Kong should be placed under United Nations auspices. This, with China's insistence on sovereignty, was a non-starter. He serves as Honorary Consul of Honduras in Macau.

Second to the Ho family in power and wealth among Eurasians, and connected to it by marriage, is the Lo family, mentioned in Chapter 1. They have distinguished themselves in the legal profession and have had members of every generation, since the turn of the century, sitting on Hong Kong's Legislative and Executive Councils.

Lo Tak-shing CBE, born in 1935 in Hong Kong, also sat on both government Councils as well as on other major committees. A big man with a commanding presence, he was packed off to boarding school in England and later went up to Oxford. Nevertheless, he still maintains he feels very Chinese, with 'seeds implanted especially during World War II'. He plans to remain in Hong Kong. Himself a lawyer, owning the oldest law firm in the Territory, he is convinced communism and capitalism can co-exist and that 'One country, Two systems' can work.

Because the British Government refused to bestow full British citizenship on all Hong Kong people, he resigned in protest from all his government committees. Bearing in mind his family's strong links with the British over generations one must sympathise with his convictions. A copy of the document which the Hong Kong Government gave to Sun Yat-sen, refusing to allow him sanctuary in the Colony for fear of spoiling Chinese-British relations, hangs in Lo's study. 'The British Government demonstrated as much courage now as it displayed then, in 1897,' he maintains.

In 1984, until when he had been staunchly anti-communist, he established 'Hong Kong Freedom of Movement and Right of Abode Limited' and himself provided funds to offer assistance to anyone who wanted to emigrate. He, like others, advocated Britain should provide an island somewhere which could be settled by local people and turned into a second Hong Kong. Lo accepted a position on the China Basic Law Consultative Committee. He also offers hawkish advice to leading People's Republic figures by whom he has been described as 'counter-revolutionary' and a 'man of vision'. Some believe he is still destined for high office, perhaps even front runner for Chief Executive after Hong Kong returns to China. T.S. Lo is the owner and Chairman of *Window*, the magazine with the imperial-yellow cover that boasts 'it knows what China thinks'. He has been chided on the odd occasion for not handing back his decoration, Commander of the British Empire, to the Queen.

In eastern England, where I come from, we are a harmonious blend of Celts, Saxons, Romans, Vikings, and possibly Picts and Greeks. Similarly, Chinese believe, with Mongols, Manchus and other minority groups being absorbed over the years, 'All rivers running into the China Sea turn salty'. After 1997, all Eurasians will become Chinese, they say.

Stephen Fisher, in *Eurasians in Hong Kong a Sociological Study of a Marginal Group*, looks at twenty-four life histories. Himself a Eurasian, the author of this thesis maintains that, being of mixed blood is very much a state of mind. If a taipan or a Westerner in a good social position kept a 'protected woman', because it was not accepted for them to be seen together, it would often be a case of 'love them and leave them'. Any offspring would be brought up by the mother, take her name, wear Chinese dress and lead, largely, a Chinese life.

Conversely, if the father was of supervisory grade, or, say, a jailor or a policeman, he probably 'went bush', as it was termed, and lived with his common-law Chinese wife. In such cases children probably took their father's name and, to some degree, followed European working class customs. However, they would also have a Chinese moniker and would switch to it if it was advantageous to do so.

But whether following largely the European or the Chinese path, Eurasian children, because of appearance, were still not accepted as genuine members of either community. This was even if, over two or three generations, the degree of marginality had been reduced, and, by then, the person might have been partially absorbed. Years ago, few passed into the 'true-blue' European camp and had much idea of what real European traditions implied. Similarly, not many Eurasians were deeply moved by the passions that sweep China, such as the Sino-British Opium Wars, or when approaching a million Chinese demonstrated in Hong Kong, many with tears in their eyes, in the aftermath of the Tiananmen Square Massacre.

Whether Eurasians are able to mix freely with either Chinese or Europeans depends mainly on their desire to assimilate, language ability, financial position, appearance, dress and social grouping. A Eurasian is labelled either 'Chinese' or 'Western' if he or she conforms to the ethnic norm. With increasing numbers of mixed marriages, obviously, Eurasians will not disappear.

Fisher, in his thesis, goes on to explain that, unfortunately, 'half-castes' were often distrusted and regarded as less capable than pure stock. They were considered 'racial hybrids', inferior and unacceptable socially by both Chinese and Europeans. Bestselling author Han Suyin wrote: 'I am Eurasian and the word evokes in some minds a sensation of moral laxity.'

A sinologist, E.T.C. Werner, British Consul at Foochow, stated in 1928: 'Offspring of parents of widely different races inherit the worst characteristics of both sides.'

Similar views were held by authors like Somerset Maugham who described Eurasians in derogatory overtones.

It is however precisely because they are not properly accepted and appreciated, together with divided loyalty to two antagonistic cultures, that this ambivalence comes to the fore. Fisher continues that Eurasians are sometimes accused of being highly strung, moody, weak-minded and of having irrational, fluctuating temperaments. They were, undoubtedly, often labelled indiscriminately. Nevertheless Betty Wei states, in *Shanghai, Crucible of Modern China*, that Eurasians were treated better in Hong Kong than they were in Shanghai. Treatment meted out to Eurasians in Malaya and Singapore was also frequently unfair. 'I am afraid to marry,' C.H. Crabb writes in *Malaya's Eurasians – An Opinion*, 'for fear of bringing more Eurasians into this world.' He also suggests that 'Water and oil don't mix', like two different races inter-marrying.

There is, of course, an obverse side. There are those who insist that Eurasians are 'uniquely beautiful', complex and intelligent. Ho Tung, Robert Kotewall and M.K. Lo were all knighted as 'Queen's Chinese', and bedecked with medals. Countless others of mixed blood have led outstanding careers and contributed significantly to Hong Kong's development. Many of the successful insist that Eurasians should live their lives as 'personalities' and not as 'nationalities'. They should avoid complexes and be themselves. Unfortunately some 'upper-crust' Eurasian families, those that looked almost European, sometimes refused to acknowledge family members who resembled Chinese.

A further drawback was that 'toffee-nosed' English, many of whom were conscious of self-imagined superiority (which exasperated other nationalities), perceived Eurasians as deviants and a threat, and as marginal people for whom it was difficult to find a niche without upsetting the social order. It was traditional, until lighthouses were automated in the 1980s, for them to be manned by Eurasians. Until the 1950s, the Hongkong Bank only employed Chinese as 'minor staff'. Its clerical, typing and secretarial posts were filled by Eurasians and Portuguese.

The study of Eurasians, many of whom try to expunge the past, has not been well documented. It follows, nevertheless, very much the story of racism in Hong Kong, where, for the first fifty years on the Star Ferry no Chinese was allowed to ride first class and no European could ride second class.

Typical English reserve and the pattern of social relationships that applied in Britain, with a strict, implied code between master and servant, was transferred to the Empire, but even more so, with the English living more grandly than they did at home. Thus, with British arrogance and Chinese indifference 'lower-echelon Englishmen', such as supervisory staff and shopkeepers, as well as lower ranks in the armed forces, were treated as inferiors by taipan society, especially up to World War II.

As Sid Coomes, a British soldier posted to Hong Kong in the 1930s, is quoted as remarking, in *Hong Kong Military History Notes*, issue 7, all the most beautiful places, like the Peak and Repulse Bay, were out of bounds to other ranks. Even on the Peak Tram, Coomes says: 'There was a little brass plaque instructing [you] where to sit. In other words apartheid.'

Up to 1926 most passengers travelled first class; policemen and soldiers (who were 'as despicable as a gang of thieves and villains' according to one of Swire's agents) second class; and caste-conscious hierarchies of servants third class. Anyone with a load such as coal, ice or food lugged it up on their shoulders. There were separate waiting rooms for Europeans and Chinese.

Working class Europeans, 'lacking breeding', lowered the status of Whites in the East. There was the danger they would 'let the side down'. Like the Englishman who demonstrated alongside Chinese communists at North Point in 1967. He was immediately flown back to Britain. In addition, the Chinese can treat their own labouring classes terribly, although in some ways they are more tolerant than Europeans. All this meant that Hong Kong society, up to the Japanese Occupation, consisted of numerous divisions and subdivisions. There was appalling snootiness and feuding at various levels.

Sir Paul Chater (1846–1926), an Armenian Christian, was a famous businessman and philanthropist. He was also a devout royalist, an Anglophile and a Mason. However, until his death, his Nordic wife, Lady Christine (1879–1935) was never invited to Government House. Some speculated, rightly or wrongly, that this was owing to her dubious background. Snobbery in the Colony, in what has been likened to a village in rural England at the time, was self-energising and self-perpetuating. It filtered down.

Yet in some ways the Territory was not so colonial as Singapore or Malaya. The oft repeated saw had it, 'Hong Kong was run by "The Bank", Jardines, the Jockey Club and the Governor, not necessarily in that order'. Commerce played a vital role, as in Shanghai. What was good for business was good for Hong Kong. Being taipan of a large *hong* meant the burden of *pro bono publico*. 'If Jardine does not pull its weight nobody else in the community will,' the Governor insisted in the 1970s.

After World War II, Chinese bonded and hereditary servants came naturally to an end. Neither was it possible for the British to put the clocks back even if there was a reluctance to pursue Japanese war criminals who had murdered Asians as opposed to Westerners. The police, however, still held tremendous authority in Hong Kong. One visitor from England relates, in a letter to the *South China Morning Post*, how, in 1949, he saw police wielding *lathi* sticks (still used in India) to drive back spectators in the Territory so they did not obstruct the path of parading troops.

Yet by the mid 1950s, although 'Hong Kong village' had taken its first steps to becoming an international city, it remained colonial in numerous ways. There was the 'charmed circle', comprising largely senior government officials (mostly British), *taipans*, consular corps staff and high ranking members of the armed forces. By then it included rich Chinese and Eurasians, such as 'dynastic families' like the Ho Tungs, some of whom were western-educated. After World War II well-to-do, established, Eurasians were, of course, an integral part of society at all levels.

Signing the visitors' book and receiving an invitation to the Government House Garden Party, on the Queen's Birthday, 21 April, demonstrated one's standing (like being invited to New China News Agency gatherings today). It was, nevertheless, important to know your place. 'We shouldn't invite them to lunch, dear,' a woman told her engineer husband in the Waterworks Department. 'He's only an inspector.'

But even for junior expatriates, with the odd wife who was once in domestic service in England herself, it was still a privileged life. Friendships often centred around sports clubs, one's church, or, to a lesser extent, the workplace. Conversations included grumbles about amahs or cookboys, who addressed us as 'master', although few expatriates had employed servants back in Britain after World War II. The expiry of the New Territories lease in 1997, was rarely discussed. European guest lists seldom included Chinese, although one might invite one's staff for a 'duty party', at home, once a year.

If reciprocated this would normally be in a restaurant. Chinese seldom invited Europeans to their homes, which, in most cases lacked creature comforts in those days and were cramped. This caused some resentment. 'He's even got a separate room for the dog!' a Chinese colleague once complained about our mutual English boss. But still the two races lived reasonably contentedly side by side. Separation was more often due to unfamiliarity, with very different customs and lack of language ability, rather than to extreme prejudice.

Although by the 1950s segregation on the Peak was long past, and 'spilt water could not be gathered up', deep-seated, long-standing feelings still meant most Europeans and Chinese were happier among their own kind. Most Whites did not want closer acquaintances with Asians. 'It's his fault,' I overheard a colleague say about a Welshman who was not invited to a party. 'He's mixed too much with Chinese!' Suddenly, when a young Englishman came East and he was ushered to the head of a queue by Chinese in a government office, or a car parking summons was quashed, as easily as that, by a senior traffic policeman who had been in Stanley prisoner-of-war camp with the offender, you soon learnt what the 'old-boy network' meant. In turn, suffering and death was supposed to come naturally to Chinese. 'One Chinaman less won't make much difference!' a colleague regularly remarked. Yet all the time the 'Confucian-hearted' knew, living in the centre of the 'civilised world', that everyone else was inferior.

My old boss tried to dispel it by making out no-one on his staff was a bigot. But inwardly, he was as racist as they came as could be gleaned from circumlocutory remarks he let slip and a lack of sensitivity to 'things Chinese'. 'I've never had a Chinese cross my threshold as a guest,' another Old Hong Kong Hand who could not count beyond three in Chinese, used to boast. 'Never know what they might do!'

Of course there were exceptions to left over, Victorian attitudes. The late K.M.A. Barnett (a senior goverment servant) was a remarkable man who started courting his Chinese girlfriend before World War II. He had a prodigious brain that could polish off cryptic crossword puzzles in ten minutes and allowed him to play chess in his head. Derek Davies, at the time chief editor of the *Far Eastern Economic Review*, wrote on Barnett's death, in 1987, in the Royal Asiatic Society, Hongkong Branch, Journal: 'Perhaps his occasional sourness could be traced to a resentment that his (most happy) marriage to a Chinese had blocked his promotion.'

Although I know from my own experiences intermarriage was not welcomed in those days, I am not entirely convinced Davies was correct. Nevertheless, it was certainly agreed among 'charmed circle' members that marriage to a Chinese reduced a European's standing just as a Eurasian was unlikely to have a 'good marriage' – namely to a European. For those in the *hongs* or the banks it was probably more of a reality, with greater chance of spoiling career prospects, than in government service.

Yet even if my wife, as a young girl on leaving college in 1956, was unable to join the Hongkong Bank as a secretary, because it only employed Chinese as janitors, Bill Brown, with his Japanese wife, did become Chief General Manager of the Chartered Bank in Hong Kong in the 1970s. Also Sir Piers Jacobs, with a Chinese spouse, was Government Financial Secretary in the 1980s. Nevertheless, a close friend of mine was cautioned by a well-meaning English lady, as late as the 1970s, that he would be 'ill-advised' to wed his Chinese girlfriend. Eventually, they married and have lived happily ever after. Today, coincidentally, like having a Chinese partner in business so you are 'in the web', a Chinese wife can work in your favour.

So much changed after the 1967 Disturbances. Gradually Chinese, who previously imagined they might one day return to their native village on the Mainland, began to think of themselves as 'Hongkongers'. The two races had also come closer, by natural evolution, and an edict was issued in government circles stating that, except in a historical context, the word 'colony' should not be used. Remnants of upper-class Edwardian attitudes, which had become frozen in Hong Kong decades after they had melted away in England gradually disappeared in the Territory. Yet even today mixed marriages can raise eyebrows and are still not acceptable to many of both races, just as an oriental girl and a foreign man, together, can cause heads to turn.

'People can be cruel and judgemental, and make a lot of sarcastic and disdainful comments,' wrote Rebecca Woo in *Asia Magazine* in 1986.

She went on to say that mixed marriage goes against social norms and only results in unhappiness. Why should 'half-ghost' children, 'symbols of disgrace', have to bear the brunt of their parents' selfish selection of a marriage partner by breaking homogeneity of race? We live in a practical world. Life is easier if we face up to reality, Woo insisted.

Although expressions like 'hybrid', 'half-breed', 'half-caste' and a 'touch of the tarbrush' are, thank goodness, no longer common, the term *gwailo*, meaning 'ghost person' (loosely translated as 'devil person'), as a synonym for foreigner, is still common usage. In early days it was understandable. To them, 'pale' Westerners with fair hair looked so different. Today, most Cantonese insist that '*gwailo*' has become a neutral expression and no slur or negative connotation is intended. Depending on the context in which it is used, and the tone of disdain, many are prepared to accept this. Well-known journalist Frank Ching, however, in the *South China Morning Post* (13 July 1990) wrote: '[*Gwailo*] reflects feelings deeply rooted in the Chinese psyche. To say it is not derogatory is to deny the obvious.'

Ching maintains it is a modern, vulgar way in which his fellow countrymen express ancient prejudice. Having fought with the Eighth Army in North African deserts I am proud to call myself a 'Desert Rat'. Similarly Europeans, in self-mockery, frequently describe themselves as *gwailo* today.

In the 1990s, Hong Kong is a vastly different place to forty years ago. Just as Australians get a kick from being descended from convicts, banished from Britain perhaps for being hungry and stealing a loaf of bread, so it is gratifying that most Eurasians born since the 1950s have few hang ups. They are just as well-adjusted and happy as offspring of single-race marriages. In fact one Chinese woman with grown-up Eurasian children insists that being Eurasian – or even Chinese – in today's world is a cachet. Now, even if many northern Chinese consider themselves superior to southerners, and a few old-fashioned Shanghainese still warn their children, when going overseas to study, not to marry foreigners or Cantonese, things are vastly different. That is in spite of a young American scholar who had been living with a family for many months in Shanghai, learning the language, telling me in 1993: 'I still sense Hong Kong is a racist place.'

In 1989, the Eurasian grandson of the late Sir Y.K. Pao, the shipping magnate, was Head Boy at Eton College in England. At the time of writing, a Eurasian with an English father and a Shanghainese mother, is Deputy President of the Legislative Council in Hong Kong. A Briton with a Chinese wife is President of the prestigious Hong Kong Club, which, not so long ago he would not have been allowed to join because of his mixed marriage. A Chinese New Zealander in Hong Kong speaks fluent medieval Scottish and medieval Italian and is married to a British government servant.

A tall, well-adjusted, Shanghainese girl springs to mind. 'How on earth could my husband marry a Chinese,' she sometimes exclaims. 'He's so English!'

After considering my question, she felt that she had never really been slighted, as a Chinese living in England, even if, when the couple were seen together, people imagined they were having an affair.

'Mixed marriage makes the world spin round,' she insists.

'When first wed you adapt and are on your best behaviour.' Later facades are stripped, cultural differences begin to show, less desirable elements emerge and partners become outspoken. Not entirely understanding nuances of language and culture causes conflicts. Although children are innocent and racially 'colour blind', having a number of foreigners at the school in England, which her two sons attended made it less difficult for them to adjust. Being impervious to scorn and insults means it is easier to be successful. When they are teased about their Asian-like features, she taught them to say, 'Yes I'm Eurasian. I have the best of two worlds.'

CHAPTER EIGHT

ENTERPRISE

T HE 328-foot-long by 30-foot-high 'Citizen' watch advertisement, which is claimed to be the world's longest neon sign (97 feet longer than a 747 jumbo jet), still towers on top of Elizabeth House, even if there is no other city on earth in which the skyline alters so rapidly. But in spite of change in this city of label worship, that afternoon as I wandered around Causeway Bay two weeks after returning to Hong Kong, I felt I had never been away. Where I strolled used to be the waterfront, in the mid 1950s. Today, with over fifteen square miles of seabed reclaimed, land area has increased by just under 4 per cent since the Territory was originally ceded.

'By hard work and effort this tiny state hopes to prosper,' the slogan read on the back of a lad's T-shirt as he elbowed in in front of me. Like many 'Honkies', as we occasionally call ourselves, he was taking full advantage of the opportunity, although his ilk is not guilty of acts of vandalism on our underground railway as is common in many parts of the world. Yet he knows, if he does not squeeze in, he will be left standing on the platform.

'With fractured English, one-in-three don't make sense,' a researcher, after surveying the proliferation of gibberish printed on apparel, once assured me. With my jaywalking adversary, however, the maxim, 'hopes to prosper', according to my understanding of the 'T-shirt test', seemed, for the most materialistic people anywhere, appropriate.

Since Karl Friedrich Benz, the German engineer, launched his first petrol-driven car in 1885, personal mobility has become an in-satiable desire. Even though Hong Kong has had massive road con-struction programmes, with no respite in new car registrations, there are on average well in excess of 400 vehicles for every mile. One wonders how long it will be before the urban area becomes as bad as Bangkok.

It is not only roads but pavements too, with crowds surging forward and perspiring pedestrians jockeying for position, just as a couple of entrepreneurs do when engaged in business transactions. The saying, 'One mountain cannot contain two tigers,' holds good for much of Hong Kong life. That Mid-Autumn Festival eve, with a throbbing pulse in the atmosphere resembling the approach of a typhoon, there was still a tireless pace. The frustration of getting from A to B in Hong Kong contrasts with a brisk, unimpeded stroll in cool, rural England. Stomach ulcers run in families. There are 300,000 cases a year in the Territory – around average for a city of this size. Yet many people are diagnosed as contracting them at forty, ten years earlier than in most western countries.

But even in a place like Causeway Bay there are degrees of activity. Restaurants on the sunny, northern side of Lockhart Road, where there is constant chatter, can be described as *yang*. Contrarily, establishments on the shady, quieter, southern side assume negative polarity and are labelled *yin*. 'Contrasting phenomena not only rea-son,' an astute businesswoman once convinced me.

'We Cantonese enjoy *it naau*, activity, noise and bright lights, in large doses.'

'Within a culture of "consumption", you are what you con-sume, business attracts business.'

There is no exact translation for *it naau*. It means more or less 'bustle'.

There was no stopping my exemplar when she was on her hobbyhorse. 'Here, you register a business in the morning, open in the afternoon, make profit by evening.'

Hong Kong is now a 'mega city'. But its people were previously not well off although a barefooted man is not poor unless he has always worn shoes. In the mid 1950s, when it rained, as canny street traders rushed out into the streets to sell umbrellas, pedestrians rolled up their trouser legs, carried their footwear and walked bare-foot. Shoes were precious. Those pioneering days with absence of environmental planning have long since disappeared. Governor Sir Alexander Grantham (1947–57) vowed to transform Hong Kong into the most modern city in the East. New, squeaky-clean, glossy housing estates, light years from the old resettlement blocks, have sprung up. The Territory has become one of Asia's most advanced, artistically creative and free societies.

Now, what was once 'barefoot' Hong Kong has more than one telephone for every two inhabitants (China has one for 120). There are more international calls made per person than anywhere else in the world. The Territory has become the world's tenth largest trading entity. 'Hot lines' and electronic banking exist on a massive scale; pagers sound off in eating houses; Chinese yuppies turn corners with one hand on the steering wheel while conversing furiously on telephones. Technologically, Hong Kong is an electronic town and the largest purchaser of mobile telephones in the world, even if shouting over these in public places does not conform to most expatriates' idea of acceptable social behaviour.

With meagre natural resources, apart from its deep-water harbour and its purposeful people, the Territory achieved what was probably the highest economic growth in the world with hardly any of the benefits of external aid. With a population of six million, less than 1 per cent of bureaucratic India, free-wheeling, free enterprise Hong Kong – with its free port – exports twice as much merchandise as the world's largest democracy. It is its vibrant commerce that makes Hong Kong so successful. To Singapore's Lee Kuan Yew, all Hongkongers (the last 'treaty-port Chinese') believe, as risk-takers, they have it in them to become millionaires. Singaporeans, according to Mr Lee, are less adventurous.

Even the humble Hong Kong clerk, who has not a Vietnamese in a detention camp's likelihood of making it, is prepared to chance his luck. When you give him a tedious job he still says, 'I'll do my best.' Of course, inwardly, the same ambitious Cantonese expects, in the long run, there will be something in it for him.

Like gold diggers in the old American West, getting rich quick, and spending it, is a long-standing Hong Kong ambition. As Bob Hope quipped, 'I've been poor and I've been rich, and rich is better.'

Nevertheless it is often an unjust society, with coolies weighed down with shoulder poles. But with skill, hard work and the luck of the gods you may hit the jackpot. You are what you earn. Charge what the market will bear. Enrich yourself before China takes over.

Accumulating a fortune can become a passion, or even a mania, in a state where social and political infrastructure lag behind economic development. In such an atmosphere, rather than bemoaning their lot, seeking 'filthy lucre' and ostentatious social status become palliatives, symbols of power. In such an environment the all-consuming mission for 'high rollers' is work. The Territory, in some respects unfairly, has become infamous for its religion of money grubbing and mercenariness. But life is riddled with uncertainties:

like the takeover by the People's Republic, which (even if its cadres were raised on Marxist beliefs) cannot wait to get its hands on Hong Kong's wealth. Meanwhile, for Hong Kong yuppies there is still time to eat, drink and make money. Who knows what will happen tomorrow?

To be fair, in a place which is awash with foreign and local capital, it is not all take and no give. Wandering around Hong Kong one can observe many buildings named after exalted, generous benefactors: 'White cranes in the clouds' like Sir Run Run Shaw the Shanghainese film magnate, and the late, likeable but eccentric, Sir Tang Shiu Kin. Sir Run Run has always maintained, 'You can't take it with you.' Since the establishment of the Shaw Foundation, in 1973, he has handed over HK$1.3 billion to charitable projects in China, Hong Kong, Singapore, Taiwan, Britain and the United States.

To people like Shaw and Tang, and countless others, philanthrophy is a way of life. Education and social services are favourite recipients. Although 'scaling the heights' does a great deal for the benefactors' ego they are sincerely grateful for their good fortune and make a point of returning some of their wealth to the community. Li Ka-shing, the sixteenth richest man in the world, who actually lives modestly, admits that he had a lot of money he did not know what to do with.

'Not only does giving bring blessings to donors and their families in this world, but also in the life hereafter. Yet although rich men look to the future, while poor men are more concerned with the present, it is not only the well off who are generous. The citizens of tiny Hong Kong donated more than HK$468 million for flood relief in China in 1991, more than all other nations in the world put together. One Hong Kong businessman, Lee Chia-chen, gave HK$62.4 million. Taxi drivers promptly handed over one day's takings.

Yes, the Territory where poverty can be a mortal sin, even if it is at times stubborn and bigoted, is, in many ways, a blessed city. With the Territory's rampant capitalism, however, the higher the mountain the deeper the valley. 'Tumbles' are not uncommon. Although life in Hong Kong has been likened to a trip on its own Star Ferry, the finest ride in the world, rewards are not always shared equally.

How did the Colony start? Just as Westerners, largely Britons, built Shanghai out of an arid mudflat, so Hong Kong owes its beginnings mainly to British companies. Among them Jardine, the 'Princely Hong', Gibb Livingston and Watsons the Chemist, all established in Canton, pre-date the Territory.

But it took more than the efforts of private enterprise to make Hong Kong emerge from the ruined port that it had become after World War II. The international trading and financial centre that we see today could not have happened without superior government. Like good cooking, this meant the 'less stirring the better', although Sir Philip Haddon-Cave, Financial Secretary in the 1970s, insisted his policy was 'positive non-interventionism' rather than laissez faire. Nevertheless Hong Kong, because of ties with Britain, has enjoyed first-class government, sound administrative and legal systems, and adequate infrastructure. Respect has been shown for basic individual and collective human rights. Foreign leaders like Zhou En Lai, Ho Chi Minh and Jose Rizal have all sought refuge and planned their revolutions in Hong Kong.

In contrast to most Asian states the Mother Country, Britain, provided Hong Kong citizens, 98 per cent of whom are Chinese, with a relatively peaceful and stable atmosphere. Even so, in addition to the labour unrest in the 1920s and the turmoil of the Japanese Occupation, Hong Kong has survived many crises. These included pestilence, droughts, typhoons and riots. There was the 'great bank run', on the Hang Seng, Kwong On and Ming Tak banks, in 1965. But the most ludicrous of all 'bumps along the road' was the run on branches of Maria's Cake Shop, in 1984, when customers with attacks of the jitters queued for hours to secure their share of HK$10 million of pre-paid cake vouchers.

When Confucius visited the holy mountain of Taishan in Shandong Province, he was told by an old lady that her relatives kept being eaten by tigers.

'Why on earth do you stay?' the Sage asked.

'Because the government here is not bad,' she replied.

'Ah,' said Confucius, 'so bad government is worse than fierce tigers.'

Because Hong Kong administration is 'not bad', in spite of exigencies, many Chinese preferred life under the Union Jack. Although they appeared to be offering allegiance to a foreign power, they stayed because business thrived.

'How was it that ... Englishmen could do such things ... with the barren rock of Hong Kong, within seventy to eighty years, while China, in 4,000 years, had no place like [it]?' Sun Yat-sen, acknowledged as the Father of Modern China and revered by both Nationalists and Communists, asked this question when he spoke, in 1923, to Hong Kong University graduates. Orderly calm in the Colony, where he had received much of his own education, impressed him.

'Where and how did I get my revolutionary and modern ideas?' he continued, 'I got my ideas in this very place ...'

It is now fashionable to apologise for imperialism. Yet had Hong Kong not been taken back by Britain, in 1945 after the Japanese Occupation, the place would have finished up as just another back-water port on China's southern coast. As such, it would have been of little use as a catalyst for the People's Republic's 'open door' economic development programme.

The United States President, Franklin Roosevelt, planned that at the end of World War II, Britain and other European countries should no longer enjoy 'special empire rights' in cities like Hong Kong, Canton and Shanghai. In 1943, President Chiang Kai-shek abolished all standing, unequal treaties yet left those applicable to Hong Kong untouched. Nevertheless, his troops stood by ready to march in to receive the surrender from the Japanese at the end of the war. This move was forestalled by Colonial Secretary Franklin Gimson who quickly set up an interim British Government, without real opposition from Nationalist forces, after his release from Stanley prisoner-of-war camp. Rear-Admiral Harcourt's fleet arrived fifteen days later.

Since the British first occupied Hong Kong it has always been a fine place to make money. Chinese businessmen have not been so successful in the West. Examples include the late Shipping King Sir Y.K. Pao's rescue bid for Standard Chartered Bank when he rallied round and bought a massive number of shares to act as 'White Knight', in 1986. Other hardly illustrious cases include Movie Mogul Sir Run Run Shaw's flutter with Macy's, in the United States, and Hong Kong's richest man, Li Ka-shing's investments abroad including in Husky Oil, in Canada. Much of the success of entrepreneurs in Hong Kong, even if competition is keen, is due to the business environment.

The 19,000 Indian community is responsible for a remarkable 10 to 12 per cent of Hong Kong's exports. 'We prefer to get on with the job of making money rather than filling in multiple forms as one has to do in bureaucratic India,' they tell you.

Few citizens, whose Third World countries exhaust treasuries not long after independence, are willing to admit they were better off under colonial rule. Old China Hands and the elderly Chinese one meets now chatting by the run-down, once elegant, buildings along the Bund in Shanghai, often recall with nostalgia the glory, and to be fair, the horrors (with starvation, narcotics, extortion and prostitution on gigantic scales) where East met West.

The British took over Weihaiwei, at the time of China's Hundred Days Reforms in 1898, and turned it into an enclave of free trade and a sanctuary from the rest of what was then turbulent Qing China. This tiny territory on the Shandong Peninsula became a Royal Navy base. But, after eight years of protracted negotiations, Britain agreed to lower the Union Jack in 1930. Despite pledges to the contrary, shortly after taking it back China introduced a long list of taxes and duties. The United Kingdom administered the territory with a staff of twelve. China increased this to fifty. The handback of what is now called Weihai was not a model on which the return of Hong Kong, sometimes cynically depicted as a bride marrying beneath her, should be based.

Weihai and the former 'Paris of the East', namely Shanghai, are examples of what happened when China got its hands on vibrant, international cities. Yet if the communists had not ruined Shanghai Hong Kong would probably not have replaced it and become a success story. The People's Republic put dogma first. Everyone was demoted to the same level. In competitive Hong Kong everyone is not equal. China has finally comprehended what it failed to grasp when it was too busy denigrating Hong Kong. In addition to being profitable the quality of life here has its attractions.

With rule under communist China to look forward to, Hong Kong may not need to worry that the 'sky will fall'. But, as one emigrant bound for Canada said, with seemingly little concern about being thought unpatriotic or making the People's Republic lose face: 'Can we trust China to provide stability and prosperity when its own inhabitants have never had it themselves?'

'Remember the famine of 1962? Thirty million people died. We had to send food parcels to Mainland relatives so they could survive.'

'We owe the British our character as a modern city gained through continuous exposure and response to the world,' wrote Margaret Ng, *Hong Kong Standard* columnist. Britain has much to be proud of.

'The Hong Kong Government with all its warts has never been involved, since I've worked for it, in any underhand dealings,' said Elizabeth Wong, senior Administrative Officer.

Some have argued that if Hong Kong had been colonised by the United States, with its cultural blitz against which the rest of the world seems to have little defence, the Territory would have been even better off. When making such hypothetical statements one is reminded of poverty among Blacks in the United States, not to mention gigantic financial deficits and cities with the highest crime rates on earth.

On approaching Causeway Bay traffic roundabouts, strains of *Que Sera Sera Whatever will be will be* whisked me back, momentarily, to 1955. Then, although Imperial decline was well on its way, Britain was still held in relatively high esteem.

'Too expensive,' I remember saying to a North Point stall owner about a tape-recorder.

'Not Japanese,' he retorted. 'Best quality; this British.'

With memories of pomp and glory, Winston Churchill's words: 'I have not become the King's First Minister in order to preside over the liquidation of the British Empire,' sprang to mind.

The 1950s saw spectacular military parades on the Queen's birthday in Hong Kong, even if we proud 'Brits', a few sporting bowlers and furled umbrellas, were occasionally chided by less fortunate (and jealous) Europeans as 'big fish in a small colonial pond'. Nevertheless, everyone thanked God there was still a 'pimple' on the soft under-belly of 'Red China' which (we hoped) would remain forever a 'tiny piece of old England'.

Four decades on, with Hong Kong no longer dependent on cheap labour, while absorbing developed countries' technology and mimicking much of the West's lifestyle there is no longer the invincibility of the white face. Among trading nations Britain's position is downgraded, year by year. Since the latter half of the 1980s more United States' citizens have resided in Hong Kong than Britons.

In 1875, Britain's slice of Hong Kong trade with China amounted to 74 per cent, with both American and German shares standing at 4 per cent. In 1993, not only were there more Mercedes and BMWs – let alone Japanese cars – on Hong Kong's roads than Jaguars and Rolls-Royces, but the United Kingdom's share of Hong Kong imports dropped from 12 per cent in 1953 to less than 4 per cent in 1990. The latter figure compares with 11 per cent for the United States (the only country it seems with any real influence on China) and 24 per cent for Japan.

Britain is now relegated to seventh place for countries exporting to Hong Kong, even trailing behind Taiwan (8 per cent) and Singapore (6 per cent). China, where much of Hong Kong's food comes from, fluctuates between 20 and 26 per cent. Nevertheless, with only 5 per cent of global trade, 4 per cent of GNP and 1 per cent of population on the world stage, Britain, with a seat on the five-member United Nations Security Council, continues to punch above her weight. Yet in an Asian Commercial Research poll conducted in 1993, only 30 per cent of Hongkongers would have preferred the Territory to continue to be ruled by Britain.

By that same year Hong Kong, in per capita GDP terms, had

caught up with its erstwhile colonisers, the British, and other developed countries like Australia, and had overtaken New Zealand and Spain. The average Hongkonger also bets more on the races annually than 'old one-hundred names' (Mr Average) in China earns over the same period. Hong Kong also has the twelfth largest foreign exchange reserves in the world. One of the greatest challenges for economists is to analyse the extraordinary success of Southeast Asian 'Tigers' where incomes have quadrupled over the past thirty years.

THE scrawny neck of the old man gossiping with the watchman, in the block of mixed domestic and commercial accommodation, was partly circled by vertical, red streaks. These were self-inflicted, where he had kneaded the skin to bring up vicious-looking blood blisters. Plucking opens pores, stimulates nervous systems, acts as an anti-irritant and relieves headaches. Boarding a lift on the ground floor (first floor in Chinese) must indicate something about human nature. Impatient shovers frantically try to enter before those inside squeeze out. Whether waiting your turn for transportation or doing business, the nice chap, unfortunately, so often gets left behind. As we strangers ascended, packed like sardines in the lift, unobtrusively everyone avoided eye contact pretending to concentrate on ethereal things. Bereft of the pushing on the underground railway at rush hour, Confucian courtesy functions reasonably well once inside the confines of an elevator, even if the odd cynic claims that the day you surreptitiously press the 'close door' button, when you know someone is sprinting for the lift, is the moment you become a true local.

My wife's property consists of a salon where cosmetics are sold and beauty treatment given. There is a classroom for training beauticians and a plate-glass entrance door. Carpeted, chromium plate, aseptic off-white paintwork, with modern equipment; apart from Goddess of Mercy bamboo for *feng shui* effects, it is the kind of accommodation you find in Los Angeles, London or Luxembourg.

As I arrived my mother-in-law came out from the kitchen. 'Wela!' she called, 'Denny [*sic*] come.' Like many Chinese, as she summoned my wife, she pronounced 'V' as 'W' and 'R' as 'L'. Ma then brought me a cup of 'dragon well' tea. In rural China spring water is superior to well water, and well water is better than river water for brewing tea.

'If you're invited to "drink tea" and you reply, "Don't stand on ceremony", they think you're just being polite,' a friend once quipped. 'It arrives just the same!'

Nevertheless, with the world going mad with skirmishes and rumours of skirmishes, being welcomed with refreshing, steaming-hot tea, even if it is made from tap water, contributes to gracious living.

My mother-in-law is a tiny woman. Marriage was decided for her at sixteen over a mahjong table. In China, where at one time men and women did not sit in the same room, hang their clothes on the same peg or pass objects from hand to hand, marriage was too important to leave to two inexperienced youngsters. Selecting the right partner for one's offspring required conscious, pragmatic choice, correct dates and hours of birth and proper planning.

> Let wooden gates match wooden gates, and bamboo doors match bamboo doors!

With the blessings of the gods the two would fall in love after marriage.

Male births outnumber female births all over the world. But in addition in China, with its one-child policy, enforced abortions in final stages of pregnancy and compulsory sterilisation, everyone clamours for a son. Consequently with infanticide, 5 per cent of baby girls are unaccounted for, according to their 1990 census (although China's statistics are not always accurate). Changing 5,000 years of conservative Chinese culture is a slow process.

Accordingly my wife's father, continuingly threatening to take a concubine, was bitter that his wife could bear only daughters. He did not accept Chairman Mao's saying: 'Women hold up half the sky.'

To have no sons, along which the family line passes, is to have failed. The fact that Father considered 'Girls no use, money invested in them wasted' spurred Vera on. She set up her own business in 1965. Even though Father died in 1959 the desire was firmly implanted to prove 'Women as good as men any time'.

Selected in 1974 as one of the 'Ten Outstanding Young Persons' of Hong Kong, an event organised annually by the Junior Chamber of Commerce in countries around the world, Vera was employed by the British Chartered Bank of India, Australia and China (now Standard Chartered) for over thirty years. This once very colonial institution was established by Royal Charter in 1853. Having worked in such an environment it is natural that, like countless Hongkongers, she should be influenced by western management methods.

Many argue that, in a city-state which is really part of China on nationalistic grounds, the medium of instruction in educational institutions should be Chinese. No doubt in the future, speaking Mandarin will carry influence with our Peking Masters and, before long, we shall all be surprised how Chinese Hong Kong has become. But if Hong Kong goes largely monolingual, multinational companies will find it difficult to operate. There will be fewer English speakers to answer telephones. Even in a small firm like my wife's, with its overseas commitments, at the centre of each network business depends on some person who speaks reasonable English.

In addition to language, the British have also undoubtedly left their mark in other ways.

'Hong Kong impressed me a great deal because there was orderly calm and artistic work was being done without interruption.' So stated Sun Yat-Sen when he addressed Hong Kong University students in 1923.

With British colonial traditions Singapore is again a better-managed place than most Chinese communities, for instance Taiwan. One can also compare Hong Kong or Singapore with the hurly-burly of China's Shenzhen Special Economic Zone, with all the excesses of nineteenth-century capitalism, including half-finished roads, layers of mud and stifling Chinese bureaucracy.

'When I discuss problems with head office in the United States,' a Chinese told me, 'we are good friends. In spite of nationality differences and cultural conflicts I try to appear westernised. But with "people management", in my Hong Kong branch, Chinese methods play an important part. We think differently.' He looked slightly puzzled. 'You could phrase it "Western technology, Eastern ethnics",' he went on.

To earn an expatriate's trust you win his mind. With a Chinese you must win his heart. Such differences, with eastern rules of sincerity, can get Westerners into trouble.

Much of Chinese management, as with life in general, places emphasis on ritual and symbolism. These are combined with control by individuals and personal factors rather than formal hierarchies and rule by law. There were no lawyers, as such, in China before the Nationalists came to power and the country was ruled by *Qing* law. By 1949, however, there were about 60,000, although, with the Communists coming to power, by 1952 this number had fallen by 70 per cent. During the mad excesses of the Cultural Revolution the legal system was virtually dismantled.

Serious attempts have been made more recently to establish a new legal system. A criminal code was enacted in 1979 and a civil code in 1986. Some scholars, nevertheless, doubt whether common law, as now practised in English in Hong Kong, will endure long after 1997. Certainly criminal law is bound to be dispensed in Chinese. This is natural. Cynics claim that the Court of Final Appeal, the Privy Council in London, will in the future consist of four men in crumpled uniforms in a room in Wan Chai. Even though the People's Republic is trying hard to set up a legal system of sorts the danger is it will be politicised. China's laws state, for example, that no subject shall be detained for more than two months without being charged. That is fine in theory yet, in actual fact, several Hong Kong citizens have been imprisoned in China for more than two years without a charge being laid against them.

Because the People's Republic lacks an independent judiciary and a sound legal system, Chinese have traditionally preferred to avoid contracts and to deal with acquaintances or, better still, friends who they think they can trust. In Vera's World I spotted an assistant sorting business cards. These play an important role out East, where, until a card is proffered – with two hands to show respect – you are a 'non-person'. But as soon as the small, magic piece of cardboard, that reveals something of a person's lifestyle, is presented, suddenly you are provided an entrée and given face. Does he work for an important company? What position does he hold? The card should be studied to show the donor respect and not pocketed hastily. Per square inch, it is probably the most effective item of communication.

'Graft, to grease business wheels, and *karaoke* (a sing-song session in a bar with colleagues) are the keys to success,' a middle-aged, Taiwanese entrepreneur announced when addressing a gathering in Hong Kong. Others insist it is more important to be 'in the web'. Certainly 'being reciprocal' has always guided Chinese – and Hong Kong – business behaviour.

The Territory's Upper crust consists of well-off people like the late ninety-four-year-old Lord Kadoorie, Hong Kong's first peer. Then there are the Lees of 'Lee Garden' business fame, who are one of the few really old Hong Kong families. Although membership of the Hong Kong Club has always been based more on status than wealth a modest person like Li Ka-shing, the world's wealthiest Chinese, with limited qualifications apart from the ability to make money, can electrify a reception as much as the Governor. It is mainly hard work over long hours and good joss that has allowed Li to forge ahead. 'Why was it,' Lee Kuan Yew asked during his visit to Hong Kong in 1992, 'that Hong Kong could produce such entrepreneurs as Li Ka-shing and Singapore could not?'

In the Orient, instead of a rigid legal system of rights and obligations, relationships are more personal. Business cannot be conducted in a vacuum. ' If you haven't built up good networks by the time you're thirty-five you're in trouble,' I was once chided.

'If you plant melon seeds you get melons, if you plant beans you get beans.' You have to make a conscious effort to create relationships.

To clinch a deal it is important to know someone in the right position. You cannot 'clap with one hand'. Although strict dichotomy between Asian and western methods can be dangerous, with *guan xi* (networking) among Chinese around the world there has to be an 'optimum market structure'. Namely, a workable combination in which the 'old-boy network' plays a profitable role as opposed to competition. Cantonese and Shanghainese textile firms in Hong Kong do not break one another's rice bowls. 'Do not destroy a worthy business competitor.' Examining a taxonomy of businesses, with the trend towards more small firms being established and the importance of complex linkages, in what proportions does one mix economic, sociological, political and geographical ingredients in order to achieve maximum success? It is the stuff of a good thesis.

Old Chinese scholars provided Chairman Mao with guerilla warfare strategy which brought victory in 1949.

> The enemy advances, we retreat;
> The enemy encamps, we harass;
> The enemy tires, we attack;
> The enemy retreats we pursue.

Some businessmen swear they learn from the Classics.

The *Tao Te Ching* (The Way and the Virtue) advocates: 'To remain whole, yield; to remain straight, bend; in order to contract, first expand; in order to weaken, first strengthen.'

Some communists will tell you that because they are not well-versed in the art of compromise, they are often unable to resolve differing opinions. Certainly Hongkongers at one moment can be firm, stubborn and tenacious, willing to wait with oriental patience for others to give in. But they can be realistic, too, ready to retreat slightly, depending on human reactions. Just as the *Tao Te Ching* advises, they can be both unyielding and highly adaptable.

When 'blunt, insensitive Westerners' negotiate with 'evasive, duplicitous Chinese', if they come to an impasse, perhaps because symbols are not understood clearly, it is better to 'retreat' a little and come back and talk next week rather than confront. Otherwise, cultural difficulties compounded with emotions can create major problems.

During the political manoeuvres of the Sino-British negotiations in 1992 and 1993, misunderstandings emerged with China taking an aggressive stance and negative code words apparent. With changes in British policy Governor Patten brought a western approach and an occidental mind to a Chinese situation. These differing postures, with Hong Kong having to live with the consequences, took on proportions not always appreciated in London. Making the opposition lose face is not the way to succeed. Under such circumstances, it was hardly surprising the People's Republic insisted the spirit of letters and articles of understanding be adhered to. These are the rough equivalent of what a businessman agrees to in a teahouse. Britain conversely maintained they were only preliminary documents and formed no part of the firm agreement.

In China people meet, get to know each other and then express a wish to do business together. Much of this drawn-out process seems unnecessary to Westerners who prefer a get-up-and-go approach. There is, of course, some common ground.

Sun Tzu in his book *On the Art of War*, the oldest military treatise in the world dating back two-and-a-half millennia, states: 'The control of a large force is the same in principle as the control of a few men: it is merely a case of dividing up numbers.'

Sir Percy Cradock, previously China-advisor to the British Prime Minister, quoting from *Sun Tzu*, said:

> Know yourself,
> know your enemy;
> And you can fight a hundred battles
> and never be annihilated.

Other businessmen quote maxims from the *The Analects* of Confucius, such as: 'Only women and petty men are difficult to handle. Be close to them and they are not humble, keep them at arm's length and they complain.'

Just as Germanic efficiency and Swiss fastidiousness have been ingredients of success, so Confucian values have been important 'software' that helped make Hong Kong's 'hardware' effective. That is in spite of claims fashionable earlier this century that Confucianism and its ancient traditions and beliefs were to blame for many of the 'ills' of China. Undoubtedly the 'little (often intangible) traditions' have played an important part in Hong Kong's development. They include clan and family cohesion, filial piety and the drive for education. There is also the powerful work ethic (until 1971, workers in Hong Kong laboured seven days a week), not to mention the propensity to be frugal and save. Hongkongers also display a markedly Confucian sobriety, national pride and a respect for authority. They also believe very much in looking up to an educated elite whilst displaying a strong desire to compete for wealth and position. The Hong Kong Chinese possess an innate familiarity with the marketplace.

As Lee Kuan Yew, who constantly inveighs against a drift to western values and Singaporeans losing touch with eastern ethics, hypothesised about Confucianism: 'Could it be that some religions inculcate a tougher spirit in their disciples and a willingness to strive and slog against unfavourable dispensation of providence?'

Even if the Confucian creed is more likely to appeal to elderly Chinese autocrats, such values are not so different from those prevailing during the Victorian era in Britain. These included the Calvinist work ethic. The Protestant Reformation provided intellectual and moral bases for business. Usurious Catholic restrictions were renounced. Many Westerners still admire the dynamism and paternalism of the Victorian age. Both qualities constitute established pillars of Chinese management today.

But whether industriousness will appeal to the same extent to future generations of Chinese, is questionable. Lee Kuan Yew sees the danger and insists, 'A more relaxed lifestyle is the road to ruin for Singapore.' In the age of 'self-propelled adults' some principles need reformulating rather than hanging on, willy-nilly, to what may be out-dated dogma.

Wang Gungwu, Vice-Chancellor of Hong Kong University, rightly maintains excessive claims have been made for Confucianism which glorified the scholar-bureaucrat. You could say that Adam Smith, with his *Inquiry into the Nature and Causes of the Wealth of Nations*, published in 1777, has been a better mentor for Hong Kong.

My wife is old-fashioned enough to believe that while 'great riches come from providence, moderate wealth comes from diligence'. If asked to quote verbatim the tenets of Confucius (the Great Teacher) she might have difficulty. But, while Vera's World employs a pragmatic mix of eastern and western management methods, on closer inspection one would need to retract the statement made earlier that the accommodation is 'entirely international' in character.

Patron gods are of universal appeal in most Chinese communities and a common feature of most professions and trades. Because the crimson-faced *Kwan Kung* (the Duke of Kwan, sometimes known as *Kwan Tai*) is a symbol of power, loyalty and devotion to duty, he is a great ally in a tight corner. You find him in his red shrine in every police station throughout Hong Kong. As a Chinese blend of Robin Hood and King Arthur he is often seen in other establishments, such as restaurants and even brothels. Although strictly Taoist, because of a large following, long ago he was also adopted as a Buddhist divinity. And after one has prayed to the gods and spirits for assistance in business one repays them by a ceremony or by making a donation.

Vera's World has its shrine – to 'invite gods to the premises'. There are two images, as well as the 'five ritual objects': two vases, two brass candlesticks and a central lotus-shaped receptacle in which sickly-smelling joss sticks smoulder. Although in this techno-logical age red, electric-light 'candles' have advantages over their old-fashioned, messy wax counterparts, recent trends in 'electric joss sticks', the purist insists, are 'totally unacceptable'. Tiny cups of Chinese tea and offerings of tangerines and apples also decorate Vera's World's shrine.

One of the divinities – you guessed it – is none other than the Goddess of Mercy. The second deity is a 'territory god', wearing bright yellow robes and holding a heavy, gnarled stick. A red sign, translated, reads: 'In five directions (the Chinese compass includes 'centre' and the four cardinal points) Dragon-God, back and front Territory God and *Ts'oi Shan* offer protection.' Understandably the last, the 'God of Wealth and Financial Services', has become espe-cially influential in recent years.

In money-oriented Hong Kong considerable attention is paid to the Chinese almanac when conducting business, however much owners may deny this to Westerners. Apart from being consider-ably thicker and more comprehensive, it is something like the *Old Moore's Almanac* Mother kept on the mantel shelf in Norfolk. *Tung Sing* the Imperial Calendar – probably pre-dating 2205 BC – which guides people on important occasions in their daily lives, is thought to be the oldest continuous publication in the world. It is still a best-seller. Every year approaching one million copies of the Hong Kong version are bought. The stylised format remains similar to the fifth-century edition. Many are sold abroad, including in Britain. There used to be an English language translation.

Although it includes information on subjects like *feng shui* and palmistry, much of the contents of the Almanac concern the 'science of date choosing'. It is important not to 'upset men or gods' when selecting 'good days' for opening a new branch or carrying out repairs. You have to watch out when changing the goldfish water or crossing a river by boat. Even more personal matters have their good and bad days:

'Not tonight, dear, it's not propitious!'

A variety of lucky charms are listed to counteract affliction, such as stomach ache, attacks by wild animals and buzzing in the ears. Although flexibility is one of the main keys to the success of Chinese businessmen, following advice from the Imperial Calendar and the fortune teller can obviously cramp dynamic management style just as tradition can hamper evolution.

At Vera's World moles and warts are removed not only for appearance and health reasons. Cosmetic surgery can change one's luck. With the adage, 'There isn't a good mole on the face,' physiognomy is regarded as an important science. Blemishes here, supposedly, reflect what is in the heart and most warts and moles on the face are associated with unpleasant meanings. Close to the eyes, at the sides, signify an unhappy marriage. An exception is blemishes on the ears. These imply wisdom, kindness and respect for parents. Although a few beauticians deny this, some even allege moles come in pairs. With a wart on an ear there is likely to be a second on the buttocks. Defects near eyes may be linked to counterparts on the breasts.

A long-time Chinese friend maintains the most effective medical treatment is that which has been proven in the land where the patient resides. Although not everyone suffers bouts of sneezing, or breaks out in a rash immediately after eating certain food, the West does not seem to have real answers to allergies. Even if there is a diminishing gap between oriental and occidental medical science, acupuncturists are still often described by western medics as quacks. One wonders how much is professional jealousy. With 367 meridian points to exert pressure on, or to insert needles into, conveniently located all over the body in the most unlikely of places, this supposedly 4,500-year-old skill, invented by Emperor Huang Ti, does provide some solutions.

The Chinese practitioner who treated me on my wife's premises was trained in both eastern and western medicine. 'Date of birth?' was his first question. So often this crops up in Chinese culture.

'Your skin troubles partly caused by overactive lungs out of balance with liver,' he informed me.

'Yes, my nails split easily,' I admitted.

Treatment consisted of inserting and agitating acupuncture needles into feet, knees and elbows, at pressure points connected to the liver and gall bladder. A small 'skin inside' needle was inserted in my back and masked with plaster. This was removed on my next visit. At the end of the treatment I was given a drink of hot water, my body was covered with a blanket and I was left to sweat it out for twenty minutes, not unlike western treatment. Small, black Chinese herbal pills were prescribed. Treatment concentrates the mind. Before dozing I reflected briefly on the possible effectiveness of acupuncture for anti-aging and the common cold.

There is an old Chinese saying, 'Great fortunes have no third generation', much like the English version, 'Clogs to clogs in three generations'. Unlike with the Japanese, inheritance for the Chinese is based on primogeniture. On death they divide estates up among sons. In the past there were usually many. It was therefore considered wiser for relatives to turn a third generation entrepreneur into an opium addict rather than to let him squander the family fortune on gambling, women and unprofitable business ventures. With my wife having no children, I mused as I lay there soaked in sweat, inheritance was not a problem we had to face.

Only people who have unusual and interesting jobs reach any real fulfilment. It would be a pity for Vera to give up her business and for us to return to England. For a Chinese – or even for a 'colonial retread' such as myself – getting a job in the West, where there is high unemployment, often means receiving a lower income, or indeed not obtaining professional employment at all.

In the early 1990s, Hong Kong and South China are among the few places where significant economic growth is taking place. With the recession countries like Britain, in Churchill's immortal words, 'Just keep buggering along'.

It is a hypothetical question, but what would have happened if there had been two identical Hong Kongs, one occupied by Hongkongers and another by a like number of people from somewhere else? Which other nationalities would have given the Territory's Chinese a run for their money? Certainly the Lebanese and the Jews, to name just two, would have provided good accounts of themselves. Undoubtedly not the Russians, though. Have you ever met a successful overseas Russian apart from ballet, opera and circus stars?

Milton Friedman, the Nobel Prize winner for economics, while lecturing in Hong Kong, would not commit himself on the future of his favourite city where free market forces have not been hampered by government intervention. 'It all depends on China,' Friedman quite rightly pointed out. 'And who is bold enough to answer that?'

There are others like Wong Man-chiu, *feng shui* consultant, who predict that submissive Hong Kong, while surviving 1997, will fade from the international scene shortly before the 'One Country, Two Systems' concept comes to an end in the year 2047.

In the mid 1990s, Hong Kong is the source of two-thirds of all investment in China. More than one-third of China trade passes through Hong Kong. With terrific potential for development in the People's Republic, where workers earn in a year what their counterparts take home in a month in Hong Kong and, with the latter's position as the crossroads of Asia, this must augur well for the Territory's future. However, it is unlikely that the euphoric growth of the past, where the Colony learned to use people, capital and technology so efficiently, can be maintained. 'The golden age is over,' many economic buffs would have you believe.

Nevertheless, be it at Vera's World or in some other organisation, if a person possesses innate intelligence and business acumen; if he or she has strong genes and is prepared to work, Hong Kong should still be a splendid place to do business. Accompanied by good luck and continuing high growth, Hongkongers can expect a standard of living comparable with the United States by the early part of the twenty-first century.

Probably of all territories Britain has relinquished, Hong Kong is the best qualified to be master of its own destiny. That is in spite of Mrs Thatcher, while still Britain's Prime Minister, allegedly describing the Legislative Council as 'Hong Kong County Council employing toytown politics'. Ironically, for historical, geographical and political reasons, the Territory is not to become independent. For the first time, a capitalist society is being handed over by treaty, without any revolutionary struggle, to the faceless bureaucracy of what remains of a communist regime.

Hardly suprisingly, in Hong Kong, amid suspicion, mistrust and inertia generated between the People's Republic and Britain, rumours, gossip and lack of confidence continue. Predictions range from Old Hong Kong Hands with unabashed affection for the place maintaining that China's 'future colony' will cruise along into the twenty-first century becoming more prosperous than ever. Others anticipate irreparable chaos. They include an old government colleague of mine who, along with many others, forecast in early 1991, that by the end of that year property prices would have dropped 25 per cent, emigration would have snowballed and there would be widespread industrial unrest. His other prophesies of gloom were also completely wrong. 'Pessimists are doing their best to muck Hong Kong up for themselves,' a Chinese senior government servant protested.

Many people are convinced that it will remain an eternal reproach against Britain that some form of democratic government was not established in Hong Kong. The formation of a fully representative, elected municipal council was, in fact, approved by the United Kingdom Cabinet in 1952. However, with the Communists coming to power in 1949 and the Korean War at its height, Hong Kong's Executive and Legislative Councils maintained that, with tension just across the China border, the time was 'inopportune for constitutional change'. The largest nation on earth was not prepared to accept another 'China' on its underbelly just as it has never recognised a separate Taiwan. The then Governor, Sir Alexander Grantham, agreed. Moves towards independence were curtailed. The Colony remained a 'benevolent dictatorship'.

Hong Kong, nonetheless, enjoyed many features of a democratic society without employing a formal political structure or one-man-one-vote. The public has always expected efficiency from its government officials and it is probably the only Chinese society with, for the past century, no fear of the midnight knock on the door. It is also the only place in Southeast Asia where, with freedom of speech, no restrictions have been placed on the press. It will not be easy to convince China, after the takeover, that a journalist who reports facts or unfavourable events is not anti-China.

Apart from members of a few pressure groups, Hong Kong citizens generally, in spite of what many try to tell you now, displayed limited interest in democratic representation. Turn-outs at Urban Council and District Board elections were abysmal. People were more concerned with earning a living. Also the Government tended to perceive factional party politics, with its disparate interests and acrimonious voices, as an impediment to speedy, rational decision-making. This process was effected largely by small, tightly knit groups of experienced, senior (mainly British) civil servants, advised by businessmen and technocrats. In such a climate, with comparative stability, judged by Asian standards, Hong Kong accomplished its economic miracle.

After 1997, autocratic China will appoint Hong Kong's Chief Executive. 'It will put its own "monkeys" in power,' is how a Shanghainese friend of mine phrased it.

Like most Hong Kong businessmen, China considers it more important for the Territory to be an economic success rather than a political liability. The People's Republic is keen to preserve the city-state as a capitalist enclave within its own socialist system. However, in keeping with the rest of the western world, the desire for democracy is spreading. Many more Hongkongers now want to be responsible for their own destiny. Previously, the Territory was all

about business. Now it is about business and democracy. The latter
can clash with Asian values.

In a free world every citizen has a right to be treated humanely
by his or her government. The tragedy of the Tiananmen Square
Uprising left Hongkongers in a state of shock. Those on the Mainland had seen it all before. 'Never be surprised at anything the PRC
does,' remarked one Chinese political commentator. But the whole
calamity of Tiananmen was shoved into the background and seemingly forgiven by many much more quickly than expected. A few
even commended the People's Republic Government for bringing
back stability to the country so soon. Since then, China has been
eager to depict itself as a law-abiding member of the world community.

But persistent campaigns of verbal shadow-boxing between
China and Britain continued. These consisted mostly of racist abuse
and rhetorical gong bashing. There was no attempt to follow the
age-old adage, 'You give me one foot and I'll give you ten feet,' or
to seek the 'Golden Mean' – the middle road. Both the British and
the Chinese like to talk in their own colourful metaphors. But, as it
says in *The Analects*: 'If names are not correct, language is not in
accordance with the truth. If language is not in accordance with the
truth, affairs cannot be carried on to success.'

Governor Patten maintained China would, on taking over
Hong Kong, receive the 'biggest dowry since Cleopatra'. The People's Republic representatives took a more indecorous and confrontational stance. Some remarks would have done Joseph Goebbels,
the German Nazi propagandist, proud during World War II. China
always feared a British conspiracy that would leave a *de facto* pro-
United Kingdom government in Hong Kong after it had made off
with the family silver. Patten was described in catchphrases which
often sounded ponderous when translated into English and could
have come from a comedy series. He was likened to a serpent, a
prostitute and being disgraced in history for a millennium. Much of
this rhetoric was unworthy of 5,000 years of continuous civilisation.
At one stage during the megaphone diplomacy, with obfuscation
and the two sides viewing things quite differently, Britain was told:

> You think there is a problem.
> We don't think there is a problem.
> If you think there is a problem
> then it's your problem.

Nevertheless forceful protests by China to Governor Patten's modest proposals for democratic reform made many Hongkongers real-

ise what the Territory is in for. As a Shanghainese friend explained: 'We can't fight China, she's too vast.'

Nevertheless many were pleased that, with Patten's Political Package, at last an attempt was made by Britain to stand up for Hong Kong. 'Any attempt by China to violate the "One Country, Two Systems" concept, with Hong Kong people ruling Hong Kong, must be resisted,' the politically active, quite rightly, insist.

'The PRC likes to bully.' My Shanghainese friend went on. 'With its inferiority complex it is never wrong.'

But if the Tiananmen Square revolt had succeeded, Hong Kong could have been swamped by multitudes of illegal immigrants from the Mainland.

Such conjecture brought back memories of the 'trial run', in 1962, when China's Communist border guards stood back and allowed – and at times even directed – 70,000 illegal immigrants, including men, women and children, to stream over the twenty-four-mile-long Hong Kong-China border during a period of twenty-five days. The tide was stopped by the Canton authorities just as suddenly as the flood gates had opened. The whole episode appeared to be a threat: 'If Hong Kong doesn't play shuttlecock this is what we'll do.'

With so many of our resources, including water and victuals coming from the People's Republic, in those days at cheap rates with relatively no inflation, it was very serious. Today, catastrophe could still be brought about by China 'exporting' a few million surplus inhabitants to neighbouring, recalcitrant countries.

Although the People's Republic is attempting to find its soul as the West tries to make it a member of the international community, China is still on many country's 'bad guys' lists. With more than usual duplicity it made a fortune selling arms to both Iran and Iraq during their eight-year war.

Many believe China has no intention of fully honouring the spirit nor the letter of the 1984 Sino-British Joint Declaration, which grants a high degree of autonomy for Hong Kong.

'The People's Republic will do as it pleases with or without UK's co-operation,' they say.

Although there are differences of opinion, China seems comfortable with a capitalist enclave on its doorstep and insists, after 1997, it will be 'business as usual'. Other commentators are convinced the 'One Country, Two Systems' concept will never be properly implemented. Hong Kong will never enjoy fifty years of untrammelled autonomy. The Social Democrats insist the only way to ward off 'commie tyranny', and safeguard Hong Kong's lifestyle, is to make the Territory as international as possible and introduce democracy. But, no matter what, the world will never be prepared to go to war over Hong Kong.

Although ideas are changing, whether it be in the government of a state or the management of a firm, many 'round-eyed Westerners', who are incorrigibly alien, see things quite differently from the average Chinese. Although the 'tremble and obey' age may have passed locals tend to believe more in iron fists, albeit in velvet gloves, and benevolent dictatorships. Most businessmen were indignant in 1992 and 1993, when China's resistance to the 'Patten Package' resulted in that well-known affliction: Hong Kong jitters. A dramatic fall on the stock market resulted. This followed what had been described, unfairly, as a lame-duck led government which refused to fight for Hong Kong's interests.

'Nothing should be allowed to interfere with Hong Kong's prime task of maintaining stability and prosperity,' say many businessmen. They see political battles as debilitating.

In a blatantly commercial city, even if some entrepreneurs now welcome a degree of democracy, in no way are most willing to sacrifice love of making money.

'We must have a good working relationship with China at all costs,' many believe. Activists, many of whom are trade unionists with working class backgrounds, who want capitalism to have a 'softer edge', accuse businessmen of 'shoeshining' (bootlicking). The People's Republic instructs Hong Kong businessmen how they can frustrate 'imperialist plots'. 'All Chinese are as close to one another as "lips and teeth",' Peking insists.

China has been very successful in 'reminding' Hong Kong businessmen where their future interests lie and in appealing to grassroots sentiment and seeking support for its actions.

With more emphasis needed on topics like social justice and safeguarding the environment, many businessmen are now accused of being turncoats to protect their own vested interests.

'What is at stake is the Territory's survival,' they retort, 'not righteousness.'

Many businessmen believe if the Territory, in spite of bouts of turbulence, is an economic success, with more Mainlanders coming here we shall be able to influence and persuade Peking, in the longer term, to see our viewpoint about democracy.

'The Chinese Communist dynasty is coming to an end,' Hong Kong businessmen insist. 'The Old Guard are "falling off the bough". They are now as keen as we to make a buck.' They quote one entrepreneur from China who said: 'Who the hell gives a damn for socialism. You can't make money in China. Given the chance I'd leave tomorrow.'

Gradually, with slow evolution, the government of one-fifth of the world's population will change. The People's Republic cannot be rushed. 'Wading across a river you need to feel the stones under your feet.' There has never been democracy in either China or Hong Kong. Politics should take second place. Where Westminster-style government had been introduced into ex-British territories, in Third-World countries like Uganda, Nigeria and Fiji, it has been notably unsuccessful.

Communism is dying fast in China, although Karl Marx's half-baked theories were never taken too seriously. The People's Republic, with its mixed-market economy, will probably continue to modernise without democratising all that much. However, with the old guard (who sacrificed their everything to establish communism) dying off, the country will progress to a kind of one-party state, on the lines of Singapore. The last personality cult and 'son of heaven' syndrome will disappear with Deng Xiaoping.

B EFORE leaving Vera's World, that Mid-Autumn Festival evening, I was given half of a golden-brown moon cake stuffed with lotus seeds, nuts, bean mash and the yolk of a salt egg. 'Sustain you for festivities,' Ma insisted.

Six hundred years ago, on the night before the Han Chinese uprising against the hated Mongol oppressors, each mooncake contained a tiny paper message. The rest is history. Centuries later, the previous night of our festivities included 'welcoming' the moon. That particular evening as I walked the streets was the second day of the festival, a time for contemplation and appreciating what corresponds to the Harvest Moon in the West. The third evening we 'chase' the moon as it starts waning.

It was a perfect, cloudless, Moon Festival evening with the full moon high in the heavens. Across in Victoria Park crowds of doting parents minded teeming, clamorous children who held brightly coloured, flickering lanterns aloft. These came in a variety of shapes and designs. Butterflies 'fluttered', goldfish 'swam', sinister figurines cast ominous shadows and spaceships did whatever spaceships are supposed to do. All were exquisitely made with coloured paper stretched tightly over cane frames bound with wire and lighted with candles.

A couple of good cricket-ball throws away to the east, at Tai

Hang, the ferocious Fire Dragon would shortly slither his way through what used to be a peaceful Hakka farming and fishing settlement. Years ago, a villager killed a mighty serpent one stormy night. But the next morning its remains had disappeared. A few days later a plague spread causing many deaths. A village elder then saw Buddha in a dream. He was instructed to arrange a fire-dragon dance for three consecutive nights during the Mid-Autumn Festival and to burn fire crackers. The sulphur in these drove away the pestilence.

Accompanied by drums, clashing cymbals, banners and children carrying lanterns, the 220-foot-long Fire Dragon is a benevolent 'spirit of the waters'. With head erect, on a cane frame, its thirty-two segments are filled with 'pearl grass'. In addition to the crowds, the monster, pierced by thousands of incense sticks, is surrounded by 120 dancers. Preceded by two dancing 'dragon pearls' it has succeeded, over many years, in banishing disease. It has brought good fortune to a community where many top-class footballers were raised. Since 1880, apart from during the Japanese Occupation and the 1967 Disturbances, the parade of the Fire Dragon has been an annual event.

Until fairly recently, female participation was limited to little more than collecting the grass. They were not allowed to touch the Dragon nor admitted into the Kwan Yin Temple when it paid its annual visit. Women who have only given birth to daughters, can however pass under its long, scaly body to help them bear sons.

'Collect dragon cakes from temple,' a villager instructed a woman.

A scramble to retrieve incense sticks from the body of the dragon followed later that evening. These were seized by villagers, and, together with the cakes, offered up to ancestors on home shrines. At the end of this long established, community festival, with village traditions right in the heart of what is now overbuilt, urban Hong Kong, the poor old Fire Dragon with his 'spirit of the waters' is regularly disposed of in Causeway Bay Typhoon Shelter. There its remains float, in its natural element, together with a great deal of other rubbish. This practice of disposal was followed long before most of the world adopted the same, short-sighted, weakness of becoming a 'throw-away' society.

Before the night finally ended, however, for me it was a one-hour drive, together with friends from the Royal Asiatic Society, to Wo Hang Village, on the Hong Kong-China border. There, villagers were launching hot-air 'balloons'. The first lantern, approaching thirty feet high and six feet in diameter, was being made on the concrete slab where rice was threshed. With twine, wire and glue the frame, made with large hoops of flexible, green bamboo, was assembled and covered with rice paper.

After an hour's work, accompanied by bantering and everyone shouting advice to someone else in the twelve-man team of building it, a large ball of cotton wool soaked in paraffin was placed at the bottom of the 'missile'. This was then lit, and, with the heated air rising, the whole contraption ascended skywards accompanied by the roar of fire crackers together with the banging of cymbals and gongs.

Up and up went the paper cylinder, drifting away over the mountains of southern China where they are offically banned because of the danger of fire. At approaching 3,000 feet it seemed to hang in the sky.

'They used to say lanterns touched by females won't go up!' a Chinese girl, who had studied for twelve years in Canada, spat out in perfect English.

Today lanterns are still sent on their way, not only for pleasure, but occasionally to celebrate a joyful event – like the birth of a son.

Joseph Needham refers to the 'ancient pastime' of setting off hot-air balloons in his volume *Science and Civilization in China*. They were said to have been invented shortly after AD 200. Similar contraptions, some shaped like dragons, were used by armies for signalling. This 'balloon' custom could, in fact, be older than the Mid-Autumn Festival itself.

CHAPTER NINE

CONTEMPLATION

T HE further east one travels in Asia the less seriously, theologically, religion seems to be taken. This impression comes, probably, because eastern religions are more silent and contemplative. Their many gods dwell on the same plane as man. Religions of the West with the Supreme Deity, conversely, are more vociferous and active. For early Europeans arriving in Asia, the profit motive was important. But many carried swords in one hand and Bibles in the other. Few at that time shared the views of a Hungarian religious man, Emil Torday (1875–1931), who wrote:

> Never scold a man,
> always show respect towards
> objects or acts connected
> with native ideas of
> religion ... remember,
> you are an intruder for
> colonisation, itself, is
> an injustice.

Nobel Prize winning author Pearl S. Buck wrote that she was afraid to invite childhood Chinese friends to her home for fear they would be preached at by her missionary parents.

Before Buck's parents came East, the big-headed, erudite Reverend Doctor Karl Friederick August (also known as Charles) Gutzlaff dreamed of 'Europeanising' Chinese culture and converting the Middle Kingdom populace. As the first Lutheran missionary to China he preached hell-fire and brimstone salvation to the strangest people in the most unlikely places. He also worked as an interpreter for Jardines on their opium runs. Although Prussian, and a paradox of Christian piety and materialistic conceit, Gutzlaff served for a time as a Hong Kong government servant.

On visiting Europe, however, after an absence of twenty-three years, the man some labelled a 'pious old fraud' was applauded by one journalist: 'Perhaps no foreigner of the age has more thoroughly identified himself with the [Chinese] people.'

But limited change took place in China and Gutzlaff died a disappointed man. His remains have lain in a ponderous, granite tomb in the Colonial Cemetery (renamed Hong Kong Cemetery and now close to a busy flyover), between a lebbeck and a bombax tree, since 1851.

Down-at-heel Gutzlaff Street in Central District, is too narrow for vehicular traffic. Like its namesake the thoroughfare is intriguing. There are workshops, stalls and shops trading in a variety of products. They include '100-year-old' (preserved) eggs, with crinkled, muddy shells, and medicinal herbs and insects, as well as dried scorpions, snakeskins and wasps' nests. Like many street vendors, barbers are an itinerant breed. The one in Gutzlaff Street clicks his scissors in a semi-open stall and provides not just 'short back and sides'. He also shaves foreheads and grubs out wax from ears.

Not only did Protestants like Gutzlaff fail to evangelise the Middle Kingdom, whose ancient empire contained more subjects than the Catholic Church worldwide, but the vast country also eluded papal grasps. Jesuit priests, starting with the Italian Father Matteo Ricci (1552–1610), who put their roots down where they worked, were welcomed as savants of invention, astronomy and literature. Another Jesuit of forceful personality, the German Adam Schall (1592–1666), became a friend of emperors and mandarins. He also became as Chinese as possible in dress, behaviour and occupation. Such efforts bore limited fruit.

In some cases, however, the Holy Father was successful. Hong Kong's Yim Tin Tsai lies two miles east of Sai Kung. High up on the wall of its tiny, Italian-style church is painted: 'Hall of the Lord of Heaven'. All inhabitants of the isle bear the surname Chan. All are Catholics. First baptisms were conducted in 1867, when, as the island's name 'little salt-fields' signifies, many residents were employed extracting that vital commodity from sea water by evaporation. A number now work in the catering trade overseas.

Fervent Christianity is not normal for the average Chinese, many of whom see religion, like many things, as a commodity best hedged. After all, with a judicious combination of Christianity, Buddhism, Taoism and primitive folk religion, if one doctrine does not succeed in 'brightening a person's soul', another may. If you live on a precipitous mountain and pass Catholic and Buddhist shrines every day who can risk not making the sign of the cross as well as bowing?

'Rice Christians' were not uncommon when Hong Kong was less affluent. It is still easier to obtain a good grave space if one has been baptised. In materialistic Hong Kong pragmatism is important. Our parish priest relates with a smile how he received a request for a supply of holy water so a woman could brew coffee and, simultaneously, reform her husband.

Many believe 'one Christian more is one Chinese less'. 'Grandmother caught me in Church when I was a schoolboy. She threatened to disown me,' a retired dentist, told me, laughing. The old lady was afraid, as a Catholic, the lad would not be a 'true Chinese'. Customs to her were important and 'vital commodities', as they have been for 'sons and daughters of the Yellow Emperor' for millennia.

There are eight sites, including Lantau and Cheung Chau Islands, and Big Wave Bay on Hong Kong Island, where two or three thousand years ago Yueh prehistoric man hacked abstract, magical symbols onto rocks. These were possibly to invoke protection from forces of the ocean. Since then many animistic objects, superstitions and even sorcery, with manifestations large and small, have become assimilated into Chinese culture.

Supernatural power does not depend just on one Supreme Being as in the West. Destiny can be influenced by lucky numbers. Changing one's given names (one's family name is never changed) and thereby altering the number and angle of strokes in characters can also have a big effect. Also the layout (*feng shui*) of buildings can produce positive or negative results. If people meet a priest when going to the races it is unlucky. In spite of many of my comrades carrying lucky charms during World War II the average Westerner newly arrived out East often wears 'cultural blinders'. He or she is used to totally different customs. In an alien society where many Chinese insist their beliefs can produce as good a solution as praying to a western supernatural being, where does religion end and superstitions begin? Such thinking is similar to autosuggestion – if one really believes something is beneficial, as with a placebo, there can be positive psychological effects.

With the mystic art of 'Beating the Small Person', an adversary is represented by a paper 'cut-out' on which is written the name and birthday of the antagonist. This is then struck with a 'weapon', such as a shoe. Pins are stuck into effigies to exorcise the devil. On certain days of the month these practices are carried out by old women (being *yin*, females are more easily able to contact spirits than men), under the flyover near what was Wan Chai's Bowrington Canal, long since slabbed over.

What European in Hong Kong has not had his fortune told by Chinese astrology, face reading (a high forehead means a greater chance of living far from one's place of birth), palmistry or other means? Long ago, I was advised I would have power and authority over others; I would live a long life, and I would travel. I was told that I would not do well if I remained close to my home town. All predictions have come true – not so surprising, perhaps, since I am an Englishman living in a colony.

Periods of uncertainty, like the takeover by China, always stimulate the clairvoyancy business. Clients need guidance. Some fortune-tellers move with the times, 'improve their product' and provide 'macro-readings'. These give an overall forecast for the next cycle. If detail is required then 'micro-readings' are available.

With campaigns like the Cultural Revolution, denouncing and destroying the 'Four Olds' (similar campaigns were run earlier by the Nationalists), one would have expected superstitions and 'feudal beliefs' to have disappeared. But most revolutions have not inwardly changed China all that much. In spite of remonstrations from the communist press after the 'Open Door Policy' commenced in 1978, for many burning incense and the placing of votive offerings on altars began creeping back into daily life – albeit 'surreptitiously and with sideways glances'. Today in China, even the lighthearted have second thoughts before sticking a cigarette in the hand of the Goddess of Mercy, as many flippantly did during the Cultural Revolution.

Of two things which divide much of the world, religion and the 'rule of the road', the latter could cause more people greater concern. The British Colony drives on the left, but, after the Americans persuaded Chiang Kai-shek to change in the wake of World War II, China has driven on the right. But in spite of religious strife in some countries, in places like Northern Ireland for example, for the most part, apart from the odd war now and again, different denominations co-exist reasonably well.

In the Third World, in spite of some 'missionary bashing', churches have, in concert with evangelism, pursued programmes of 'practical Christianity'. In Hong Kong, schools, hospitals and social welfare programmes have been established and run by over 200 organisations. Hundreds of thousands of citizens have benefitted.

The Baptists run a drug rehabilitation scheme on idyllic Long Ke Beach, overlooking the South China Sea, where the power of prayer combined with 'cold turkey' has proved an effective cure. With withdrawal symptoms and no guards or barbed wire fences some inmates abscond. But this spartan life-style, Baptists claim, has a higher success rate than government methadone treatment.

One would expect zealous Hong Kong to have a competent and forward-looking church. In fact, the first female Anglican priest, Lei Tim-oi, was ordained of necessity during World War II by far-sighted Bishop Hall. In 1971, the Reverend Jane Hwang and the Reverend Joyce Bennett followed. The latter, after serving as a Hong Kong Legislative Councillor, returned to London in 1983 to work among Chinese at Saint Martin-in-the-Fields.

Emphasis on the 'Fatherhood of God', with Jesus as 'Elder Brother' ('brother' alone sounds crude: Chinese have different titles for all relatives), appeals to Chinese family instinct. Yet with resistance from some quarters to western influence, moves have been made towards greater 'enculturation' in Hong Kong. The Patriotic Catholic Church in China, which until fairly recently still celebrated Mass in Latin, is more westernised in several ways than the Roman Catholic Church in Hong Kong. There, efforts have been made to encourage 'indigenisation', promoted at the Second Vatican Council (1962–65), although priests have always worn cassocks which look something like Chinese *cheung saams*. Customs like the 'three bows' and the 'last glance' at the corpse before a coffin is closed all make it easier for Chinese to accept Catholicism.

Of course the dynamics of religious groups sometimes go awry, as during the Inquisition or today in the Middle East. But in spite of animosity, like when a Jesuit in Stanley Prison Camp during World War II refused to lend his chalice to an Anglican priest, the different denominations in Hong Kong get along reasonably well. In Oi Kwan Road one can see mosques, temples and synagogues in close proximity.

A New Year Message in the press in January 1992, wished all 'flocks', among other things, 'good health and blessings'. This came from leaders of the 'Six Religions', comprising Buddhists, Taoists, Confucians, Muslims, Christians and Catholics. In Hong Kong 'Christian' is synonymous with 'Protestant'. 'No, I'm not a Christian, I'm a Catholic' is not an unusual expression.

Although sometimes classified as a 'religion', Confucianism is more concerned with earthly things, like filial piety and obligations to the family, than with the afterlife.

Lai See, writing in the *South China Morning Post*, referred to the basic philosophies of Hong Kong's 'Six Religions':

> Buddhism: if bad joss happens it isn't really bad joss.
> Taoism: bad joss happens.
> Confucianism: Confucius said, 'Bad joss happens.'
> Islam: if bad joss happens it is the will of Allah.
> Protestantism: let it happen to someone else.
> Catholicism: bad joss happens but I deserve it.

In addition to the 'Big Six' there are, of course, other faiths in Hong Kong, such as Judaism, Hinduism, as well as non-conformist churches. There have also been break-aways. *Chun Hung Kau* is more akin to Taoism than Buddhism. With *hung* meaning 'emptiness' their temples have no idols and no incense is burned. When the People's Republic came to power in 1949, many clerics, who were spared incarceration for their beliefs, were forced to leave China. All religious orders were made welcome in Hong Kong, including the ethereal Trappists who attend 3.30 a.m. Mass and follow ascetic practices, including solitude, silence and seclusion. They retire at 8.00 p.m.

In the 1950s and 1960s, the growth rates of the Territories' churches were among the highest in the world. Many converts had escaped from communism. Hong Kong prospered. With talk of camels and needles the gospel has always held more hope for the poor. For many, as they became affluent their religious zeal waned. Of the quarter of a million or so Catholics in the Territory, now less than a quarter attend Mass regularly.

During the run-up to 1997, emigration, for which there are no restrictions on the quota for clerics, has taken its toll. Surveys have forecast up to one-quarter of the clergy will emigrate. Because of uncertainty and an 'atmosphere of unhappiness', many priests in the mid 1980s, like Father Laszlo Ladany, although assisting people to emigrate, had hoped to see people again 'turn to God'. 'The size of our Catholic flock could double!' he once predicted. This has not happened.

Some academics, like Canadian Dr Greg Chernish who visited China in 1990, feel that Hong Kong has developed a 'spiritual illness and an existential crisis', just like the People's Republic. There has been a decline in moral standards.

'In the past Confucianism, Buddhism and Taoism, yes even Chairman Mao, were guiding lights. Today, there is spiritual emptiness,' Chernish maintains. 'Youngsters with clans and extended families disunited have nothing to believe in, apart from the quest for materialism.' In the last thirty years, China has gone through a period very similar to that of post-Vietnam America. The effects of the Cultural Revolution, the demise of the Democracy Wall in 1980 and the hopelessness in the wake of the Tiananmen Square tragedy, have all contributed to create a mood of pessimism and soul-searching. 'But each time ferment returns, seeds for the future lie within it,' Chernish insists.

Although religious freedom is guaranteed in the Sino-British Joint Declaration Hong Kong Protestant churches will, no doubt, eventually become part of the Church of China. Naturally, the Catholic Church wishes to retain links with the Holy See of Rome. In this capacity, it may be able to serve as a bridge between the Vatican and the People's Patriotic Church in China. Both have matured over the past two decades. Religious freedom in the People's Republic is now more liberal with the state providing funds, in some cases, for church and temple restoration. Yet Hong Kong's Catholic Bishop Wu was not allowed to say Mass during his 1986 visit to China. There are still, Hong Kong church officials maintain, cases of Christians being fined, arrested and even tortured, in China.

W HEN on leave in England with fewer distractions than in Hong Kong and influenced by the Chinese concept of *uen* (predestined connection), I habitually retired early to seek 'spiritual revitalisation'. But no matter how introspective one tries to be, with the 'umm' mantra vibrating through one's cranium, the mind still 'rears' like an unbroken horse.

I would visualise the two-foot-tall, grubby, golden Goddess of Mercy with the enigmatic smile. She stands alongside a child inside the 'Temple Overlooking the Sea', with which I have special affinity. It is situated among the clutch of tiny, ramshackle buildings painted bright red, green and yellow just off Hatton Road, half way up 'High West'. I would try to recall *Kwan Yin*'s benign composure and the folds of her garments. Spasmodically, there were illusions of colour. Proportions changed. My mind would dart directionless, like a kangaroo stepping into a hornets' nest. I would struggle to bring myself back, gently but firmly, to the formidable task of meditation.

Possessed of inner peace I levitate on 'clouds of the unknown', just as an aura of light appeared behind an enlarged Goddess of Mercy. High above Victoria Peak's carpet of greenery my soul floated serenely on, over the Kowloon Foothills, towards Tai Mo Shan. Beyond the Territories' highest terrain, with always another mountain beyond the next mountain, I observed lofty ranges over the border in China. Fine, red dust swept down at high altitude, blown by northerly air streams from the Gobi Desert.

Minds produce random thoughts when allowed to roam free. The next thing I knew I was entering a stately room, with lincrusta wallpaper and a clock on an oak mantelpiece. Was this really an apparition from a previous life?

Moving slowly, concentrating on deep breathing, I levitated back to Tao Fong Shan, at Sha Tin. The power of meditation was lost. I lay in bed, in England on leave, staring at the ceiling. With 'guru trips' the closer you journey towards the horizon the more it recedes. Yet to experience the inner peace such expeditions can bring, or the frightening effects of inner space, can be as testing – one can speculate – as the ultimate, supreme voyage.

With 'spiritual visits' to this 'Locus of the Soul' while on furlough, it was not surprising that, on returning to Hong Kong, I should want to go back to Tao Fong Shan where the founder 'knew providence had prepared for (his) future work'.

On completing the forty-five-minute journey, first by Mass Transit Railway and then by Kowloon-Canton Railway, I found myself staring up the hill at the huge cross. Minutes later, I strode up the gentle slope of the winding, peaceful road, past 'Ascension House'. As a 'pilgrim', to board a taxi would have meant missing magical moments along well-wooded slopes which hide the retreat from the town below. Clumps of drooping, bright-red, sleeping hibiscus, known as 'turk's cap', brightened the route.

Listen! Yes, there it was! The unmistakable, soft cry to the Goddess of Mercy.

I should have expected distressed persons to call the gracious lady here. She, who was so filled with love and kindness for all mankind that she took a vow to help anyone, anywhere, who needed her. The top of the 500-foot-high Tao Fong Shan (Hill of the Logos [or Christ's] Wind), depicted by a mosaic mural in Chinese style, was an obvious location for the Goddess.

This is where Christianity and Buddhism flourished side by side. Here broad-minded Protestants, Buddhists, and even a few Taoists thrown in for good measure, lived and worked in harmony. The complex of uncluttered buildings, with clean, simple, Chinese architecture, was established during the years of the Reverend

Ronald Owen Hall. Until 1950, his Bishopric took in South China and its population of around seventy-seven million souls. His diocese stretched as far as the border with Burma. He was Bishop from 1932 to 1966 and, in the late 1950s, became Chairman of the Tao Fong Shan Study Centre.

The beautiful, white-walled 'Christ Temple', is an octagonal building with red columns and a 'swept' roof clad with blue-black Chinese tiles. One feels compelled to contemplate awhile. A bell hangs outside together with a plaque to the memory of Johannes Prip-Moller, the Danish architect. He had the vision to design this Christian centre which took eight years to complete. The corner stone was laid on 28 July 1931.

Obviously faith, which unlike many things in Hong Kong cannot be 'bought', does not just mean sitting on a mountain and praying. Mercy and charity both play parts. Yet to run a centre like this one has to balance spiritual and material things. Thus, in addition to the church and other buildings, including dormitories and the pilgrims' hall, a porcelain workshop staffed by two artists from China was added in 1947. Although not exactly the 'big bang of business', crockery with fine, bibical patterns helps raise funds. Wandering monks and the handicapped can work there.

God summons some men with a vision, others with music and some with a command. Karl Ludvig Reichelt a Norwegian missionary, the son of a sea captain, was born in 1877. All remarkable mountains have spiritual influence over the affairs of mortals and he conceived his idea on a visit to Weishan Monastery, on one of China's sacred mountains near Ninghsiang in Hunan Province. He records: 'I got a glimpse of a peculiar and exclusive world, a world charged with deep religious mysticism, a world full of tragedy and heartrending, but also marvellously rich in points of contact and sacred religious material.'

Hong Kong, an outpost of empire before World War II, has for the past half century been a meeting-point between capitalism and communism. In the early 1930s Reichelt selected the Crown Colony as the location for his study centre: in the jargon of today, 'to examine the interface between socialism and Christianity'.

Although criticised for 'going native', he understood the value of Buddhist piety. Although a chasm often separates a melange of Chinese and western attitudes, it is still a fertile combination, despite the Chinese saying that 'well water and river water should not mix'. He believed Christ's touch influences non-Christian religions. This was the message he passed on. During its 'golden years' thousands of Buddhists stayed on Tao Fong Shan where they attended programmes run by the Norwegian and his colleagues. With its red lacquered altar, the smell of incense, together with the cross, lotus and swastika, Buddhists felt very much at home. A number not deeply rooted in their faith were baptised. Some became Lutheran pastors. Others secured secular jobs, like working in factories.

'And God spoke to the almond tree and the almond tree blossomed.'

But now, sadly, it has withered. Nonetheless, the day I visited the Centre it was not deserted. A local crew was shooting a film. An attractive young lady was being made up in a pavilion. Selfishly, I should have liked to have had the whole place to myself. I wandered past the propped-up boulder and the bamboo clumps, then walked along the 300-yard-long path to the 40-foot-high concrete cross. It is spotlit at night and can be clearly seen from the valley below.

Beyond the hills near Tsuen Wan stands another scholarly meeting place which attempts to combine religions. With its 'Hall of Three Teachings', like the three legs of a tripod, the Yuen Yuen Institute is modelled on Peking's Temple of Heaven. On its upper floor are statues of Buddha, Lao Tzu (founder of Taoism) and Confucius.

Somewhere across the valley, out of sight towards Kowloon, stands Amah Rock. Resembling a woman with a baby on her back it is one of the Territories' many examples of animism. Hong Kong is chock-full of devils, fairies, folklore and fables. Joss sticks are frequently placed at the foot of boulders like Amah Rock, as well as against special trees and grottoes in which spirits dwell. Some are kind and some malevolent. People of all ages light candles and offer sacrifices. The more reverent the bow the more likely the supplication is to succeed. Legends like those surrounding Amah Rock date back centuries and were later grafted onto eastern religions.

Years ago, a dutiful wife went each day to watch for the return of her fisherman husband. He never came. One day in a thunderstorm, on the bruised, dark range of hills, mother and child were struck and turned to stone.

From where I stood, with my back to the giant cross, my hands clasped Buddhist fashion, gazing upwards, I muttered: 'Please let me stay on in Hong Kong!'

From that vantage point, in the rapidly changing New Territories, I could spot the temple I used to visit in the early 1960s. You may recall a Chinese girl whom I mentioned in Chapter 5. She married an American-born Chinese and went to live in the United States. Her dad was a fervent Buddhist and became 'a monk for a weekend'. Dressed in white and wearing sandals, I can still hear him chanting as he walked around the altar in procession with other disciples. 'Part-timers' are excused from having heads shaved or scalps burned by lighted joss sticks.

Looking down at the New Town, where the population grew 328 per cent in the ten years up to 1991, when it stood at over half a million, it is not easy to recall what Sha Tin Village was like in the 1960s. It is even more difficult to visualise it as it must have been in November 1947, when Bishop Hall sent a hastily scribbled message, together with a scale drawing of a six-inch-diameter pug mark. 'A large cat, probably a tiger, walked across my garden!'

The odd tiger from China occasionally visited Hong Kong up until the 1950s – or even until the early 1960s some old-timers insist. G.A.C. Herklots, described as Hong Kong's first naturalist, appeared to accept this. But, he records in *The Hong Kong Countryside*: 'Many were sceptical even of a bishop's evidence.'

Tigers' organs are used in Chinese medicine. Some are said to be good for curing rheumatism, ulcers and typhoid. They are also supposed to be good for stopping malaria, dysentry and burns. Because of hunting, the South China tiger population was believed to have been reduced, by 1993, to about fifty. Unless drastic measures are taken it will be extinct shortly after the turn of the century. Similarly, in parts of the New Territories there is now little farming and few villages. The days of rural Hong Kong are numbered. The Territory is fast becoming nothing more than a concrete slab on the edge of the China Sea.

Looking over the now developed Sha Tin valley, which will see no more 'large cats', I turned and stared at the cross. I have been a Christian with fluctuating degrees of fervency all my life. I believe in the mysteries of the universe which we cannot always comprehend. Science does not provide all the answers; other forces are at work. If we accept belief in the existence of a 'facilitator' as the basis of faith for any Christian, Buddhist, Jew or Muslim, are we not right then in assuming that their Gods are but varying countenances of one Supreme Being?

In a similar way, principles such as tolerance and gentleness apply to all religions. Have you ever seen a stern-looking image of Buddha? Many are smiling and benevolent: some almost lustful. Cannot people of all faiths learn from the wonderful compassion that comes from Buddhism? It teaches that this compassion, along with loving kindness, sympathetic joy and equanimity, constitute the 'Four Highest States of Mind.' The Buddhist 'Noble Eightfold Path' comprises right understanding, right motives, right speech, right action, right means of livelihood, right effort, right mindfulness and right concentration. This is not intended to define right from wrong as with the Christian Ten Commandments. In this context 'right' is intended to mean, rather, that which is wholesome and leads to enlightenment.

Certainly Jesuits, since first coming to China in 1583, have been influenced by the work of Confucius. A few were even accused of betraying their faith. Christianity and Confucianism have much in common. Even today the odd Catholic priest quotes the Chinese sage in his sermons.

As a student of oriental religions was Reichelt a renegade? Although it is 'easier to make the sun shine at night than to baptise a devout Buddhist', he believed if similarities between the two faiths are highlighted Buddhists will aspire to convert to Christianity. Also, like Eurasians with their command of eastern and western languages and intimate knowledge of two cultures, a varied religious background can enrich one's life.

After strolling for five minutes I arrive at Tao Fong Shan cemetery. Reichelt died in 1952. Unlike many headstones which are hewn from Italian marble, as one would expect his is of Hong Kong granite. On it, a Christian cross springs from a Buddhist lotus. Juniper and elephant-ear trees grow close by.

Probably more than any other missionary to China the Norwegian sought common ground between ideals of Buddhism, likened to the 'great ropes of a net', and Christianity. He was ahead of his time. According to his so-called Johannine method, one person's superstition is another's culture. Yet, in spite of what others saw as 'perverse elements marring non-Christian religions', 'Grains of truth and beams of light are to be found there', he insisted.

The Tao Fong Shan Ecumenical Centre has become largely a meeting place to suit changing times and needs. There, lectures and seminars are held to discuss contemporary local and international Christian issues. The institute is no longer involved with evangelism and conversion. Nevertheless, lodgings are still available as they were for pilgrim monks half a century ago.

'Intolerance, bigotry and xenophobia make an inter-faith programme even more necessary now than in the past.' These views were expressed by Saint James's Church, Piccadilly, London, in their '1990–2000 – A Vision for Ten Years'.

There were differences between the deeply held ideas of the legendary Reichelt and the Norwegian Missionary Society whose members found his ideals antagonistic to accepted Christian teachings. Consequently, he frequently trod a lone furrow.

Half a mile away from Reichelt's Ecumenical Centre stands the commercialised Temple of 10,000 Buddhas. There are actually 12,838 gold-painted statues of varying forms. Adjacent temples also house effigies of other gods. The Reverend Kok Kwong, leading Buddhist in Hong Kong, maintains that superstitious practices are not truly part of Buddhism.

'Everything will turn out good if people think good and do good. There is no need to consult a fortune teller.' Unhappiness will end, he insists, when the fuel of excessive desire no longer feeds flames. We must cease to want. Then, true happiness will emerge.

The late Abbot of 10,000 Buddhas, Yueh Chi, tried to reconcile his work at the garish temple with that of Reichelt at Tao Fong Shan. The Abbot described this Centre as 'the place that specialises in destroying Buddhism'. Although both men's remains lie on the mountain they loved, even in death they fail to strike a common chord.

The Norwegian is buried in traditional European fashion. By contrast, Abbot Yueh Chi, realising his body was destined to be revered, fasted unto death in 1965. He was eighty-seven. His corpse was buried in a coffin, in a seated, cross-legged position. The body dried into a leathery, hard mass of skin and bones. After eight months, as he had instructed, the 'fleshy body' (signifying immortality) was exhumed. Hardly any decomposition had taken place. A mark on his lower right ribs was shaped like a tiger. Another on his breast resembled a human head.

Yueh Chi, honoured by Buddhists with the title, 'Perceiving the Cause of the Universe', always maintained there was a tendency to look down on non-Christians. Thus, divinely inspired to enhance the Buddhist faith and raise funds, he decreed his body should be venerated. When I visited the temple several of his followers were burning joss sticks and making generous donations.

The Abbot's tiny, brightly gilded body is clothed in a yellow robe with a red sash and surmounted by a five-leaf, *vairocana* crown. This is a Sanskrit word meaning 'belonging to the sun'. Yueh Chi was enthroned in 1966. His lotus throne is a reminder that any person can rise up, pure, from tainted surroundings. The body sits in a glass case in front of a twenty-five-foot high Buddha. The benevolent influences exercised by Yueh Chi during his lifetime, his followers insist, are still present. Offerings of pomelos, oranges and apples were piled on the altar. Although both he and Reichelt proffered 'love in their hearts' to all mankind, they were ill-disposed towards each other. Conversely, dogs at the Temple of 10,000 Buddhas – as at all Buddhist temples – are placid, unlike many on hillsides in surrounding villages.

IT was approaching midnight after my long day at Sha Tin. Vera and I were getting ready for bed when the telephone rang.

'Ma's suffered a heart attack!' was the message. Although the journey to the hospital took barely fifteen minutes, it was too late. As one of the first Taoist writers, Chuang Tzu, phrased it: 'We are born from a quiet sleep, we die to a calm awakening.'

Nobody can outlive destiny.

At such times, mute dejection does not satisfy. Close relatives, especially females, are expected to display grief. My wife, her two sisters and two nieces stood in line and wept together for five minutes, although the clamour was interrupted by cries, such as, 'Ma, I love you!', in indistinct speech.

After the funeral of the serving Governor of Hong Kong, Sir Edward Youde, in 1986, a group of well-educated Chinese expressed tacit disapproval. They had found the pomp and circumstance impressive but, while they had not expected ritual wailing, they did feel that there should have been some weeping. 'Brits are brought up to keep a stiff upper lip,' my friend, who is more westernised than the others, explained.

The three daughters, on Ma's death, certainly shed tears. But they also expressed profound relief when authorities confirmed no autopsy was necessary. One should not inflict harm on one's 'heavenly body', not even hair and skin, because it was inherited from one's parents, they believe. Neither should the corpse be mutilated by surgical incision. It needs to go complete into the next world ready for reincarnation.

Ma was no different to most elderly Chinese. She was raised on the moral precepts of Confucius. On occasions such as funerals, even for those who do not profess a faith, this usually means participation in Buddhist services and its dogma of rebirth. Taoism, the only indigenous Chinese religion, is the 'way of naturalness and non-coercion'. Folk religion, the burning of offerings, fortune telling and folklore, are also part of life. However, with Eldest Daughter attending a church school it was neither surprising nor unusual, in the perplexing 1950s with the takeover of China by a communist government, that Ma should have been baptised a Catholic. But for a person who spoke no English and understood little of western ways the Christian faith did not satisfy. A few years later, with an insatiable desire to burn joss sticks again, she left the Church.

After the deceased's spirit departed her body as visible vapour it was said to be in limbo, 'wandering about'. A non-Christian ceremony was appropriate for this lapsed Catholic. Like most Chinese she would expect a good 'send off'. It epitomises filial piety. Close relatives do not eat meat, fish and eggs, or engage in sexual intercourse during mourning. They are also unlikely to haggle over costs. Not only is a Chinese funeral noisy, it can also be an expensive social occasion. This is unlike many Europeans who prefer simple interments. Foscolo, in his Italian poem, *I Sepolori* (graves), describes elaborate obsequies as *inutil pompa* (useless pomp).

However, nineteenth-century British Prime Minister William Gladstone (1809–98) contended:

> Show me the manner in which a nation or a community cares for its dead and I will measure with mathematical exactness the tender sympathies of its people, their respect for the laws and their loyalties to high ideals.

We see ourselves in the monuments we erect for the dead. Since the establishment of Hong Kong countless Britons have been buried in the Colony.

Years ago, many bigoted Westerners insisted that Chinese funerals, with mourners knocking foreheads on floors, were 'devil worship' more concerned with superstitions than with religion. Although Chinese still follow different customs to Westerners, attending such a funeral – even if it is of a person who has achieved just the simplest goals in life – can leave a mourner with a warm glow. Moving experiences like this can actually strengthen one's own Christian beliefs.

We arrived at the 'Hong Kong Hotel' (slang for the multi-storey funeral home) at three o'clock on the day before the funeral. The long service is sometimes dubbed the 'complete menu'. Two large 'blue lanterns' hung outside the hall. Actually they have white backgrounds, with the family name in large purple characters and the age of the deceased written in smaller red characters. The age is done by Chinese reckoning, making a person one or two years older than with western calculations. In addition three years: one for heaven, one for earth and one for mankind, had been added. Because the old lady was over seventy it was considered a 'happy funeral'. She had lived through one complete sixty-year 'cycle of Cathay' which corresponds to our century.

The interior of the funeral hall was lined with wreaths wired to slender, bamboo frames some eight or nine feet high. Chinese are nothing if not pragmatic, and the walls were draped with blankets and lengths of cloth which were presents from many considerate friends. These were later divided among immediate mourners. Many such gifts carried messages in large red, white or gold characters. One proclaimed, 'Picture of her lives in minds of women,' and another, 'Everlasting life in heavenly kingdom'.

Surrounded by smouldering incense, a sixteen-by-twenty-inch photograph of the deceased hung over the altar. A certain amount of hedging was apparent so as to get the best of both worlds. Both Chinese and western candles were flickering, along with offerings like rice wine, vegetarian food and chopsticks. There were also fruit, cakes, her favourite home-made cookies and cigarettes. Many were convinced, when a butt was found in an ashtray on the altar, it had been smoked by Ma's spirit.

All friends who came to pay their respects at the funeral hall were given a hankerchief to dry tears, as well as an envelope containing lucky money and a sweet. Mourners bowed three times to Ma's photograph, in time with the Master-of-Ceremonies' commands. They then bowed once more to us, the immediate relatives, as we stood to the left of the altar, clad in cheap, unhemmed white clothing with surcoats of sackcloth. I wore a white headband with a red spot on it to counteract evil. Such clothing symbolises that the family has relinquished all earthly wealth to pay for the funeral. After sitting and reflecting a while visitors left. They disposed of the envelope because it could bring them bad luck if it was taken home. Then they ate the sweet so as to 'take away the bitter taste of death'. As for the lucky money, it was used to buy more sweets.

The heavily made-up cadaver, straight, stiff and stern, had been put in a coffin. It lay behind a glass screen in the 'farewell room' at the back of the hall. As I stood in silence looking at Ma I recalled how she had once looked at me, with my 'strange', western features. Shocking in her stillness, she was different to how I remembered her. Years ago in the tropics the stink of the corpse was conspicuous in an atmosphere heavy with incense, candles and sandalwood smoke. Today, even if nature still recycles bodies back into the earth's system, refrigeration and embalming retards decomposition. Ma wore four upper garments and three pairs of trousers. The latter, pronounced *foo* in Cantonese, sounds similar to the character for 'riches'. No fur, leather nor rubber were employed for fear of reincarnation as an animal.

'The cult of death started when civilisation began and man was no longer a primate,' Foscolo wrote. A bronze talisman, a custom dating back 5,000 years to *Liangzhu* culture, had been placed in the mouth of the corpse. This prevents body spirits escaping and acts as a safeguard, some believe, against rapid decay.

Objects Ma treasured, such as delicate pieces of jade and cassettes of catchy Cantonese songs, as well as 'necessary' items, like powder compact and cigarettes, had been placed in the coffin. Spectacles were omitted. With cremation, glass could splinter and injure the body. Two 'lamps', made from bowls of peanut oil with wicks of dried seaweed, glowed on the floor. These would 'lead her on her way'. There were also chopsticks and cooked rice, to placate fierce dogs en route to heaven.

Accompanied by five Buddhist monks chanting sutras, to the sound of flute, gong and cymbal, female mourners and children folded tinfoil into 'gold and silver ingots'. These, together with imitation 'hell banknotes', 'dead men's' notes, mixed with a few United States dollars, were burned in a stove. This process went on, assiduously, until midnight and continued after the all-night vigil the following morning. Money is needed in the next world – not least, for bribing officials!

Funeral day dawned. Along with the hour for the ceremony it had been selected by a soothsayer. Many mourners came. Again, shaven-headed Buddhist monks in colourful, flowing robes chanted mantras. 'The law of Buddha is boundless.' Among the congregation there was the muffled ring of a portable telephone. As the body in the coffin was wheeled out we were warned over a loudspeaker: 'Those born in Year of Monkey or Rat no look.' If they did not avert their eyes until the bier came to a standstill bad luck could be caused. Towards the end of the ceremony mourners filed around the coffin, some holding up children for the 'last glance'. Many people were sobbing. A few took care not to walk too close in case they were 'possessed'. Finally the lid was secured.

After the funeral service we, the immediate family, boarded cars. With eldest daughter in the front seat of the foremost vehicle, holding Ma's photograph and 'spirit shrine', we wended our way through heavy traffic to Pine Shade Buddhist Hall. One of her three souls now reposes there. Pine frightens away evil, such as ghouls that prey on corpses. Although views sometimes conflict, a second soul is supposed to reside in the columbarium and the third in heaven.

Cremation took place two days after the funeral because the previous day was inauspicious. Only close family members attended the simple ceremony. In addition to the coffin, parphernalia such as her 'spirit shrine', made of rattan and colourful paper, were burned. Burial was traditionally preferred to cremation, where the body can remain in contact with the earth. But overcrowded Hong Kong is short of space.

On the twelfth night after death the closest relatives waited in Ma's flat for her spirit to return. First, the table was set with her favourite dishes and, of course, cigarettes. She would, many believed, invite demons to that meal, including one with a cow's head and another with a horse's face. These two could be obstreperous.

Western candles and incense sticks were lit outside in the passage. The sticks were placed in clusters of three: one for heaven, one for earth and another for mankind. A pair of scissors, a Cantonese pun on words symbolising both 'weapon' and 'gain' or 'profit', was placed on the floor near the door to prevent unwanted spirits entering. Copies of a powerful Buddhist prayer, usually placed in strategic positions like on bedside tables to ward off evil, were removed from the flat. It could keep the dead person's spirit away.

Like children in the West hoping to catch a glimpse of Father Christmas, we all did our best to stay awake in Ma's home in overbuilt Hong Kong. But then, in the early hours, even the most steadfast dozed off.

'Even if it didn't, it is better to believe it happened,' Second Sister told everyone firmly the following morning. It was rather like not seeing Santa Claus as a child, much like a firecracker not going off because it was damp. I felt very disappointed – especially since the spirit of my old Chinese colleague's father returned to visit the family and left marks depicting bamboo, which he loved to paint, in incense ash dusted in readiness for possible evidence in the doorway.

Throughout Ma's mourning period all family members wanted, so badly, to do the right thing. They thus took refuge in customs in which they felt secure. They certainly gave the impression they believed, absolutely, in what they were doing. To these ends tradition has it that, holding a ritual once every seven days, for seven weeks, will help the spirit of the dead person 'negotiate the underworld'. Of these 'weekly rites' the most important is the final ceremony. Before leaving for the Buddhist hall close relatives bathed in water purified by floating pomelo leaves. Up to the forty-ninth day sexual intercourse was still forbidden.

Immediate mourners wore the coarse, white clothing that they had on at the funeral, except for sacking surcoats which had been burned. There was the same picture of the deceased on the altar. Many maintained that although she looked stern when they first arrived, she cheered up as rituals progressed. As for most ceremonies there was an impressive spread on the altar. This was so she could invite spirits of other, long dead, family members to the feast. A group of six Buddhist nuns, led by a monk, chanted prayers. Again friends attended all, or came in for parts of, the six-hour ceremony. Many helped fold tinfoil into 'silver' or 'gold ingots'.

These were later incinerated and 'despatched' to the next world.

A 'charade' was acted out by close family members. The dead person's soul had to pay 'spirit money' in order to cross 'demon gate barrier' by the 'gold' and 'silver bridges' which span rapids and whirlpools. Enormous snakes reside in murky waters. To the accompaniment of a lament on a flageolet and clashing cymbals, Second Daughter went through the motions of washing poor, dead Mother inside a tiny, paper bathhouse.

In England, most would think me deranged for taking part in a ceremony with, what they would describe as, 'archaic absurdities'. Yet after living many years in Hong Kong much was meaningful, appropriate and natural. One felt chastened and compelled to make amends for one's inadequacies according to Buddhist karmic belief. Tomorrow, our life in the next world will be fashioned out of our actions performed today. Ma was the kindest of persons. She had done no evil and, consequently, had not been punished by a long-drawn-out death.

Much that befalls us, even the way we die, emanates from our conduct on earth. Although what proportion of a person's fate one fashions for oneself, by morality, abstentious behaviour and Confucian ethics and how much is shaped by the Almighty, is not easy to deduce. We should live a life of moderation and kindness, like Ma, priests tell us. Some day, if we learn to evaluate our impressions and thoughts properly, we shall understand.

Afterwards, everyone went up to the flat roof of this multi-storey temple to burn the considerable quantity of 'spirit money' and tinfoil 'ingots' which had been folded with loving care by deft Chinese hands. Effigies of people and things considered important in the hereafter, like a maid, television set, chauffeur and car with the lucky registration number, 888, all went up in flames. A friend telephoned from Canada to say that, in a dream, Ma had requested her to 'consign' a doll, which the emigrant had given the dead woman a few years previously. This was, in fact, already 'airborne'.

Among other duties, relatives are expected to transmit money, goods and food to a dead parent. In return for ancestor reverence the living require the departed to mete out generous supplies of blessings, including prestige, wealth, moral order, fertility and health. Chinese rites are based to some extent on fear. For non-compliance, the living accept punishment. The whims and pulsations of *feng shui*, in the positioning, among other things, of graves, spirit tablets and niches for ashes, play a part, with man, earth and nature seen as one. Moving a relative's remains may alter a family's luck.

Rituals have therapeutic effects on mourners. Burning a domestic helper made from paper, fake money and other 'necessities' are indicators of serious intent. Cash, the lack of which the poor see as the reason for hardships, has power to solicit and secure worldly and spiritual favours and goods. With abundant imitation money the dead can be looked after in a style usually not possible on earth.

As I stood on the flat roof of the temple watching the sparks rise, dodging the choking smoke amid the burning process, I pondered why no one, openly questioned to what degree the whole funeral operation, seeking a suitable place in the afterworld, would be successful. Simultaneously, I visualised barbaric days when live slaves and real household items were buried in elaborate tombs to serve their dead, imperial owners. One could imagine pretty, young concubines being dragged away screaming to their fate.

After this, the last of our weekly ceremonies, about fifty people attended a Chinese banquet in a happy atmosphere. All concerned had done their duty to the dead person. We were finally able to eat meat again. The few specks of soot encountered during incineration were of little account as we drove home to take our second bath of the day. This time, not only pomelo leaves but also wampee leaves had been added to the water. I tried to compare the effectiveness of these additives with that of a priest describing the Cross in the air with his right hand and blessing tap-water to produce Holy Water.

After bathing, lucky packets were opened. Besides money they contained sprigs of hibiscus, *foo paak*. In Cantonese this is a homonym for riches, so important in materialistic Hong Kong. A second lucky packet, in addition to coins, contained a needle and thread and a hairpin. *Kat lei* can be interpreted as meaning pierce or sharp or, alternatively, as lucky or profit.

Anything that could bring bad luck, including black objects, had been burned. Items brought home, for good luck, included white mourning shoes, white clothes and a piece of 'blazing-red' material, about eight-and-a-half inches square, cut from Ma's shroud, which I treasure.

All was not over. The day following the last weekly rites we, the immediate mourners, went to the funeral home to collect the ashes. They were 'fairly white', which was construed as a good omen. From there, we went to Ching Chung Koon temple complex. Here the local soil is good and the trees and *bonsai* luxuriant. We asked the door gods to give us permission to enter and paid our respects by bowing three times. Oranges were placed on their shrines.

Ma's interment was conducted in one of the halls of the

columbarium by a Taoist priest wearing a 'squared hat'. He carefully poured her ashes into a white cloth, spread around the neck of a funnel. This was then put into an urn. The deceased's gold bracelet and a piece of jade were also deposited inside, although in the West an urn is sometimes seen, as a vessel in which, symbolically, tears are collected. After tying the top on with a red ribbon the dead person's name was written on the urn with a brush dipped in 'lucky vermillion' paint.

Then there was more bowing; flowers were arranged in vases; joss sticks and paper rosettes were burned. The last had been 'blessed' by an old lady who burnt a small hole in the centre of each sheet with a joss stick, making up a rosette. Prayers were chanted. Food was laid out in front of the niche. This was done after the door, which also serves as a memorial tablet, had been sealed with plaster. The site of a person's remains, and going back to one's origins the natural and proper way, can influence future generations. A vegetarian lunch for all mourners followed. With retribution always possible, charitable work is important in most religions and relatives were told by a fortune teller it would help the dead person enter the 'extremely happy world' if good deeds were performed. A donation was made to help a poor watchman with his medical expenses.

Mourning lasted 100 days and another ceremony, this time not so elaborate, was held at which everyone was in good spirits. Some chatted to the deceased person's photograph. 'Hullo Mummy, how are you?' As always, there was food. This was, first of all, placed on the altar in Second Sister's home. Later, it was consumed by members of the family.

Rituals demonstrate resolution. The most important dish, in services for the dead, is golden-brown, crisp-skinned roast pork. This is believed by some to replace, ritualistically, the flesh the deceased loses with decomposition. When placed on an altar, in which a person's spirit dwells, pork takes on magical qualities. Some insist it is similar to the Host consecrated at the Eucharist. According to Roman Catholic Church dogma, handed down from medieval times, with transubstantiation bread and wine become the actual substance of the body and blood of Christ. Together, we celebrants become one with Christ in a mystery we cannot fully comprehend.

It is important not to starve Chinese ancestors and to keep their memory alive. By eating pork, 'food fit for the gods' which has been ritually 'shared' with ancestral spirits, the spiritual essence is passed on to living descendants. Celebrants are able to fortify their 'cosmic breath' and inner strength (*chi*) and even capture magical powers. Some 'golden pork' is occasionally pressed into mouths of babies barely able to masticate. 'Ah Git is better behaved, cough gone since he ate his pork,' a mother was heard to exclaim. Whether true or not, exchanging pork between the dead and the living renews the symbolic union between two worlds. To receive blessings the living know they have a duty to worship ancestors.

The cult of death, in which symbolism, homonyms and colour play important parts, is complex and clearly defined. Although there are regional variations Chinese have been 'honouring urns' in a similar fashion since the Chou Dynasty (1122–255 BC). Probably more than any other nation they are obsessed with their dead.

The dividing line, however, between mourning and celebration, is not always easy to draw. *Ching Ming*, 'Remembrance of Ancestors Day', and *Chung Yeung*, the 'Double Ninth', often take the form of a picnic. Also, on the anniversaries of a person's death and on his or her birthday, they are remembered.

Some time after the hundred-day mourning period expired a close friend dreamed that Ma told her she was staying in the house of the Chan family. 'I'm to be reincarnated as a male,' she whispered. The dreamer was then introduced to an old woman who insisted: 'Ma will be easy to recognise. She will be playful and able to turn somersaults.'

A few days later Second Daughter also dreamed she saw Mother, who was 'neither happy nor sad'. She then disappeared. A handsome young boy stood in her place.

CHAPTER TEN

FINALE

I TS clear, blue-green waters lap Hong Kong's shores. It fans out, far away, comprising nearly 40 per cent of the water on this planet. The deepest of the 'Seven Seas' cradles about fifty countries, large and small, developed and developing, housing half the world's teeming population. It washes the beaches of China, the Russian Far East, Central and South America, Australasia, as well as the coasts of the superpowers – Japan and the United States. Its balmy waters embrace countless islands, including Melanesia, Polynesia and Micronesia. Yet in spite of romance and impressive statistics, throughout history, the Pacific has been rated by Westerners of less importance than the Atlantic.

Up to the start of this century Europe strode the world like a colossus. Then, one night in 1984, more jumbo jets flew over the Pacific, with its considerable untapped off-shore oil and mineral wealth, than over the Atlantic. By the beginning of next century the United States Pacific trade will probably be double that of its Atlantic counterpart. The Far East has become the world's 'economic cockpit', in terms of growth. Its 'chopstick belt' depends largely on the advanced technology of Japan, the dynamism of the four 'Asian Tigers' (Hong Kong, Singapore, Taiwan and Korea, the most successful wealth-making countries ever known), and the cheap labour of places like China and Vietnam.

Although the term 'Asia-Pacific Century' has become almost a cliche, there has been a population explosion in numerous countries. This has brought about excessive urbanisation, overcrowding and poverty. Each of these has added to problems such as poor sanitation, traffic congestion, pollution and a lack of pure water. In spite of amazing achievements Japan is still a partially 'closed' society and not yet entirely 'internationalised'. For years to come regions like North-West China and other areas of its interior will form part of the Third World. The future pace of growth of Asia could have been over-estimated.

Traditionally, cultural and trade pressures have been exerted by the West upon the East. But with the United States overstretching itself and experiencing difficulties, single-handedly coping with its role of world's policeman, this is changing. The third millennium, beginning in 2001, will be more and more influenced by the Far East. The new era will be less predisposed towards Whites.

In the last century, the Chinese were restless, flexible, pragmatic settlers dreaming of a better life; today they would be classified as unwanted, economic migrants who could create a nationalistic backlash. Over a century ago they were seen as heroic, hardy pioneers. Known as *Nanyang* (southern ocean) sojourners, many sailed from Hong Kong, the main sea outlet for Guangdong Province, and emigrated to the Malay Peninsula, Burma, India and Ceylon. Others made for the Philippines, Indochina, Thailand and Indonesia. Other Chinese wandered farther afield, to faraway countries like South Africa, the Seychelles and Mauritius. Many travelled still further west, to the Caribbean and South America. The British encouraged them to open up sparsely populated terrain in their colonies. When Sir Francis Light and his party landed on the uninhabited island of Penang in 1786 and started to clear undergrowth, the first Chinese settlers arrived that same afternoon.

Considerable intermarriage with local populations resulted in the mestizos, Peranakan and Baba Southern Ocean, 'mixed blood', Chinese of today. A few married into royalty or aristocracy. Their main aim in emigrating was trade, not conquest or political intrigue. Fortunes waxed and waned alongside colonialism. Any Chinese who wore a jacket and carried an umbrella, could, it was said, obtain credit from a British banker.

In the second half of the nineteenth century many coolies were shanghaied and shipped overseas in appalling conditions, in what was known in Chinese as the 'pig business'. Because of harsh treatment, insanitary conditions and overcrowding, up to one quarter or more of indentured labourers died en route. Descendants of these bold frontiersmen are the rubber, pineapple, sugar, and even 'Tiger Balm' ointment 'kings', of Southeast Asia that we know today.

Loke Yew arrived in Singapore as a poor boy of eleven in 1858.

The story goes that, starving and desperate, he went to the temple to pray for guidance. He was instructed to take money from the poor box and proceed to the gaming table. This he did with considerable success. Entering business, everything he touched 'turned to gold'. Years later, he became the Andrew Carnegie of the Far East giving away millions. Hong Kong University's Loke Yew Hall is named after him.

Up to 50 million Chinese now live outside China proper. Many have settled in countries like North America, particularly in 'Old Golden Mountain' (California) and 'New Golden Mountain' (Australia). There are Pacific cities with strong ties to Asia. Greater Vancouver has a population of 1.6 million, including 130,000 Chinese some sporting 'Hong-couver' or 'Van-kong' T-shirts. Other Canadian cities with large Chinese populations include Toronto and Edmonton. Hong Kong's Li Ka-shing's Husky Oil Group's headquarters are in Calgary.

Within this wealth-making web Chinese 'networks', with concentric circles consisting of relatives, kinsmen, business associates and old classmates, continuously increase their 'economic reach'. The Lees, a typical extended family who profess to 'love China', but apparently from a distance, have members at the end of numerous telephone lines around the world. The Jewish diaspora gives tiny Israel, through its overseas lobbies, disproportionate political clout. Likewise, in the twenty-first century China will wield immense power capable of yielding considerable hard currency.

As I threw a stone into the South China Sea that afternoon I imagined ripples radiating outward, around the Pacific, to the many Chinese 'colonies' about the globe. From Clear Water Bay, one of twenty-one parks occupying 40 per cent of Hong Kong's land area, one can gaze across the largest ocean, with its peculiar, 'heaped-up', cumulus cloud formations, towards the Ninepin Islands. Thank God not every square mile of the Territory's countryside is occupied by multi-storey housing estates.

It was twenty-five years since I had last driven the nine miles from the Star Ferry to Land's End, where the South China Sea ends and terra firma begins. In those days, except on special occasions like Mid-Autumn Festivals, only the odd courting couple and a family out for fresh air went there. In the late 1960s, it was a beautiful, desolate spot. Now, vegetation has been planted and paved areas, an exhibition hall and a cafeteria have been constructed, all against a backdrop of scrub-covered, arid-green hills. But apart from crowds at weekends, on a weekday most of the park is peacefully still.

The one exception is the kite-flying area. There is incessant chattering and guffawing from old and young. As those earthbound mortals went about their passion, with their ill fate being borne away up strings into the spirit world, 'Up, up ... and up,' the kite buffs seemed to cry. They flew beautiful butterflies, dour dragons, fierce frogs, colourful, dragon-headed centipedes and other fearsome creatures, some with moving tails or paws.

The Chinese started flying kites in the fifth century BC. They were made of bamboo, silk and natural glue. A musical variety, with bamboo tubes through which the wind whistles, has been flown since AD 600. They were sometimes used for psychological warfare when they wailed: 'Protect the Han (Chinese)'. According to Needham's *Science and Civilisation in China*, manned kite flights, forerunners of aerodynamic experiments, started as early as the sixth century. Hapless convicts were strapped in and sent aloft, from the fortress 'Tower of the Golden Phoenix' in North China, to entertain the Emperor Lao Yang.

Wandering alone along the coastal path in the park, among tallow trees, wild coffee, screw pines and horsetail trees, I pondered the pace of change. Southward, on Tung Lung Island, stand the ruins of a seventeenth-century fort built by the Chinese to suppress pirates on a busy trade route. Twenty-five soldiers were stationed there, commanded by a sergeant. Eastward, I spotted two pleasure craft and a marine police launch. Closer to shore, two large floating platforms were used for raising fish for the table.

These clear waters used to be haunts of freebooting, swashbuckling pirates, like Koxinga (Cheng Ch'eng-kung) the pro-Ming patriot who drove the Dutch from Taiwan to establish an anti-Manchu base. He also attempted, from his main lair in Amoy (now Xiamen), to wrest power from the Qing Dynasty. But one man's pirate is another man's freedom fighter and Koxinga, born of a Chinese father and a Japanese mother, has more recently been lauded by the People's Republic in a re-write of late seventeenth-century history.

Today, the Hong Kong Marine Police and the Royal Navy, which in the last century were awarded prize money, keep constant vigil for smugglers. Part of this illicit trade is conducted by wayward, unscrupulous elements of local government in southern China. 'The mountains are [still] high and the Emperor far away.'

To my south, in the distance lies Wagland Island with its rugged beauty and colony of white-rumped swifts. Its 1893 state-of-the-art, cast-iron lighthouse was constructed by Barbier and Company of Paris for the Chinese Maritime Customs. Although many of

Hong Kong's lighthouses were manned by Anglo-Chinese the senior posts were filled by Europeans. Wagland Island was one of 235 ceded, together with the New Territories, by China to Britain, in 1898, on a ninety-nine year lease.

This important New Territories' hinterland, of which Clear Water Bay Country Park forms a part, amounts to 92 per cent of Hong Kong. Sir Cecil Clementi, Governor from 1925 to 1930, wrote in 1936:

> As I cannot believe that the British Empire will ever acquiesce in the retrocession of Hong Kong to China, it behoves us to offer, and the sooner the better, terms upon which the Chinese can honourably agree to the cession of the New Territories in perpetuity to Great Britain.

Some Old Hong Kong Hands argue that, had this been done, the Territory's major reservoirs, airports and other vital infrastructure would have been sited on land which would not have had to be returned to China in 1997. The truth is, however, that today's few remaining colonies are anachronisms. It is no longer appropriate for the Union Jack to fly here. Like it or not Hong Kong, as part of 'Greater China', belongs to the Chinese.

With vast natural resources, including on- and off-shore oil reserves, the terrain of China varies considerably. The area south of the Yangtze River, stretching south to Guangxi Province and Hainan Island, and east to Fujian Province, housing in excess of 283 million people (more than the United States), has developed most rapidly. Shops are crammed with goods and customers. Billboards line streets. This growth in southern China has been spearheaded by Guangdong, the fifth 'Economic Dragon', with a population of about 66 million – more than either Britain, France or Italy. A superhighway leads down to Shenzhen, adjacent to Hong Kong. This is the most developed of China's ten major Special Economic Zones and probably the fastest growing city in the world. This trunk road could, one day, be the start of the long dreamed of 'Great Asian Highway' wending its way to Europe.

With China seen as an opportunity, not a threat, Hong Kong, with her buccaneering, freemarket system and know-how, effectively took over Shenzhen from its inception in 1978. Beyond 1997, with China previously changing direction at intervals, there will, one day, be a seamless border between the two territories. Already, with Hong Kong subsidiaries employing over three million people in materialistic, southern China, instead of the People's Republic taking over Hong Kong it is 'annexation' in reverse.

Hong Kong executives in business suits soldier on into the hinterland. With everyone making money 'Birds now sing and all under heaven is bright'. Middle-level communist cadres are no longer ideologues. They too are keen to get in on the act. In their terribly patient way the Chinese have remoulded communism and made China great again by renouncing Marx and Engels and, instead, approving policies like those formulated by Marks and Spencer. Hong Kong residents are the chief buyers of real estate in China. Land prices in Shenzhen Special Economic Zone, born of a Hong Kong economic father and a Middle Kingdom socialist mother, increased ten times in the two years up to 1992, due to rampant inflation and the spiralling cost of living.

Shenzhen is where yuppies spend more on a dinner than snooty Peking government officials, who Southerners maintain look down on their Cantonese cousins, earn in a month. It is this neo-colony of the Guangdong hinterland that has allowed Hong Kong to grow fast in spite of a world recession. The Territory has expanded outside its physical boundaries. It has become a catalyst city.

Back in the days of undiluted communism, in 1964, Chairman Mao repeatedly exhorted: 'Learn from Tachai!' This was a model agricultural village in Shanxi Province. Now, with wealth accumulating in the China hinterland as the result of business know-how and capital emanating from over the border, the cry has changed to: 'Learn from Hong Kong!'

Early in the twenty-first century, the Hong Kong-Shenzhen Zone will form a metropolis of ten million, linked by mass transit railway and super highways, much like the Tokyo-Osaka district of Japan. The whole region, stretching on to Canton and the Pearl River Delta, will become the equivalent of California with Hong Kong as its Los Angeles. Hong Kong, a cash-cow ripe for exploitation by China, will be comparable to New York (or Manhattan Island) as the services, communications and financial centre of the 'China Economic Circle', where millions are moved on computer screens at the touch of a button. China, debilitated by the Cultural Revolution, has played a weak hand to advantage. It will advance from regional power to regional super-power. It could replace the United States as Japan's biggest trading partner. With over a fifth of the world's population it must be pivotal to a peaceful and stable world.

As ties strengthen the whole area could unite. The People's Republic, Taiwan (which China has not renounced using force to overthrow), Macau and Hong Kong – even Singapore – could become partners. These states could develop by peaceful evolution into the long-standing dream of a 'Greater China'. Already the odd, far-sighted businessman prints this on his visiting cards. Indeed the economic circle could develop still further, led by Japan, or, in the more distant future even by 'Greater China', into an Asian trade alliance. This would compete with the two other major economic blocs, Europe and America.

There are those who insist Hong Kong will become still more successful within another generation, largely because old enmities will have made way for a 'Chinese Economic Community' (CEC). There are others, however, who believe Hong Kong will not remain the 'Brussels of China' but that, as development gradually pushes further north, where land and labour are cheaper, Hong Kong will be partially replaced by places like Shanghai, Shandong and Dalian, and by Hainan in the south. The big test will be whether Hong Kong can remain an international financial centre. Moody's Investor Services, a leading credit rating agency, predicted in 1993 that China will put an end to the Territory's role by meddling in its affairs. History has not treated kindly 'free cities' like Venice, Trieste and Tangiers. They have all been absorbed by large countries.

Hong Kong could eventually become just one more southern China seaport. Changes usually take time, though. Yet twenty-five years ago, who would have thought the 'Four Young Dragons' would emerge as they have today? However, the greatest economic take-off in history, for a large country, is taking place now, in China.

In 1993 the International Monetary Fund, using revised methods of calculating Gross National Product (GNP), figured the United States and Japan have the world's largest economies. But, owing to sheer size, China follows not far behind. Even some China-watchers have yet to grasp that the People's Republic is a great economic power. If it does not tear itself apart, and continues to grow at an annual rate of nine or ten per cent in spite of some 'overheating', by the second quarter of the twenty-first century China could have the largest economy on earth.

Although the country which was the scene of the Tiananmen Square Massacre has the wherewithal to clutch the rainbow, in the mid 1990s, on a per capita basis, it is still one of the twenty-five poorest nations on earth. In remote provinces like Gansu, Guangxi and Guizhou its people are inadequately housed. Toil is unremitting. With a generation missing out on schooling during the decade-long Cultural Revolution much of the population is not well enough educated to cope with the continuous technological change of the twenty-first century. But, with the will, great strides can be made in a short time. There was not a primary school place for every child in Hong Kong until 1971. The phasing in of nine years of compulsory, free education started seven years later.

Certainly China is far from being a stable country, and, with memories of warlordism and imperial conquest, the People's Republic Government is wary of releasing control from the capital. It loves to demonstrate its authority. In 1990, China brought the Macau airport project to a standstill. In addition to complaints about financing it claimed reclamation work was causing pollution further up the Pearl River, which has contained toxins for years anyway. After the People's Republic held up work for half a year, made its political point and demonstrated who was really in charge, Macau was permitted to continue constructing its runways.

Although China sometimes acts in ways which are not easy for Westerners to comprehend much of the world is slowly moving closer together. With 'globalisation', the pundits tell us risks with 'alternative communities', such as China armed with nuclear weapons going in one direction and the main stream of countries in another, will be considerable. Even if the People's Republic appears bent on peaceful transformation, fifty years from now she may still not have entirely accepted western-style human rights.

As recently as 1993, a People's Republic official was reported as saying: 'What human rights? We've trouble enough feeding people let alone giving them human rights.' Decades earlier, Chairman Mao phrased it more poetically: 'We don't need flowers on brocade but fuel in snowy weather.'

After 1997, Hong Kong will no longer be shielded from turbulence in China by Britain. However, although there will continue to be mini and major crises the country is unlikely to disintegrate, as has happened in Eastern Europe with the demise of rampant communism. Up to 80 per cent of the population still live in the countryside. Although there are frustrations which sometimes explode into local incidents, as long as standards of living improve there appears to be no strong urge for the masses to unite in a common political cause. Within a few relatively small, radical factions in cities, however, democracy has sold like hot cakes.

With more, often hyped, news and information from the outside world rebounding off satellites this must have significant effects, especially with retaliatory moves by the United States as it links human rights to 'Most Favoured Nation Trading Status'. As much as some American politicians would welcome the overthrow of the government in China, this would obviously have terrible consequences. A lesser danger is the preaching of the

American way of life (which, unfortunately, includes its frightening crime rate) through compelling advertising. It now appears to have almost taken on the qualities of a new religion. Seems vaguely like the Crusades when Christians marched off to fight in the Holy Land.

Some Westerners today agree that not everything Chinese is outmoded. Their 'art of living' and 'practical philosophy of life', not to mention things such as alternative medicine, are areas where the Chinese can make valuable contributions.

THE sun had already dipped as I drove away from Land's End, feeling hungry. I thought of my home town, Watton, with its emblem of a hare (wat) jumping over a cask (ton). There, twilight lingers longer than in the tropics and hues change after a cucumber sandwich tea. Then shadows lengthen and a mantle of peace descends well before sunset. There is still time, during the rare heat wave, to drive out to Fowlmere, or, as we did as children, cycle down to Loch Neaton for a swim in its murky waters. Finally, on reaching home we strolled around the garden and paddock before darkness fell – which in midsummer is approaching ten o'clock. There, in the fading light one could smell flowers, the newly-mown grass and the honeysuckle which has climbed up our house for five generations. Although parts of the country have become ugly, squalid and disagreeable there are countless things I still love about England.

Here in Hong Kong I drove home in the gathering dusk along the Clear Water Bay Road. Junks, now motorised, no longer rely on patched sails for power as they did in the 1950s. On my left a few picturesque, 'bright-light fishermen' netted catches attracted by kerosene lanterns shining from their small craft. The lunar calendar is remarkably accurate. With the Mid-Autumn Festival behind us it had already turned slightly cooler and less humid. Important Chinese holidays occur when there are likely to be major weather changes. 'He has "passed over" the Mid-Autumn Festival' is not an uncommon saying concerning the infirm and the elderly who are prone to die at such times.

Wait ... surely there it was! Yes, I could hear it distinctly. The plaintive call to *Kwan Yin*, saviour of the afflicted who hearkens to the cries of the world.

I gazed from my car across at Xianggang Island. What is it going to look like with red flags flying from roof tops where the

Union Jack previously flew, and with People's Liberation Army soldiers in sloppy, green uniforms with red stars on their caps marching in the streets? Symmetrically shaped 'Grandfather Fisherman Hill' was coming up on my left.

'It's worrying,' a Chinese architect friend had confided in me. 'Twenty years from now will we wander the streets, in the twilight amid run-down buildings, sighing for a bygone age? In a police station or before a court of law, under the British system, you feel you will receive a fair hearing.'

In 1956, when Chairman Mao made his famous, 'Let a hundred flowers bloom, let a hundred schools of thought contend speech,' he urged comrades to express opinions and vowed full protection for freedom of thought. The People's Republic populace acted with uncharacteristic fervour. Mao responded with brutality. A vicious, anti-rightist campaign was launched. Thousands were marched off to labour camps.

The Communists had a long record of broken pledges when they negotiated with Nationalist Leader Chiang Kai-shek. They promised to forsake communism and to espouse Dr Sun Yat Sen's 'Three Principles of the People'. Winston Churchill was adamant. 'Any agreement made with communists is not worth the paper it is written on.' Post-World War II history is replete with reversals of Chinese policy at short notice.

After the Hong Kong takeover by China will living standards drop and the Territory deteriorate? Will public toilets stink? To what extent will Hongkongers be ingeniously brainwashed about communism and subtle pressure applied to solicit donors for 'good causes' for the Motherland? Just as our forebears expectorated in Victorian times, will China's supreme leader hawk contemptuously into a spittoon while he receives visitors just as Deng Xiaoping, who was put into 'cold-storage' twice before he became China's elder statesman, does now?

'Nobody knows whether this is for effect or whether he is just a vulgar old bugger,' one British diplomat is reported to have commented. Certainly the few hard-line communists that are left try hard to hang on to unpopular ideology as there is a personality cult around Deng as there was around Chairman Mao.

While awaiting the 1997 handover, in retrospect the odd historian has even quoted the 1644 Manchu Conquest when people were afraid 10,000 Chinese would be slaughtered at Yangzhou, in Jiangsu Province, to 'honour the Manchu flag'. Appalling carnage did in fact ensue. Few Hans survived. The Manchus then tried to block information. Massacres (like Tiananmen Square in 1989) are not uncommon in Chinese history. China has an appalling record in repressing its citizens. Afterwards, rulers try to be conciliatory and rule from behind the scenes using local officials as front men. It is not suggested that history will repeat itself in Hong Kong at the end of the twentieth century. A few have questioned, however, whether there will be an analogy of any kind after the People's Republic takes over.

But with the *yin-yang* complementary principle the heat of summer invariably follows the cold of winter. The People's Republic has passed through bitter seasons during half a century in power. Shortly after 1997 (which optimists explain add up to twenty-six, and these two figures total eight, which in Chinese is a homophone for 'blessings'), with major changes in direction every seven years or so, reformists could by then be in power. That more liberal winds will blow in the People's Republic is assured. Only the timing is uncertain.

'I sometimes tease Hong Kong friends by telling them there are six million people in Tibet – the same number as in Hong Kong,' the Dalai Lama was quoted as saying.

No one expects the Pearl of the Orient to share that unfortunate land's fate. Tibet used to have 3,000 temples and autonomy based on the sixteen-point agreement with China made in 1951. The latter promised non-interference and recognition of their common border, although to be fair, until then Tibet was a backward, poverty-ridden, dark-age society. Children were packed off for life, by parents, to become monks. Yet still it was our 'lost horizon', a mystic land close to heaven, cut off from the rest of the world. Then, in 1959 our 'Shangrila', where the air is crisp and colours distinct, was annexed. Its leaders and lamas were shot or imprisoned. Religious persecution and the rape of Tibet had begun.

Hongkongers' predictions, about their own fate, varies from: 'I don't trust China, I'm afraid it won't fulfil its promises,' to 'The 1984 Sino-British Joint Declaration is better than nothing.'

The working man frequently sighs: 'I'm a small "kernel". My main concern is a steady livelihood.'

Many citizens express no opinions about China's promises to keep Hong Kong's social, economic and legal systems basically intact until 2047. Meanwhile, People's Republic bureaucrats spout propaganda no matter what they themselves, inwardly, believe. Although the Chinese Constitution is one of the best ever drafted, with seemingly many legal safeguards, few officials pay too much attention to it. Can China, the communist lion, really lie down with Hong Kong, the world's most errant capitalist lamb?

Britain held no aces leading up to the 1984 Sino-British Joint Agreement. Now, most concede the more Hong Kong can be internationalised the better chance it stands of China keeping its word. Undoubtedly, the People's Republic wants the capitalist lifestyle to continue in Hong Kong and for the economic gem to retain its lustre. But there is a difference between 'wanting' and 'achieving'. However, the healthier the 'golden goose' the less likely the communists will be to kill it. Yet the degree to which China is interfering in Hong Kong's internal affairs, even during the twilight of British rule, is unnerving.

China even considers itself an authority when advising on Hong Kong's new, '24-carat', airport when the People's Republic's only airport approaching international standards in their whole gigantic country is in Peking. Really, however, the long drawn-out, airport dispute, although on the face of it concerning finance and planning, was basically more about trust – like other disagreements between the two parties.

Appropriately, Wong Kin-bun wrote to the editor of the *South China Morning Post*: 'China, could you please honour the Joint Declaration which promises us a high degree of autonomy in accordance with the concept of two systems under one country?'

If such a policy is faithfully implemented, coupled with continuing, sensible management and Hong Kong's accepted resilience, it is hard to see how our city-state, with good joss, can falter. In fact, if there are only two survivors after World War III, both will probably stagger with blackened faces towards each other, through settling dust, speaking Cantonese.

In many ways Hong Kong is a far better place today than before World War II. Then, few crossed the Chinese-Western divide. Any European who was anyone lived in comparative isolation from the local community. Now, aided by modern technology, the average Chinese not only enjoys a high standard of living but everyone also has the added advantage of the two races mixing and enriching each other's lifestyles.

Most expatriates have long ceased being members of a privileged minority in a colony that is forced by history and circumstances often to pretend it is not one. As a result of incidents like the Opium Wars, a few locals still see Whites as symbols of oppression and feel that Europeans are getting better cracks of the whip. Certainly anti-British feeling remains. The odd, enraged Englishman who has, or imagines he has been the object of racial slights has even prophesied there will be an anti-colonial backlash after 1997. With the release of pent-up frustations there was a racist ring during the 1981 Christmas Riots. Like the 1966 Star Ferry Disturbances, however, economic resentment between haves and have-nots was also apparent.

In spite of the 'fellow countrymen syndrome', and the strong pull of nationalism, Chinese do not usually forget old friends. The Bund, a major thoroughfare in Shanghai alongside the Whangpoo River, was originally a towpath for scrawny, underfed coolies. There old Chinese men in cloth caps, who in pre-1949 days worked under Westerners, are still eager to chat to elderly tourists. 'You work in Shanghai in old days?' they questioned me.

Bitter memories fade fast and pleasant ones stay. Crossing racial boundaries a few staunch alliances were formed. Ditching old friends leads to bitterness. In the next century, when British administrators have long left Hong Kong, their conduct and methods will be compared, predictably favourably, with China's counterparts.

Challenges, unsettling for the elderly, have always been present in Hong Kong. Life here is never dull. If a person is unable to live with change then this is not the place to be. Cast your mind back to the mid 1960s, if you are able to. During the coming thirty years Hong Kong will probably change at an even faster pace. International understanding will become still more important. One wonders how broad-minded we Whites will be when, one day, one-man, one-vote is introduced for some form of world government.

'CAN'T bear the thought of leaving my bones here. I want to live among my own kind,' an old colleague whispered to me.

'One's more at peace,' he continued, 'where one grew up.' With Hong Kong being little more than a 'staging post' through much of its century-and-a-half of British history that is natural. Old elephants return to their early stamping grounds to die. But retirement 'back home', does not always work out.

In an age before air-conditioning my commanding officer, a lifetime, off-shore Brit, told me, when we auxiliary policemen turned out during the 1956 Hong Kong Riots: 'I'm retiring to Scotland. Want to see the four seasons again.' After 'eating his way out of the Territory', at farewell parties, he was dead within eighteen months.

Most of us know where our roots are if even we spend decades staying as far away from them as possible. In addition to people retiring, many expatriates in various stages of their careers give up their overseas jobs, pack their bags and head for the 'promised land'. Unsurprisingly several, having emotional attachments with Hong Kong, have difficulty adjusting physically, mentally and psychologically, 'back home'. Believing the cultural clash will at last be over it comes as a surprise to find many, especially Old Hong Kong Hands, feel more alien in their land of birth than in roller-coaster Hong Kong.

After six months trying to settle they begin to appreciate living in the Territory is a unique experience which, for better or worse, changes one. With the agenda provisionally set for the twenty-first century, budding high-fliers at last realise the Far East is the place to be. After another couple of months a few of the disillusioned wend their way back to Hong Kong with embarrassed explanations to friends who contributed to farewell presents. Hong Kong has its way of keeping people.

As years roll by we Old Hongkongers who stay on become less and less English. Had I remained in Norfolk all my life I should, no doubt, have continued to run the family firm. But with 'itchy feet', for people like me the motto was, 'Go East young man!' where, on average, salaries are higher and taxes lower than in Europe. There is also the mystique of the Far East and the proximity to other exotic Asian cities. Over many years Hong Kong has become home. But I shall never be Chinese. Although it is difficult to predict what is in store after 1997, I shall retain the nationality printed in my travel document.

A month before my visit to Clear Water Bay Park, at a Government Antiquities Advisory Board meeting, we trooped into the council chamber for a group photograph. My intended path, to the centre at the back of a row of chairs, was blocked by chatting members. A few seconds later a large, heavy electric-light globe crashed down in the very place I had intended standing for the picture. My friends' hesitancy and those few seconds delay saved me.

With good fortune coming in waves, with peaks and troughs, Chinese reactions to my narrow escape varied. 'Your luck then at high ebb. Should have immediately bought sweepstake ticket!' a colleague informed me in authoritative tones. 'Luck attracts luck.'

Others maintained, 'Escape death reward for good deeds.' 'You've donated blood seventy times.' Others quoted: 'Big disaster not die later have blessings!'

'With only death and ingratitude inevitable,' a friend joked, 'when the last call comes I hope I'm holding a full hand of mahjong tiles!'

It is not only Chinese who need fantasy in their lives. It helps keep us all sane, especially with China taking over Hong Kong and glass globes tumbling down. Certainly that incident was not intended to be my Nirvana. I had not arrived at the state of bliss when mortals are snuffed out like candles, signifying final release from a cycle of reincarnation after all desires have been extinguished and passions spent on attainment of blessedness.

With Hong Kong's bright lights one cannot really appreciate the starlit heavens. Nevertheless that October evening the sky was clear and blue, arguably auguring well for the Territory's future. Staying on under China's neo-colonial rule is a calculated risk. With the best possible outcome, with good joss and getting lucky numbers right, after a few years the Territory could become truly international and far more important than it is today. If allowed to manage its own affairs, with continuing development of its sophisticated infrastructure and paying due regard to diversification, it can remain a marvellous place to do business with a driven market nurtured by a mixture of aggressiveness and anxiety over volatility.

Another possible scenario is that Hong Kong's Armageddon will be apocalyptic. The Communists naturally object strongly to any suggestion that they are incapable of managing the Territory although some Hongkongers believe, either intentionally or unintentionally they will 'run it into the ground'. But even if, like *Ichabod*, 'its glory will depart', with corruption rampant, Hong Kong will still be, at least for some time, the most developed metropolis in China and the commercial capital of Southeast Asia.

The likely outcome concerning Hong Kong's future, with time on her side and democracy spreading around the world, is of course somewhere between the above two extremes. China will gain nothing by destroying Hong Kong.

Meanwhile, down at colonial-style Marine Police Headquarters the disbanded pigeon corps, although not employed since 1926, is kept on strength. Before the introduction of radio, police launches took a few pigeons aboard to fly messages back to base. Today, the flock of about fifty birds is looked upon much like the legend of Gibraltar's barbary apes. If the birds leave, it is predicted, the British will depart and Hong Kong will no longer prosper. The pigeons disappeared during the Japanese occupation but returned mysteriously in 1945. They were watched over carefully during the 1967 communist Disturbances.

The encapsulated city-state, with no natural resources, has come of age. This has been achieved by evolution, not revolution. There is substantial real growth. Pegged to the United States dollar the local currency is stable. There is a massive programme of economic and social investment. Unemployment is low. There is virtually no central government debt.

Britain will hand over a marvellous legacy to China. Few, if any state has achieved such a rapid increase in population while maintaining a continuous sharp rise in the standard of living. Because of fear of riling China, the 150th anniversary of the birth of the Colony, the largest remnant of empire, passed in 1991 with barely a whimper. Not to acknowledge the great Asian success story was regrettable. It would have engendered pride in Hong Kong. The errors of the founding fathers of this 'barren rock' are accepted. China has a historical desire to humiliate Britain, with its below the surface guilt, to avenge opium wars and unequal treaties.

But Anglo-Chinese relations were far worse during the Korean War and again when the Cultural Revolution was in full spate than they are now. During the 1967 Disturbances, with bombs exploding in Hong Kong's streets, the colossal People's Republic's Army could easily have marched in. Cession, after the First Opium War, is regarded by many as a shabby period of history. Yet the 1997 transfer of a spit of a colony, although not receiving independence and instead being handed over to a communist power, is, in some ways, a valedictory triumph for British imperialism. It is not the squalid sell-out many would have you believe.

For over three-and-a-half centuries (almost as long as the Roman Empire) we Britons basked in the glory of Empire. For the likes of me, who fought alongside the Fourth, Eighth and Tenth Indian Divisions in the deserts of North Africa and in Italy, we harboured pangs of sorrow and bitterness when India was cast loose from the Imperial Crown in 1947. World War II sounded the death knell of western colonialism. Most Indians wanted Britain to leave. More recently, Hong Kong provided us with glamour on a smaller scale. We could still relish the same 'pride of possession' that our relatives cherished when they served in India earlier this century.

Reservations, for the Hong Kong handover, were made at leading hotels by perspective guests from around the world, starting as early as the mid 1980s. The night of 30 June 1997 will be the 'bash' of the century. Chinese will return from overseas. Tolling church bells sounds rather western but Jardine's Noonday Gun, colonial custom or not, will no doubt fire. It will be an historical moment and the sun will set on the British Empire, at least in theory for the last time. For those with no regrets there will be harbour cruises and witching hour feasts. Many Old Hong Kong Hands, who are optimists but at the same time realists, will have difficulty in jauntily waving little red flags. With the future emanating from the present and the present emerging from the past, minds will be cast back. For many who do not respect Peking officials let alone trust them –

a reciprocal process – there will be little to celebrate. Perhaps a wake would be more appropriate.

With hints of sorrow, even bitterness, one must be intimidated by China's prodigiousness, her multitudes, her feudalistic values. One can be scared, too, by her philistine, intractable Communist Party remembering the Cultural Revolution when rulers plunged the country into mindless violence. How can one not be afraid of the effects of almost monolithic bureaucracy, its impact on initiative and enterprise, and the lethargy that prevails among its gerontocracy, addressing one another as comrade? What if China, governed largely by unwritten laws, is again thrown into turmoil as had happened within the past thirty years? It would be such a tragedy, after the 1997 handover, to see it all go wrong. Perhaps it is better to 'desert the junk' before the actual transfer takes place?

Much water has flowed down the Yangtze since 14 September 1793, when Britain's ambassador, Lord Macartney, leading the first formal British mission to Cathay, stood in the garden of the summer palace at Jehol Court. It was considered a world sufficient unto itself. Surrounded by ministers, mandarins and 600 courtiers he awaited an audience with the Chinese Emperor. While others knelt, foreheads touching the ground, Macartney, with bureaucratic formalism, bowed his head. He did not kowtow. The truth is the meeting, over 200 years ago, was cordial and dignified. It was not the tragi-comedy it is sometimes made out to be. The emperor did not impose trading restrictions between two countries rich in culture.

It is ironic that the Comintern, in the 1920s, intended that this British Colony should be the first bastion of imperialism to topple. Now, 200 years after the Macartney incident, the solution to the spectre of 'Hong Kong 1997 Ltd' is undoubtedly the dawn of 1998. Come what may, a great deal in Hong Kong will not change although the place will become more regimented, like Singapore. The Chinese possess the capacity to endure. Facing up to reality they are geniuses for survival against extreme odds. Hongkongers will carry on shouldering the vicissitudes of life with fortitude and grace no matter what their communist masters hold in store for them. What does Macartney's ghost think about it all?

With the anticlimax in the aftermath of handover, Hongkongers will continue to get on with their lives instead of fretting. On into the twenty-first century they will still be beavering away, developing business networks, flying kites and appreciating the Mid-Autumn Festival moon. They are sure to be worshipping long-departed ancestors, consuming aphrodisiac dishes and paying regard to the *feng shui* of taller than ever skyscrapers. Tourists, with Japanese group leaders holding flags aloft, will continue to visit our city in droves. There will, however, be no more coveted postings for British servicemen, to what was once a crown colony, although some old soldiers back in the United Kingdom will recall naughty nights spent in the arms of buxom Wan Chai bar girls.

But in spite of the colony's passing there will continue to be openings for English yuppies, with old British *hongs*, and vacancies for up-and-coming young men from the City. Expatriates will still be posted here, on short contracts as well as on long assignments, ensconced in rent-free, plush accommodation replete with bonuses, servants, cars and chauffeurs. These same expatriates will continue to go on company-launch trips at weekends and, with glazed expressions, quaff countless pints of the local brew at their favourite watering holes. There, they will retell old yarns.

'Did you hear about the two "Golden Arrow" pullman coaches left behind in a siding at Kowloon station having arrived via the Trans-Siberian Railway?' the Old Hand will enquire of the new arrival. Hong Kong was the only colony connected to Britain by rail. In the meantime we oldtimers, hankering for the 'good old days', will look down our big western noses at newcomers. Our memories are limitless about a world they will never know.

For Old Hands, including those who are members of the satellite, expatriate community on Lamma, Cheung Chau and Lantau Islands, living in Hong Kong has been marvellous. In spite of a few elderly Europeans being afraid to stay on because they will have nobody to look after them when they go gaga, the place has many trapped. There are good reasons to remain with the fall back position of a full British passport. The least one can do is to give it a whirl.

After another 'hundred autumns', looking back, the 156 years of British rule will be seen by enlightened generations merely as a brief interlude. A place where the British 'played for a season' and then moved on. There is a misconception that 1997 is the end. It is a comma rather than a fullstop. The saga is to be continued.

T HE day had departed and the evening was far spent as, under the western calendar's 'Hunters' Moon', I sat on my balcony gazing up at Victoria Peak. A bat, with angular flight path, circled the sky. Was it a dog-faced fruit bat I wondered: those that sleep by day under the leaves of palm trees? I consoled myself by remembering all bats are symbolic of happiness and the name *fuk* is also a homophone for good fortune.

Intersecting planes of light played on the rugged face of Seymour Cliff and on massive hideous blocks of flats, comparatively recently constructed, to my left which partially block my view. Those segments of luminosity represented, so I fantasised, stages in my life: babe in mother's arms, schoolboy crawling unwillingly to school, soldier in World War II, family businessman, teacher, administrator, civil servant and now pensioner. Just inside the flat, on a glass shelf, sat the benign figure of white-robed *Kwan Yin* gazing down. Innumerable miracles have been attributed to her. I was no longer confused and had decided to stay. Post-modern Hong Kong and its people will have a great future.

A gecko (house lizard), welcomed as a guest because they keep the insect population down, remained as motionless as the Buddhist scriptures on the far wall. 'Are they lucky or unlucky?' I questioned. 'You're getting as superstitious as the Chinese.' I told myself.

With the hare in the moon looking down – not an old man as in the West – I thought of the Babes who were murdered by the Wicked Uncle in Wayland Wood, in Norfolk. Yet I knew that, just as Ma's soul was 'wandering about' somewhere out there, so a part of me would remain always on Victoria Peak. With complexities of culture, personality, experience and sensibility, I am proud to be, and will always remain, an Englishman – although in appearance I can be mistaken for a German or a Dutchman. But, married to a Chinese, I have been influenced by surroundings and environment. Although almost indecipherable street cries of itinerant, Cantonese street traders, like 'grind scissors, sharpen knives!' are not alien to me, one thing is certain: I shall never be Chinese.

Yet my marriage to a Chinese has stood the test of time, in spite of many cross-cultural unions failing because of complexities of race, language and culture. There is not the same opposition to them that there was even when we got married in 1960.

This still does not resolve the paradox of an Old Hong Kong Hand, impatient, like many Westerners on occasions, thousands of miles from his birthplace, living in what is, undoubtedly, a part of China and which will become a post-communist world. Sir William Purves, Chairman of the Hongkong Bank, in a *South China Morning Post* interview, said: 'We must give the People's Republic time.'

One day, in spite of what others insist, there really will be a modern China.

Eventually, after I have gone to bed and not woken up, the West will have helped drag China into the modern world. Democracy in some form must come. Meanwhile, for many of us, as a famous colonialist, Rudyard Kipling (1865–1936), wrote:

> And the end of the fight is a tombstone
> white with the name of the late deceased,
> And the epitaph drear: 'A fool lies here
> who tried to hustle the East.'

GLOSSARY

Amah   Chinese female servant.

Cheung saam   For females a long, sheath-like dress with high Mandarin collar and splits up sides of legs to allow movement. For males a long, loose-fitting gown.

Chi (hei **in Cantonese)**   A complex word similar to the Greek *pneuma* or the Yoga *prana*, meaning 'life-force'. It pervades everything, including mind-body organisms.

Ching Ming   A spring festival when visits are paid to family graves and tombs tidied.

Chung Yeung   Festival held on the ninth day of the Ninth Moon when Chinese climb hills and vantage points to protect themselves against future disasters. Graves are often swept at the same time.

Congee   Rice gruel.

Cumshaw   Gift of money often presented in a lucky, red envelope; gratuity.

Face   A complex word meaning prestige, reputation, dignity, honour, self-respect, status.

Feng shui (fung shui)   The principle that buildings, graves etc. should be designed so they 'reconcile' with environmental currents and cosmic principles.

Godown   Warehouse (from Malay).

Griffin   Newcomer to the Orient.

Gwailo   Ghost person, often loosely translated as 'foreign devil'.

Hong   Business house, commercial undertaking.

Joss   Idols (from Portuguese *deos*, meaning God) sometimes loosely used to mean 'luck'.

Junk   Keel-less native timber vessels of various designs (from Javanese).

Kowtow   Kneeling, bending forward and touching forehead to floor to pay respects.

Kwan Yin (Koon Yam, Kwun Yam, Guan Yin)   The Goddess of Mercy, a Buddhist and Taoist deity.

Lai see   Lucky money usually presented in a special red envelope.

Mandarin   The Peking dialect originally the language of the official classes.

Matshed   Large, tent-like structure with bamboo framing clad with rattan matting.

Nullah   Watercourse (from Hindi).

Putonghua   Standard national language of the People's Republic of China, based largely on Mandarin.

Sampan   Small boat, usually sculled, meaning, in Chinese, 'three planks'.

Tiffin   Lunch.

Typhoon   'Big wind' (from Chinese), hurricane.

Xianggang   'Hong Kong', using modern Chinese, *Pinyin* Romanisation.

Yin **and** *yang*   Basic cosmic, dualistic, negative and positive principles which apply to countless 'pairs', like man and woman, light and darkness, odd and even numbers, which complement each other rather than compete.

BIBLIOGRAPHY

Footnotes and references were not considered appropriate in a book of this nature although a certain amount of such information has been written into the text. I am, however, especially indebted to the authors and publishers of the following works, some of which may help readers pursue in detail topics I have only touched on briefly. Unless otherwise stated they are published or drafted in Hong Kong.

BOOKS

Baker, Hugh, *Ancestral Images*, South China Morning Post (1970).
———, *More Ancestral Images*, South China Morning Post (1980).
———, *Ancestral Images Again*, South China Morning Post (1981).
———, *Hong Kong Images, People and Animals*, Hong Kong University Press (1990).
Ball, Dyer J., *Things Chinese*, Graham Brash (Singapore, 1989; first published 1903).
Bond, M.H. (ed.), *The Psychology of the Chinese People*, Oxford University Press (1986).
Buck, Pearl S., *Letters from Peking*, Pan (UK, 1957).
Burkhardt, V.R., *Chinese Creeds and Customs*, South China Morning Post, a trilogy (1982; first published in 1953, 1955 and 1958).
Cameron, Nigel, *An Illustrated History of Hong Kong*, Oxford University Press (1991).
Chan, Mimi, *Images of Chinese Women in Anglo-American Literature*, Joint Publishing (HK) (1989).
Cheng, Irene, *Clara Ho Tung, A Hong Kong Lady, Her Family and Her Times*, Chinese University Press (1976).
Choa, G.H., *The Life and Times of Sir Kai Ho Kai*, Chinese University Press (1981).

Coates, Austin, *City of Broken Promises*, Heinemann Asia (1967).

Crabb, C.H., *Malaya's Eurasians – An Opinion*, Eastern Universities Press (Singapore, 1960).

Crisswell, Colin N., *The Taipans, Hong Kong's Merchant Princes*, Oxford University Press (1981).

Eitel, Ernest J., *Feng Shui*, Graham Brash (Singapore, 1984; first published 1871).

Endacott, G.B., *A History of Hong Kong*, Oxford University Press (UK, 1958).

Gascoigne, Bamber, *The Treasures and Dynasties of China*, Jonathan Cape (UK, 1973).

Gillingham, Paul, *At the Peak, Hong Kong Between the Wars*, Macmillan (1983).

Hall, Peter, *In the Web*, Peter A. Hall (UK, 1992).

Hayes, James, *The Hong Kong Region: 1850–1911, Institutions and Leadership in Town and Countryside*, Oxford University Press (1977).

————, *The Rural Communities of Hong Kong: Studies and Themes*, Oxford University Press (1983).

Herklots, G.A.C., *The Hong Kong Countryside: Throughout the Seasons*, South China Morning Post (1951).

Hoe, Susanna, *The Private Life of Old Hong Kong*, Oxford University Press (1991).

Hughes, Richard, *Borrowed Place Borrowed Time: Hong Kong and its Many Faces*, Andre Deutsch (UK, 1968).

Hunter, W.C., *The 'Fan Kwae' at Canton*, Kegan Paul, Trench (1882).

Hyam, Ronald, *Empire and Sexuality*, Manchester University Press (UK, 1991).

Ingrams, Harold, *Hong Kong*, HMSO (UK, 1952).

Jaschok, Maria, *Concubines and Bondservants: the Social History of a Chinese Custom*, Oxford University Press (1989).

Keswick, Maggie (ed.), *The Thistle and the Jade: A Celebration of 150 Years of Jardine Matheson & Co.*, Octopus Books (UK, 1982).

Kinkead, Gwen, *Chinatown: A Portrait of a Closed Society*, Harper Collins (USA, 1992).

Lai, T.C., Husein Rofé and Philip Mao, *Things Chinese*, Swindon Book Co. (1971).

Lin Yutang, *My Country and my People*, William Heinemann (UK, 1936).

The Lun Yu in English, Confucius Publishing (c. 1986).

Lynn, Irene Loh, *The Chinese Community in Liverpool: Their Unmet Needs with Respect to Education, Welfare and Housing*, University of Liverpool (UK, 1982).

Markert, Christopher, *I Ching: The No. 1 Success Formula*, Aquarian Press (UK, 1986).

Maugham, W. Somerset, *On a Chinese Screen*, William Heinemann (UK, 1922).

McCunn, Ruthanne Lum, *An Illustrated History of the Chinese in America*, Design Enterprises of San Francisco (USA, 1979).

————, *Thousand Pieces of Gold*, Design Enterprises of San Francisco (USA, 1981).

Morris, Jan, *Hong Kong, Xianggang*, Viking (UK, 1988).

Needham, Joseph, *Science and Civilisation in China*, various volumes, Cambridge University Press (UK, 1961–84).

Ng Kwee Choo, *The Chinese in London*, Oxford University Press (UK, 1968).

Pakenham, Valerie, *The Noonday Sun, Edwardians in the Tropics*, Methuen (UK, 1985).

Pan, Lynn, *Sons of the Yellow Emperor: The Story of the Overseas Chinese*, Secker and Warburg (UK, 1990).

Shang, Anthony, *The Chinese in Britain*, Batsford (UK, 1984).

Walters, Derek, *Feng Shui: Perfect Planning for Your Happiness and Prosperity*, Pagoda Books (UK, 1988).

Wang Gungwu, *China and the Chinese Overseas*, Times Academic Press (Singapore, 1991).

———, *The Chineseness of China*, Oxford University Press (1991).

Watson, James L., *Emigration and the Chinese Lineage: The Mans in Hong Kong and London*, Berkeley, University of California (USA, 1975).

Wei Tao-Ming, *My Revolutionary Years: The Autobiography of Madam Wei Tao-Ming*, Charles Scribner's Sons (USA, 1943).

Yang, Bo, *The Ugly Chinaman*, Allen and Unwin (Australia, 1992).

Yung, Judy, *Chinese Women of America: A Pictorial History*, University of Washington Press (USA, 1986).

THESES

Cheung, William Chuen-hing, *The Chinese Way: A Social Study of the Hong Kong Chinese Community in a Yorkshire City*, University of York (UK, 1975).

Fisher, Stephen Frederick, *Eurasians in Hong Kong: A Sociological Study of a Marginal Group*, Hong Kong University (1975).

Watson, James Lee, *A Chinese Emigrant Community: The Man Lineage in Hong Kong and London*, Berkeley, University of California (USA, 1972).

REPORTS AND PAPERS

Civil Rights Issues Facing Asian Americans in the 1990s, United States Commission on Civil Rights (USA, 1992).

Employment Prospects of Chinese Youth in Britain, Roundabouts International Centre and Commission for Racial Equality (UK, 1986).

Ling, Amy, *Revelation and Mask: Autobiographies of the Eaton Sisters*, paper presented at the seminar 'Asian Voices in English', held at the University of Hong Kong (1990).

Smith, Carl T., 'Ng Akew, One of Hong Kong's "Protected Women"', *Chung Chi Bulletin*, Chinese University of Hong Kong, **46** (1969).

Turnbull, C.M., *Western Colonialism and the Chinese Diaspora*, inaugural lecture, Hong Kong University (1988).

PERIODICALS

Asian Profile
The Economist

Far Eastern Economic Review
History Notes, Hong Kong
Hong Kong Anthropology Bulletin
Hong Kong, inc
Hong Kong Military History Notes
Royal Asiatic Society, Hong Kong Branch
Window

NEWSPAPERS

Hong Kong Standard
The Independent
South China Morning Post

INDEX

ABOUT THE AUTHOR

DAN WATERS was born in Norwich, city of pubs and churches, in 1920. He was educated at Thetford Grammar School. Like most of his generation he marched jingoistically off to the Second World War and fought in North Africa and Italy, including on the Beachheads of Salerno and Anzio. He suffered from desert sores, was wounded three times and was mentioned in Dispatches.

After demobilisation he rejoined the family building business, established in 1853 and, later, became managing director. He studied and taught at Norwich City College.

In 1954, when Britain had possessions on five continents and before Waters had even met a Chinese, he joined the Colonial Service; whereupon, he could have been sent to any one of fifty-two dependent territories. In Hong Kong he was posted to the Education Department, in the wake of the Korean War and the defeat of the French at Dien Bien Phu in Indochina.

'Hong Kong will be the next to fall,' friends in England warned.

The return of the pint-sized appendage to its giant neighbour, often known as 'Red China', was seldom mentioned in the Crown Colony. The world was less Americanised then. Life was a marvellous adventure.

Now, after several changes of skyline, Hong Kong is entirely different to when Chairman Mao's China was impenetrable and its people could only be viewed as tiny figures through binoculars from the Colony's outposts.

In younger days Waters was an Eastern Counties weight-lifting champion. He obtained a black belt in karate at fifty-seven and ran marathons (26.2 miles) in his mid-sixties. He served as a Justice of the Peace and was invested as a Companion of the Imperial Service Order by Her Majesty the Queen in 1981.

Although he studied earlier at Portsmouth Polytechnic and Manchester University, his PhD was conferred on him by Lough-borough University in his sixty-fifth year.

In his vintage years Dr Waters reads, writes, researches local history, serves on government committees, climbs Victoria Peak and thinks about his ancestors. He holds Hong Kong All-comers records for middle distance running in the over-seventy class.